Before the Restoration of Charles II there were no professional actresses on the English stage, and female roles had almost always been played by men. This book describes how and why women were permitted to act on the public stage after 1660, and the consequences of their arrival for the drama of the period.

There is a surprising lack of published research into Restoration actresses. Elizabeth Howe not only supplies important new facts about the women and their drama, but also opens up a fascinating subject to non-specialists. Beginning with a general account of the workings of Restoration theatre, she goes on to explain the advent of the actresses and how they were treated by theatre companies, theatre audiences and society in general. Perceived predominantly as sex objects, the actresses' sexuality was variously exploited in ways that had important consequences for drama. The remainder of the book concerns the lives and talents of the major figures, in particular Elizabeth Barry and Anne Bracegirdle, showing how their popularity, dramatic skill and public image frequently dictated the kinds of plays written for them.

The book addresses questions that are relevant to women's issues in every period: how far did the advent of real women players alter dramatic portrayals of women? Did this encourage more or less equality between the sexes? Although in one sense merely playthings for a small male élite, the pioneering actresses also represent a new female voice in society and a new place in discourse.

THE FIRST ENGLISH ACTRESSES

THE FIRST ENGLISH ACTRESSES

Women and drama *1660–1700*

ELIZABETH HOWE

CAMBRIDGE
UNIVERSITY PRESS

Published by the Press Syndicate of the University of Cambridge
The Pitt Building, Trumpington Street, Cambridge CB2 1RP
40 West 20th Street, New York, NY 10011–4211, USA
10 Stamford Road, Oakleigh, Melbourne 3166, Australia

First published 1992
Reprinted 1993, 1994

A catalogue record for this book is available from the British Library

Library of Congress cataloguing in publication data

Howe, Elizabeth.
The first English actresses: women and drama, 1660–1700/Elizabeth Howe.
p.   cm.
Includes bibliographical references and index.
ISBN 0 521 38444 3
1. Theater – England – History – 17th century.   2. Women in the
theater – England.   3. English drama – Restoration, 1660–1700 – History
and criticism.   4. Sex role in literature.   5. Actresses – England.
I. Title.
PN2592.H65   1992
792'.028'082 – DC20   91-27698   CIP

ISBN 0 521 38444 3 hardback
ISBN 0 521 42210 8 paperback

Transferred to digital printing 2001

Contents

Illustrations

Preface

In the autumn of 1660, the first professional English actress performed on the London public stage and two years later a royal warrant was issued decreeing that ever after women rather than boy actors were to play all female roles. This book is about the first English actresses and how their arrival affected both the writing of drama and theatre production in England between 1660 and the end of the century.

My study follows two major lines of inquiry:
(a) the general dramatic consequences of changing the sex of a performer of female parts from male to female;
(b) the individual influences of the various major actresses who emerged on the plays that were written for them.

In assessing the actresses' impact on Restoration drama, I have naturally also considered other influences on the playwrights, most notably the social and political background in relation to changing attitudes towards women. However, this work is primarily intended to be a study of the actresses and how their presence on the London stage affected the drama written and performed there between 1660 and 1700. Surprisingly, although the influence of the Restoration player on the drama of his time is now well recognised, there has been no separate critical evaluation of the actresses' special contribution, apart from John Harold Wilson's pioneering study *All the King's Ladies: Actresses of the Restoration* (Chicago, 1958), a useful and informative book which nevertheless seems out of date in the light of more recent research of the period and its theatre.

While this book aims to furnish the specialist with important facts about the women players and their drama, it is also intended to open up a fascinating subject to non-specialists. For this reason I have begun with a general introduction briefly outlining the history of Restoration theatre, its organisation, its audience and the production process for a play. The first chapter examines why and how the actresses came to be introduced to the English stage in 1660 – a matter on which critical agreement has not yet been reached. While the particular influence of individuals – the theatre managers, King Charles II – was crucial, the replacement of boy-actresses by women is above all a product of the changed circumstances of theatre itself after 1660. The Caroline court had supported the idea of female performers, indeed, Queen Henrietta Maria and her ladies themselves acted in private, but it was only after the Restoration that London theatre became sufficiently court-based as to allow an acceptance of actresses on the public stage. Like many of the consequences of the arrival of actresses, their introduction was simultaneously radical – in allowing women a voice on the public stage for the first time – and conservative: within a predominantly courtly, coterie theatre the women were almost entirely controlled by male managers and playwrights and were exploited sexually on stage and off. Similarly, although the profession of actress offered women a rare opportunity to earn fame as well as money in a public arena, the pay and status of the female players within the companies reflects their inferiority in relation to their masculine counterparts.

The second chapter deals with changes to tragedy and comedy created by the presence of female, as opposed to young male, bodies on the stage. The actresses were perceived predominantly as sex objects and were required, with significant frequency, to represent rape victims and to enact explicit love scenes. Again, however, the consequences of such developments can be seen as both reactionary and subversive, questioning as well as reinforcing traditional dramatic female stereotypes. While many dramatists used the body of the actress purely to titillate, the best ones – Thomas Otway, William Wycherley, Aphra Behn, Thomas Southerne, William Congreve – used the new female resource to present and explore women's sexual feelings in important new ways.

The remainder of the book concerns the contribution of individual actresses to the drama they performed. It has been shown that the talent and popularity of a player could affect radically the kind of plays that were produced: if a player proved very successful in one type of role, this would influence the playwright who then tended to write plays around him (or her) and his speciality. In fact, patterns more complex than simple typecasting took place and it is possible to trace the development of dramatic genres and conventions, as well as female character types, in relation to the actresses who made them popular. Chapter 3 deals with the development of Restoration comedy in this way, chapter 5 is similarly concerned with the actresses' impact on tragedy. Chapters 6 and 7 trace the way in which particularly successful female specialities left a strong mark on the repertory. Inevitably, the best and most influential actresses appear again and again in different chapters, while the greatest of them all, Elizabeth Barry, had an outstanding effect on almost every type of play. Any book on Restoration drama and the actress must often become simply a study of the versatile and irresistible Mrs Barry and the numerous vehicles that were written for her.

I have devoted chapter 4 to the relation between the actresses' own actual or reputed characters and the roles that were written for them. From the beginning, the public took a particular interest in the private lives of the female players, gossiped about them, even had affairs with them. The most popular actresses delivered especially written prologues and epilogues which played on this intimacy and allowed them to communicate with audiences as themselves, rather than solely in the guise of fictional characters within a play. As a result, dramatists had to take care to base the roles they wrote for a popular actress around her public image and the relationship she had with her audience.

Finally, any study of the actresses' influence on drama cannot avoid addressing certain feminist questions. Did the use of real women as players significantly alter the portrayal and treatment of women in plays? Did the presence of the actress encourage, on the stage at least, more equality between the sexes? How far can female performers be said to represent a challenge to traditional, patriarchal attitudes? While touching on these issues throughout, they are the focus of the conclusion in which the actresses' contribution to changes in the dramatic treatment of women (and, especially, of wives) is seen as part of a pattern of wider social, political and cultural change. Alongside the establishment of actresses, the late seventeenth century also saw a series of striking attacks on all traditional forms of authority (monarchist, religious and familial), a new degree of support for divorce, new laws in women's favour and a remarkable growth in publications by and for women. As has been pointed out, the struggles that characterise every aspect of English culture during the seventeenth century may not have brought women significantly nearer to sexual equality, but the end of the century left them more articulate in their own defence than ever before. Although in one sense merely playthings for a small, male, mostly royalist élite, the actresses were also part of the new female voice in society. Their talent and popular success fostered a shift from male-based drama to female and led more radical comic dramatists to write sympathetically about female problems and female rights, particularly in marriage. In this way the actresses form part of the new place in discourse, the new ability to speak, which by 1700 women had begun to achieve.

I should like to offer sincere thanks to all who have helped me with this work. I am most grateful to the University of London for giving me a research grant to enable me to study for three weeks at the Folger Shakespeare Library in Washington and to examine the Restoration prompt-books there. For help at important moments I should like to thank Professor Anne Barton, Professor Robert D. Hume, Dr Derek Hughes, Dr John and Dr Gillian Manning, Eva Simmons, Sandra Richards, Sophie Tomlinson and Dr Jackie Bratton. For their generous assistance I wish to thank many librarians, especially those of the University of London Library, the British Library, the London Library, the Folger Shakespeare Library, the Bodleian Library and the Library of Queen's University, Belfast.

My thanks are due especially to my supportive husband, whose practical experience as a theatre director and as a script editor have proved invaluable, to my parents, for minding the children at crucial moments, to my patient and efficient typist, Sue Wasley, to my editor Sarah Stanton for her unfailing advice and encouragement and above all to my Ph.D. supervisor, Professor Inga-Stina Ewbank, without whom this work would certainly never have been written. To Inga-Stina this book is affectionately dedicated.

A note on styling, dates and editions used

In the text the date given in brackets after a play is the date of its first performance as given in *The London Stage* unless otherwise indicated. I cite publication date only in notes and bibliography. If a play has two titles (for example *The Man of Mode: or, Sir Fopling Flutter*), both will be given at its first mention in the notes and in the bibliography, but in the text only first titles will be used. Prologues, epilogues and prefaces are quoted from the edition of the play (normally the first) cited in the text, notes and bibliography.

Unless otherwise stated the place of publication of all texts is London. When quoting from seventeenth-century editions the long s has been printed as s.

First editions of plays have been used where possible, unless a good modern edition is available.

I have ignored the fact that the calender year was held to start on 25 March during this period and have used the modern style of dates starting on 1 January throughout.

Introduction: the Restoration theatre

When Parliament issued an ordinance against stage plays in 1642, the professional theatre officially died in England until Charles II regained the throne in 1660. During the 1630s theatrical activity in London can be divided into three main areas: 'public' playhouses such as the Globe, the Fortune and the Red Bull, which mostly revived older plays, romances, farces and melodramas for a predominantly lower-class audience; more élite 'private' theatres like Blackfriars, the Phoenix and Salisbury Court, attended mainly by members of the upper and professional classes, from which the majority of new plays came; and the court theatre where, among others, the productions in which Queen Henrietta Maria and her ladies performed were staged. During the Interregnum most of these forms of theatre ceased, although old plays were still performed at times (sometimes in public, more often in private) and occasional new ones composed and staged. A handful of playwrights and players survived into the Restoration, but essentially the professional theatre had to be recreated, along with the monarchy itself, in 1660.

Soon after Charles II returned, he issued patents to two of his followers, Sir Thomas Killigrew and Sir William Davenant, to open theatres. In spite of opposition from other interested parties, these two playwrights, who were courtiers and friends of the king, were given the exclusive right to put on plays for profit and thus for the first time theatrical production in London was limited to only two companies. Killigrew, who was closer to the king, got most of the experienced actors available as well as a virtual monopoly on classic English plays. He formed the King's Company and began to stage plays at the converted Gibbon's Tennis Court. Davenant formed the Duke's Company from novices and less experienced players, but compensated for his disadvantages by arranging for the erection of an impressively equipped theatre with changeable scenery at Lincoln's

Inn Fields, which was opened in June 1661. The success of this theatre propelled Killigrew into building a new theatre himself, the Theatre Royal in Bridge Street, which opened in 1663.

In spite of the fact that between them Killigrew and Davenant made it virtually impossible for plays to be staged by anyone else, by 1682 the King's Company was in such dire straits financially that it was forced to negotiate with the more successful Duke's Company to form an amalgamation. A variety of factors contributed to the company's demise, including poor patronage, internal dissension, bad financial management and the disaster of their Bridge Street playhouse burning down in January 1672. (In 1671, incidentally, the Duke's Company opened the finest Restoration theatre of all at Dorset Garden, spectacularly equipped with all the best stage machinery.) Its death warrant was signed on 14 October 1682 when its leading actor-shareholders, Charles Hart and Edward Kynaston, negotiated terms with the leading shareholders of the Duke's Company (Thomas Betterton, Charles Davenant and William Smith) and agreed to act for the Duke's Company, assign it their roles in King's Company plays and promote a union of the two companies. The so-called United Company was created and maintained control of all theatrical production for the next twelve years.

Two businessmen, the lawyer Christopher Rich and Sir Thomas Skipwith, purchased control of the new company. They discreetly bought up the Davenant share between 1687 and 1690 and then proceeded to conflict bitterly with the players, reducing their salaries and juggling with profits. Increased bad feeling came to a head in December 1694 when the best players banded together and presented a formal petition of complaint to the Lord Chamberlain. Efforts by Rich and Skipwith to appease the rebels were finally made, but too late. Led by star tragedian Thomas Betterton, the angry players broke away and formed their own company. In March 1695 they obtained a licence to perform and the following month they opened their own theatre, a players' republic, in the remodelled Lisle's Tennis Court. Betterton's company played at this theatre for the next ten years. In this way the competitive two-company system returned to London and continued into the next century.[1] Only in 1709 did a third company begin acting at William Penkethman's new theatre at Greenwich and it was not until the late 1720s that there were six or seven companies performing in London concurrently.

THE STRUCTURE OF THE RESTORATION THEATRE

While the structure of the different London theatres in use between 1660 and 1700 naturally varied from Killigrew's primitive conversion of Gibbon's Tennis Court in 1660 to the impressive Dorset Garden theatre, all shared a similar design, a design which encompassed significant changes to the pre-Commonwealth playhouses. The Restoration theatre had a proscenium arch, the stage extending in front as well as behind the arch into the main seating area, the pit. There were entrance doors onto the stage for the players in the two sides of the proscenium. The forestage area in front was where the majority of acting took place: the amount that occurred behind the proscenium is still a matter of debate among scholars.[2] Extending away from the stage were tiers of boxes: side-boxes which stretched along both sides of the theatre and front-boxes facing the stage, behind the pit. Above the front-boxes and pit was a gallery, or in some theatres two galleries, the uppermost one the smaller of the two. Benches rather than seats prevailed which made the seating capacity flexible and gave the auditorium an easy informal atmosphere. Lighting was mostly by candles, the forestage illuminated by chandeliers directly above it and by lighted brackets around the auditorium.[3]

Davenant was responsible for the major structural innovation on the stage itself, the introduction of movable and changeable scenery behind the proscenium arch. Whereas in the Renaissance the action of a play was basically continuous, without breaks for different settings and backdrops, the Restoration theatre commenced the practice of transitions in the action in which changes of scene were created. Davenant developed the custom of having the curtain drawn back after the prologue was finished to reveal the stage behind the proscenium containing some kind of scene (the forestage was always exposed). The curtain was not drawn again until the whole performance, even the epilogue, was finished; all changes of scene took place in full view of spectators. The creation of each 'scene' involved, not scenery in the sense of a single backdrop behind the players, but an arrangement of sets of shutters in the wings and at the back which could be pushed shut along grooves to create a particular scene, or opened to reveal some kind of action or tableau behind. Thus when a stage direction in a Restoration dramatic text reads '*the scene opens*' it refers to the opening of a set of shutters onto something else: '*the scene shuts*' means the shutters were then closed at the end of the 'scene'. There were three and possibly even four sets of shutters to create different scenes. All were placed wide enough apart to allow players to act behind one set and in front of another, permitting a rapid succession of scenes. Scene changes were indicated by the stage manager's whistle or by ringing a bell. A bare stage usually signified the end of an act, any scene change for the opening of the next act occurring just before the action of that scene started. The intervals between acts were probably comparatively short and filled in the early years of the period by music from the orchestra and in later years by songs and dances as well. Neither company went to the expense of creating new scenes for every production. The same basic settings of palaces, groves, forests, lodgings, streets and gardens could be used over and over again.

Davenant also introduced 'machines', devices for flying in objects like chariots and angels to create fast and eyecatching illusions, particularly for operas. The machines were kept in the area behind the proscenium arch and they added further visual interest to the excitement of successive changes of scene. The simplest machines were trap-doors for raising ghosts and devils and for swallowing up evildoers, the most spectacular were the flying machines, allowing people, gods and even flaming monsters to rise and descend. In John Dryden's play *Tyrannick Love* (1669), for example, spirits bent on seducing St Catherine descended singing in clouds. The clouds parted and St Catherine was raised up in her bed while the scene changed to a richly painted paradise. Finally St Catherine's guardian angel came down, accompanied by 'soft musick' and 'with a flaming sword'.[4]

Behind the stage was the scene room where props were kept and where the players rested and waited for their cues. Above this were the dressing-rooms, called tiring-rooms, one for men and one for women, with small private rooms for the stars. These rooms may have been warmed by coal fires and certainly some of the private ones had fireplaces: on 4 May 1667, the Lord Chamberlain ordered the actress Anne Quin 'a dressing roome with a chymney in it to be only for her use'.[5] Any member of the public could enter the tiring-rooms and many did, especially men visiting the actresses. Pepys went backstage on several occasions – once 'to see the inside of the Stage and all the tiring-roomes and Machines'. He was amused by the miscellany of objects in the tiring-rooms, 'here a wooden leg, there a ruff, here a

1 Engraving of a painted 'scene' of prisoners on spikes in the 1673 edition of Settle's *Empress of Morocco*, as used in the 1673 production of the play.

hobby-horse, there a Crowne'. He visited the private rooms of two of the actors and was struck by the contrast between the fineness of their costumes on stage and their tawdry appearance close to: 'how fine they show on the stage by candle-light, and how poor things they are to look now too near-hand'.[6]

THE AUDIENCE

During the 1660s and 1670s both theatres retained close links with king and court. Charles himself visited both theatres regularly, taking a special interest in both plays and players. Courtiers and others with direct access to the king also visited the theatre a great deal, as well as writing plays for the two companies and patronising other playwrights. However, while Restoration theatre audiences were never as varied as those of Shakespeare's Globe, for example, they were by no means wholly aristocratic. The diary of the ardent theatre-goer Pepys shows that plenty of less wealthy people visited the theatre – civil servants, bureaucrats and other professional men with their wives, as well as a selection from the poorer classes, servants, apprentices and journeymen. Dividing the seating area of a Restoration theatre into four areas, the author of *The Country Gentleman's Vade Mecum* (1699) offers a vivid picture of the various types of theatre-goer. Below the upper gallery containing servants came the boxes – one for the king and royal family and others for 'Persons of Quality...unless some Fools...crowd in among 'em'. In the pit were 'Judges, Wits and Censurers...Squires, Sharpers, Beaus, Bullies and Whores, and here and there an extravagant Male and Female Cit'. In the middle gallery 'the Citizens Wives and Daughters, together with the Abigails, Serving-men, Journey-men and Apprentices commonly take their Places; and now and then some disponding Mistresses and superannuated Poets'.[7] The average audience comprised about 500 persons (the population of London at this time has been numbered at 527,600).[8]

Historians once argued that the class content of the Restoration audience shifted from largely aristocratic to largely bourgeois during the 1680s, but there is little evidence to support this – citizens as well as aristocrats visited the theatre from the very beginning of our period.[9] What did disappear, however, as the century wore on, was the direct patronage and support of the monarchy so evident at the start. While James II shared his brother's fondness for the theatre, the troubled years of his reign from 1685 to 1689 saw a general reduction in theatrical activity. Under William and Mary court support for the theatre dwindled still further: their interest in drama was minimal, as was that of their successor (in 1702), Queen Anne. This lack of court support rendered the stage more vulnerable to attacks by moralists, which strengthened during the 1690s. Indictments were gained against players for speaking licentious or blasphemous lines and Jeremy Collier's notorious diatribe, *A Short View of the Immorality and Profaneness of the English Stage* (1698) put both theatres on the defensive.[10]

Throughout the period audiences granted performers none of the reverent hush that we associate today with watching a play. The atmosphere during a performance was relaxed and informal; many spectators treated the playhouse like a kind of club and might chat, argue, or even occasionally fight duels while the unfortunate actors and actresses tried to make themselves heard. Pepys, for instance, was severely irritated when 'two talking ladies and Sir Ch. Sidly' talked so much that he 'lost the pleasure of the play wholly'.[11] Of course, fine productions kept the playhouse quiet, but players could never count on an attentive silence and had to be prepared to combat any sort of interruption.

A significant proportion of Restoration theatre-goers patronised the theatre very regularly, at least once a week, knew each other and members of both companies personally and were therefore extremely familiar with the various established modes of drama and with the types of role specialised in by different players. Dramatists wrote with this familiarity in mind, aware that they were creating plays for an audience with preconceptions they could fulfil or frustrate. Sometimes their attempts to change a formula succeeded, sometimes not. A striking example of failure was when the actor Samuel Sandford, a 'low and crooked Person' who always played villains, was unexpectedly cast as an honest man:

The Pit, after they had sate three or four Acts, in a quiet Expectation, that the well-dissembled Honesty of Sandford (for such of course they concluded it) would soon be discover'd, or at least, from its Security, involve the Actors in the Play, in some surprizing Distress or Confusion, which might raise and animate the Scenes to come; when; at last, finding no such matter, but that the Catastrophe had taken quite another Turn, and that Sandford was really an honest Man to the end of the Play, they fairly damn'd it, as if the Author had impos'd upon them the most frontless or incredible Absurdity.[12]

Ultimately power in the theatre lay with the audience on whose support the existence of the companies depended. All productions were subject to fierce, critical examination by highly experienced spectators who damned and applauded with equal vigour.

THE COMPANY

At the head of each company was the proprietor who gained the position mainly by acquiring a patent allowing him to form a troupe and put on certain plays. He assembled a group of sharing players (always male until the 1690s) who took a part of the company's profits after bills and wages were paid. Below the sharers came the players who were merely hirelings with salaries and all the non-acting personnel such as musicians, scene-shifters and machinists, prompters, treasurers, tiring-men and -women and, in later years, singers and dancers.[13]

Companies usually contained between twenty and thirty players, who were recruited from a variety of sources. At the beginning Killigrew procured various actors left over from the pre-Commonwealth theatre – the stars Charles Hart and Michael Mohun, for instance, were apprentices during the Caroline period. Some actors were drawn from the professional classes; Thomas Betterton was well educated and William Smith was first of all a barrister. On the other hand, another leading actor, Henry Harris, was a seal-cutter by profession and the comedian Thomas Doggett was brought up in the slums of Dublin. As time went on a number of men joined the theatre because their families were already in the profession. The recruitment of actresses was more problematic because no woman with serious pretensions to respectability would countenance a stage career, and yet the profession demanded more than women of the brothel class. An actress had to be able to read and memorise lines at speed, to sing and dance to some degree and to emulate a lady's behaviour. This left only a 'narrow middle stratum' of society from which actresses could be drawn.[14] The stratum included women whose good families had come down in the world, like the popular singer and comedienne Charlotte Butler, daughters of tradesmen, like tragedienne Sarah Cooke, and gentlemen's bastards, like Moll Davis. While the most obvious career for the genteel, dowerless female was domestic service, the less respectable job of actress offered better pay and better prospects.

In some ways the profession of actor was a rewarding one. During the 1660s many players were very close to king and court and throughout the period a number were held in great esteem by theatre-goers. The theatre has always been an exciting place to work and never more so than after a hiatus of eighteen years when the profession had to be revived. However, the position of player was never a secure one and an actor's or actress's social standing remained relatively low. (The particularly difficult social position of the actress will be further discussed in chapter 1.) Also, even the sharers, who had more power over their own destinies than the hirelings had, were hedged in by restrictions. Players' contracts forbade them moving from one company to another so they could not sell their services to the highest bidder. When in the summer of 1663 Harris tried to change companies, the king himself ordered him to remain within the terms of his contract.

Compared to present-day performers, the Restoration players were poorly paid. Even the sharers did badly at times, when audience numbers were low and theatrical costs increased. In addition, there were all too many times in the year when for some reason the theatres were closed so that no one was paid anything at all. Probably no players worked for more than thirty-five weeks out of the annual fifty-two. Theatres were closed for the week before Easter, on Fridays during Lent, if a member of the royal family died and when some sort of disturbance took place in the playhouse (even if the players themselves were not involved). Trade also came almost to a standstill in summer when the court and gentry left London for the country. The most difficult time of all came when the plague and fire of London closed the theatres for nearly eighteen months, between 5 June 1665 and 29 November 1666.[15]

In a working week, the Restoration players worked every day but Sunday, rehearsed most mornings, played every afternoon and possibly performed again in a private production for the court at Whitehall in the evening. If he or she failed to appear at rehearsal they might be fined a week's wages.[16] On average, each company performed four or five new plays a year, the rest of their season being composed of Renaissance, Caroline or contemporary revivals. Each theatre seems to have produced between forty and sixty different plays each season.[17] Clearly, in their spare time successful players needed to study their lines: even the best new plays or revivals rarely ran for longer than six days. A leading actor or actress might have to play as many as thirty different parts in the course of a season. During the years from 1673 to 1709 the brilliant Elizabeth Barry is known to have played 142 named parts, with presumably more in cast lists which have not survived.[18] Once a player possessed a particular part he or she was expected to be prepared to play it at every subsequent revival, no matter how much time had passed since the last performance. Sometimes when a play proved unsuccessful one day another had to be hastily substituted on the next. Not surprisingly, authors (and Pepys) often complained that the players forgot their lines or ad libbed.[19]

Although the theatres possessed fairly extensive stage wardrobes, players seem to have had to provide personal items such as hats, periwigs, petticoats, shoes, stockings, gloves and scarves. The King's Company shareholders Hart, Mohun and Kynaston made a special agreement on 6 March 1672 that they should be given articles like periwigs, stockings, hats, shirts and cravats new each year,[20] but there was no similar arrangement for the actresses. They possibly relied to some extent on gifts from admirers to sustain their wardrobes. They certainly seem to have succumbed to the temptation of wearing their stage costumes outside the theatre, for an agreement of 1675 between players and manager at the Theatre Royal stipulates, among other things, that

Whereas by Experience Wee find Our Cloathes Tarnished and Imberelled [*sic*] by frequent Weareing them out of the Playhouse It is thought fitt noe Weoman presume to goe out of the House with the Play House Cloathes or Properties upon Penalty of theire Weekes pay.[21]

If new players received any training at all this usually came either from company shareholders like Thomas Betterton, or, after 1667, from 'nurseries' for young players maintained by the companies at one of the old London theatres. We do not know how many players were trained at the nurseries nor how long these establishments continued after 1682, the last year in which they are mentioned. Barry was unusual in receiving personal instruction from her lover the Earl of Rochester at the beginning of her career. He is supposed to have decided to teach her in under six months to be 'the finest Player on the Stage'.[22] The majority of successful players seem to have appeared on the stage without previous training anywhere. But they still had to work a probationary period of 'three Monethes without Sallary by Way of Approbation' before becoming proper members of the company.[23]

Each actor and actress possessed their own particular parts, written out on scrolls of paper, which they created and retained until they died or retired from the stage (just occasionally, a senior player might 'lend' a part to another when he or she chose not to act in a

Lenten performance). When the minor actress Elizabeth Weaver left the stage in 1664 she 'brought in all her parts' and when William Mountfort was murdered in 1692, George Powell came into 'Possession of all the chief Parts of Montfort'.[24] An actor's or actress's roles tended to be of one or two specific types, like Sandford who, as we have seen, almost always played villains. While such typecasting occurred to some degree in theatre before 1641, a striking instance being the clown/fool roles of Robert Arnim in Shakespeare's plays, it happened far more in the Restoration period and especially with the actresses, since female roles were fewer and more stereotyped than male roles. (Most plays had two or three times more parts for men than for women.) When a play was cast roles seem to have been assigned according to the particular 'lines' of the players available. Most playwrights wrote their plays with a particular company in mind and fashioned roles to fit the specialities in that company. If the company contained an especially popular and talented player, then the dramatist naturally tried to include a prominent role for him or her, one which would show off his or her talents to best advantage. When the actor, dramatist and theatre historian Colley Cibber, for example, changed theatre in the mid-1690s, he rewrote his comedy *Woman's Wit* (1697) so as to incorporate the popular and talented comedian Thomas Doggett in his new company:

In the middle of my Writing the Third Act, not liking my Station there, I return'd again to the Theatre Royal, and was then forc'd, as far as I cou'd with nature, to confine the Business of my Persons to the Capacity of different people, and not to miss the Advantage of Mr. Dogget's Excellent Action; I prepar'd a low Character, which ... I knew from him cou'd not fail of Diverting.[25]

Likewise, the skilled dramatist Thomas Southerne wrote the title role of *Sir Anthony Love* (1690) for the comedienne and breeches role specialist Susannah Mountfort, 'I made every Line for her',[26] and the leading role of *The Fatal Marriage* (1694) for the tragedienne Elizabeth Barry, 'I made the Play for her part.'[27] In a letter to the publisher Jacob Tonson, we find Dryden showing anxiety over every member of the cast in two of his plays that were to be revived:

for the Actors in the two plays which are to be acted of mine, this winter, I had spoken with Mr. Betterton by chance at the Coffee house this afternoon before I came away: and I believe that the persons were all agreed on, to be just the same you mentioned. Only Octavia was to be Mrs. Buttler, in case Mrs. Cooke were not on the Stage. And I know not whether Mrs. Percivall who is a Comedian, will do so well for Benzayda.[28]

Dryden had written the role of Benzayda originally for the talented Elizabeth Boutell and, she having retired, he is taking pains over her replacement.

THE PRODUCTION PROCESS

Once a new play was accepted it was first read aloud by its author to the entire company before being cast according to the range of players available. A promptbook was then made up, indicating moments for cueing players' entrances, shifting scenes and producing special effects. Often a play had to undergo substantial alterations at this stage to be deemed performable. The prolific playwright Thomas Shadwell, for instance, 'was forc'd ... to blot out the main design' of his comedy *The Humorists* (1670) before it could be acted.[29] Since new plays were almost always staged before they were published, each player was given his or her part written out in longhand by the prompter or one of his assistants. Each part consisted of a roll of paper containing just the player's own lines and sufficient words from each preceding speech to make the cues recognisable. The players therefore had very little idea of what the rest of the play was like.

Rehearsals were called for 10 o'clock in the morning and attendance was obligatory. Rehearsals for revivals usually involved simply the straightforward reproduction of past performances; if there had been any cast changes, or any other problems arose, the prompter was consulted. The author, however, was in charge of rehearsals for a new play or, if he or she was unavailable, the company manager or a senior actor took over. The author's job appears to have been to explain obscurities in his text, to approve scenery, to oversee and criticise line delivery, blocking, stage business and general styles of acting, to control the progress of the rehearsal and to explain his play's special effects to the machinists.[30]

The greatest players, among them Thomas Betterton and Elizabeth Barry, were highly conscientious and spent rehearsals scrupulously preparing their roles and discussing with the author how the play might best be presented. The dramatist and critic Charles Gildon relates how Betterton complained about lax young players who never bothered to study their parts before rehearsals and 'come thither too often scarce recovered from their last Night's Debauch':

they vainly imagine themselves Masters of that Art, which perfectly to attain, requires a studious Application of a Man's whole Life. They take it therefore amiss to have the Author give them any Instruction ... Whereas it has always been mine and Mrs. Barry's Practice to consult e'en the most indifferent Poet in any Part we have thought fit to accept of; and I may say it of her, she has so often exerted her self in an indifferent Part, that her Acting has given Success to such Plays, as to read would turn a Man's Stomach.[31]

Naturally we can only speculate as to the acting styles used by the players. Comedy seems to have been performed comparatively naturalistically, that is, in very much the way people comported themselves in real society. There is a vast array of seventeenth-century books describing correct social behaviour, behaviour so generally accepted that it became 'natural' – and this was the behaviour reproduced on stage. Cibber tells how he once saw the brilliantly talented comedian James Nokes 'giving an account of some Table-talk to another Actor behind the Scenes, which a Man of Quality accidentally listening to, was so deceived by his Manner, that he ask'd him if that was a new Play he was rehearsing?' Cibber's story suggests that the comic style of acting was simply 'a heightened extension, a raconteur's representation of reality'.[32] Tragedy, on the other hand, seems to have demanded a much more formal, exaggerated mode of behaviour. Each emotion apparently had to be accompanied by its own stylised movement and tone of voice. According to Charles Gildon's *Life of Mr. Thomas Betterton* (1710), our main source of information about Restoration acting, the tragic actor portrayed each mood or 'passion' by a particular gesture, expression and mode of speech. The actor or actress was apparently expected to move abruptly from one stylised passion to another, although, says Gildon, there should be 'a certain agreeable Measure between one another, and at the same time answerable to that of Speech'.[33] He lists six different tones of voice, for example, for six main moods, these being anger, commiseration or pity, fear, power, pleasure and grief or trouble. Love is best expressed by a 'gay, soft and charming Voice', hate by a 'sharp, sullen, and severe one'. Joy has a 'full flowing and brisk Voice', grief a 'sad, dull and languishing Tone'.[34] The successful player harmonised his or her character, mood and speech with the correct tones and gestures.

To achieve the right gestures at the right moment, Betterton advocates practising in front of a mirror or before a helpful friend. He frequently compares effective acting of this kind with 'history painting' – painting of scenes of action where the arrangement, postures and facial expressions of the figures produce an immediate impact. The players' carefully rehearsed movements should convey the same powerful and emotive effect as a brilliantly composed painting: 'as in a Piece of History-Painting, tho the Figures direct their Eyes never so directly to each other, yet the Beholder, by the Advantage of their [*sic*] Position, has a full view of the Expression of the Soul in the Eyes of the Figures'. Nevertheless, even with the elaborate conventions Betterton describes, the tragic player's ultimate aim was still a kind of naturalism, if obviously not the kind of naturalism actors usually look for today. Betterton continually stresses that acting should be like 'nature', by which he means 'a peculiar Care of avoiding all manner of Affectation in your Action and Gesture... your Action must appear purely Natural, as the genuine Offspring of the things you express, and the Passion, that moves you to speak in that manner'. Fellow actor Colley Cibber uses the word 'natural' in a similar way when he praises Betterton and his company thus: 'these Actors, whom I have selected from their Contemporaries, were all original Masters in their different Stile... Self-judges of nature, from whose various Lights they only took their true Instruction'.[35]

Rehearsals seem to have lasted about a month. As the day of its première drew near, the new play was advertised by playbills posted outside the theatre and elsewhere, by handbills and by announcements at the end of an evening's performance. Premières most often took place on a Saturday, presumably to allow a full week's rehearsal beforehand, with Sunday to sort out first-night problems before the second performance on Monday. They were colourful and exciting occasions, extremely well attended. Pepys often complains of not being able to find a seat, however early he turns up (seats could not be reserved unless one were a person of influence). Finally, to ensure a place at the première of Thomas Shadwell's first comedy *The Sullen Lovers* on 2 May 1668, Pepys arrived a full three hours before it was due to start.

All play runs were short, ten to fifteen days at most, because the potential audience was a comparatively limited one. New plays were rarely performed for more than six days. Early on the custom developed of allowing the author the profits on the third day of his new play's being performed – his 'benefit' – so he or she had little incentive once that day was passed to press for a longer run. Successful plays were of course revived later.[36]

THE PLAYWRIGHTS

Each company possessed its own plays and retained an exclusive right to put them on. They obtained their new plays from three types of playwright – amateurs, who tended to write only occasionally and who were very much in the minority; professionals, who tended to write for both theatres but who probably tailored the roles they created to one particular company; and attached professionals, who had signed an exclusive agreement to produce plays for only one company. In 1668, for example, Dryden signed a contract to provide three plays a year for the King's Company in return for a share, and a quarter of the company's profits. Leading tragic dramatist Nathaniel Lee also made some kind of exclusive agreement with the King's Company while the prolific John Crowne had one with the Duke's Company. The author of numerous melodramas and operatic spectaculars Elkanah Settle was offered £50 a year if he wrote for the Duke's Company, but decided he would do better with its rival and 'notwithstanding his pension put his play into their hands'.[37] (The professional playwright's main source of income was his benefit.) Sometimes a playwright was commissioned to write a play, as when Shadwell was appointed to adapt Molière's *The Miser* for the stage in 1672, but most dramatists just submitted their work to the company manager for his decision. On occasion they found supporters – players, successful playwrights, other prominent figures – to intercede for them.

During the early part of the period a handful of the dramatists were also courtiers, the most famous and skilled being George Villiers, Duke of Buckingham, whose parody of tragedy *The Rehearsal* achieved enormous success in the early 1670s, and John Wilmot, Earl of Rochester. A number of others had links with the court. Sir George Etherege was knighted around 1680 and became envoy for James II in Ratisbon between 1685 and 1689. William Wycherley, author of the most famous comedy of the age, *The Country Wife*, was a law student at the Inner Temple but after the success of this play became a royal favourite and in 1679 was offered the tutorship of the king's son. (However, he subsequently lost the king's favour that same year when he secretly married the widowed Countess of Drogheda, daughter of the first Earl of Radnor.) Other dramatists earned their livings mainly as men of letters; John Dryden the Poet Laureate is the most illustrious example. Others again were actors; Nathaniel Lee and the greatest tragic dramatist of the age, Thomas Otway, began their stage careers as performers rather than playwrights, while successful actors like Betterton, Mountfort and Powell later branched out into authorship.

Significantly, for the first time women began to have their plays produced openly on the public stage and to live by their pens. This new development seems to have been caused partly by the earlier introduction of actresses to the stage in 1660 – the novelty of having women in the theatre opened the way for women playwrights as well.[38] However, the prejudice and opprobrium that a female dramatist had to face was formidable. They were felt to be automatically inferior to male writers, 'the very being a woman condemns', and they were constantly charged with sexual immorality: 'Tis hard to say – which do's the most prevail, / Women's Incontinence of Tongue or Tail.'[39]

Who were these bold pioneers? The most famous of course is Aphra Behn (1640–88). Apart from Dryden, she was the most prolific writer of the period, author of at least eighteen plays, plus poetry and prose works. Much of her youth was spent in Surinam where her father, who died on the voyage out, was to have been Lieutenant-General. She returned to London in 1664 and married Mr Behn, about whom nothing is known except that he probably died a year later. In 1666 Thomas Killigrew persuaded Mrs Behn to spy for England in the Dutch Wars, but the information she gained was considered of little value so she did not even receive the cost of her expenses from the government. In 1670, after imprisonment for debt and in severe poverty, she began to write for a living. Her first play, a tragicomedy called *The Forc'd Marriage*, was produced by the Duke's Company later that year. Thereafter she wrote plays regularly, always for the Duke's Company, until her death in 1688, when she was buried in Westminster Abbey.

Most of the other women who wrote plays in any number for the public stage came originally, like Behn, from professional backgrounds and wrote to stave off poverty. Mary Pix (1666–1709) was the daughter of a vicar. At the age of 22 she married a tailor, George Pix, and at 30 began to create plays for the stage. There are no subsequent references to her husband; she may have had to pursue a literary career in order to support herself after his death. Pix, like Behn, wrote prose works as well as eleven plays staged between 1696 and 1706. Catherine Trotter (1679–1749) was the daughter of a sea captain whose early death propelled her into authorship at the age of

14. Her first play, *Agnes de Castro*, was staged moderately successfully three years later. She married happily, wrote a total of five plays and, unusually, retained a chaste reputation until her death. By contrast, her contemporary Delariviere Manley (*c.* 1672–1724) had a scandalous public image. Born the daughter of the lieutenant-governor of Jersey, Manley was deceived after his death into a bigamous marriage with her guardian and cousin, John Manley, who settled her in London, but later returned to his first wife when she gave birth to a child. She then entered upon a turbulent and unconventional life of her own in the capital. She had a succession of lovers, including Sir Thomas Skipwith and John Tilley, the warden of the Fleet Prison. In frequent need of money, in the mid-1690s she began to write professionally, eventually producing six plays (two of which were never staged), as well as stories, contributions to periodicals, an autobiographical novel and what have been termed 'politico-erotic narratives' in which a spirited defence of Toryism is interspersed with lively sexual adventures.[40] While two female playwrights – Margaret Cavendish, Duchess of Newcastle and Anne Finch, Countess of Winchilsea – were aristocrats, neither of these wrote for the public stage and other respectable women writers, Katherine Philips, Anne Wharton and Elizabeth Polwhele, also shunned exposure in the commercial theatre.

How, if at all, was the drama changed in the hands of writers like Behn and Manley? It has been suggested that in several ways Restoration plays by women present a strongly individual and 'feminist' viewpoint. They have been shown as more likely to mock men and to protest against male oppression. They tend to give more lines to female characters than plays by men do, and to open and close more often with speeches by women.[41] However, it should be noted that 'feminist' writing in the period is by no means limited to female writers. A number of comedies by talented playwrights such as Thomas Durfey, Southerne and John Vanbrugh contain forceful attacks on sexual inequality and a strong focus on women rather than men. The overall impact of the female playwrights was also necessarily limited by the fact that they created only a fraction of the drama performed between 1660 and 1700. In contrast, almost every play staged had at least one role for the actress, whose effect on theatre was much greater. This was in any case the age of *performer's* theatre, as opposed to that of the dramatist or director: 'it was the personal glamour of the players that secured attention, not the intrinsic quality of their repertory'.[42] While the changes wrought by professional women writers were not insignificant, the most powerful female influence on drama in the period came not from them but from the actresses. *Their* remarkable impact is of course the subject of this book.

CHAPTER I

The arrival of the actress

WHY ACTRESSES IN 1660?

Some time during the last months of 1660, a professional English actress appeared in a play on the English public stage for the first time – a historic moment for English theatre. While Englishwomen may occasionally have performed in public entertainments such as mystery plays as early as the fifteenth century,[1] they were never regularly employed in the commercial theatre in any capacity until the Restoration. The exact date of the actress's debut is not known, but is usually assumed to be 8 December 1660, when it is known that a woman played Desdemona in a production of *Othello* by Thomas Killigrew's King's Company. A special prologue was written by the poet Thomas Jordan 'to introduce the first Woman that came to act on the stage in the tragedy called the Moor of Venice': 'The Woman playes today, mistake me not, / No Man in Gown, or Page in Petty-Coat.'[2] A week later one Andrew Newport wrote to Sir Richard Leveson that 'upon our stages we have women actors, as beyond seas'. On 3 January 1661 Pepys recorded his visit to *The Beggar's Bush* by the King's Company that day was 'the first time that ever I saw Women come upon the stage'.[3]

The possible reasons for the advent and public acceptance of actresses at this particular time continue to preoccupy scholars. It was certainly not the case, as some have assumed, of women being automatically superior to boys in the performance of female roles. English theatre finally relinquished a ludicrous convention many years after France, Italy and Spain (women were acting in these countries by the latter half of the sixteenth century).[4] For the twentieth-century theatre-goer, accustomed to seeing actresses, it might be easy to agree with Colley Cibber that the removal of boys playing women instantly transformed theatre for the better:

The other Advantage I was speaking of, is, that before the Restoration, no Actresses had ever been seen upon the English Stage. The Characters of Women, on former Theatres, were perform'd by Boys, or young Men of the most effeminate Aspect. And what Grace, or Master Strokes of Action can we conceive such ungain Hoydens to have been capable of?[5]

One modern commentator quotes Cibber's words approvingly, adding, 'for the first time ever, English playwrights could write women's roles for women, giving them the same weight and complexity in the overall fabric of their plays as the male characters'. Another theatre historian declares that 'the slightest imaginative consideration of the problem [of boys as women] will show that the awakening stage sorely needed a change in this essential factor'.[6] However, the Renaissance transvestite convention was in fact very successful. The parts written for boys by Shakespeare, Middleton, Webster and others suggest that these performers were highly skilled and well able to perform a wide range of leading, challenging female roles. For contemporaries, the boys seem to have been as effective in every way as we now find women. For example, a spectator watching *Othello* performed by the King's Men in 1610 was absolutely convinced and overwhelmed by the acting of the boy playing Desdemona:

They also had their tragedies, well and effectively acted. In these they drew tears not only by their speech, but also by their action. Indeed Desdemona, killed by her husband, in death moved us especially when, as she lay in her bed, her face alone implored the pity of the audience.[7]

The writer here significantly refers always to Desdemona by a feminine pronoun: '*she* lay in *her* bed', '*her* face implored' and so on. Unquestionably, boy or not, she *was* a woman to him.

With an eighteen-year gap in theatre production after the theatres were closed in 1642, there was of course a shortage of boy-actresses when they reopened in 1660. As the *Actor's Remonstrance*, a pamphlet of 1643 put it, 'our boyes, ere we shall have libertie to act againe, will be grown out of use like crackt organ pipes, and have faces as old as our flags'.[8] Nevertheless, while a lack of suitable boys may have precipitated an abrupt change to actresses, this does not explain why the change was considered desirable in the first place. The theatre of 1660 certainly possessed one outstanding female impersonator in Edward Kynaston (Pepys described him as 'the prettiest woman in the whole house'[9]) and there were several others. Had theatre-goers so desired, more could presumably have been trained. The reasons for the shift from boys to women were social and cultural rather than practical.

The acceptance of women players after 1660 has been related to a profound change in contemporary attitudes to women, female sexuality and theatre among the upper and upper-middle classes in the late seventeenth century. Whereas during the late sixteenth and early seventeenth centuries female sexuality and theatrical representation were both subject to vigorous attack, after 1660 they were positively relished: 'the infinite variety of the theater, and the infinite variety of the seductress...grew to be celebrated rather than condemned'.[10] This shift in attitude can be linked to a wider change in how relationships between the sexes were defined. As the seventeenth century wore on, a new model of sexual relations became increasingly accepted, in which the woman as well as the man was entitled to full and adequate individuality. Rather than being considered merely inferior to man, woman began to be defined as the opposite, yet indispensable sex, excluded from the male spheres of public and professional life but vital in the field of domestic management – her own private sphere of home and children. Although the working actress was an exception to the typical domestic female, she was subject to the same ideological constraints and her gender difference was emphasised (and enjoyed) by constant reference to her sexuality, both on stage and off.

However, while this theory explains the public support for actresses after 1660, it fails to take into account the fact that female actors had actually gained considerable currency and even a token acceptance in court culture during the first half of the seventeenth century. Queen Anne and her ladies took prominent roles in the great Jacobean masques of Jonson and Inigo Jones and such female activity increased after Henrietta Maria married Charles I and took to the stage in 1626. It has recently been discovered that the first time that the word 'actress' was used with the meaning 'female player on the stage' was not, as the *OED* states, in 1700, but directly after Queen Henrietta Maria's first court performance in a French pastoral on Shrove Tuesday, 1626: in a contemporary account of the performance Sir Benjamin Rudyerd referred to the queen as a 'principal actress'.[11] Women continued to act at court and in some private houses, and with William Prynne's attack on women actors as 'notorious whores' in the Puritan tract *Histriomastix* (1633), the issue became a subject of debate in a wide range of texts.[12] Prynne's condemnation was taken by the court as a direct criticism of Henrietta Maria when *Histriomastix* was published, just weeks before the queen acted in William Montague's drama *The Shepherd's Paradise*. A number of plays of the 1630s refer to the topic, usually making some kind of satiric attack on the would-be female actor, or ridiculing the affected French taste of those who would support her. For example, in James Shirley's *The Ball* (1632), a satiric comedy of London town life, the buffoon Jack Freshwater complacently shows off his knowledge of Paris and its customs by declaring that there 'women are the best actors, they play their own parts, a thing much desired in England by some ladies, inns o'court gentlemen, and others'. Shirley is clearly mocking those who favour the idea of actresses and inviting his audience to join him. 'Some ladies' presumably refers to the queen and her followers.[13]

What needs to be explained is why, although women acted during the 1630s in court privacy, they were not generally accepted and, indeed, why there were no actresses on the public stage, whereas in 1660 actresses were both introduced and welcomed in the public theatre. The answer lies in the fact that although both before and after the Civil War support for the actresses came from the court, the relationship between court and public theatre in the two periods is strikingly different.

In the Caroline period theatre at court and other theatres in London, both private and public, were emphatically separate. Although the private Caroline theatres outside the court – Blackfriars, the Phoenix and Salisbury Court – have traditionally been seen as extensions of the court theatre, that is, as a narrow, exclusively royalist milieu, in actual fact this was very far from the case. 'The theatre audiences, while not lacking strong links with the court, were themselves drawn from those same parliamentary classes from which the political challenge to Charles in 1640 would come.'[14] Although spectators at the private theatre were principally gentry, they comprised a much broader social and geographical group than did the Restoration theatre audience: they even included a number of Puritans. The difference between this audience's opinion of female players and that of the Caroline court is vividly illustrated by their very different reactions to the visit of a troupe of French actresses to London in November 1629. When these performers appeared at Blackfriars, they were apparently 'hissed, hooted, and pippin-pelted from the stage'.[15] While the dislike was probably partly due to xenophobia and professional jealousy, the violence of the reaction suggests that for many theatre-goers the sight of women acting and speaking on the public stage represented an outrageous rupture of social as well as theatrical convention. However, in stark contrast immediately after this incident, Henrietta Maria entertained the French troupe at court and then recommended to her husband that they visit Whitehall.

During the Interregnum, when the theatres were closed, Royalist support for actresses must have been strengthened, since the court spent much time in exile on the Continent where actresses had long been an accepted feature of theatre. Charles II and his court (including at various times William Davenant and Thomas Killigrew to whom the patents to open theatres were granted in 1660) spent some considerable time in Paris taking part in court masques as well as attending plays. The theatre manager George Jolly, who also went into exile, even had the distinction of introducing female players to Frankfurt, where Charles II apparently saw them when he visited the town in September 1655.[16] When Sir William Davenant eventually returned to London he used a female singer, Mrs Coleman, in a private production of his opera *The Siege of Rhodes*, some time in the late 1650s.

Thus it is not surprising to find women players being introduced as soon as the king returned to power in 1660 and granted permission for two theatres to open. Now, because the Restoration theatre was more exclusively a court milieu than it had been in the Caroline period, actresses were readily accepted by theatre audiences. Although, as we have seen, Restoration spectators were by no means exclusively aristocratic, the vast majority of them, even if they were professional men like Pepys, favoured the court and shared its attitudes and interests. Charles II was more closely involved with the public theatre, as opposed to the court theatre, than any other English monarch, and where he went his supporters followed. The Restoration theatre was a coterie theatre, not as small a coterie as was once believed, but a coterie none the less, in contrast to the more mixed theatre before 1642. It was within the select atmosphere of a particular social group that the first English actresses were introduced and flourished.

Some time around 21 August 1660, when the king granted them a London theatre monopoly, Killigrew and Davenant both seem to have recruited and begun to train a handful of actresses. A petition

addressed to the king by a group of players on 13 October 1660
mentions that they had been obliged by Killigrew to act under his
management 'with women'. Davenant's agreement with the chief
players of his company, dated 5 November 1660, included a clause
that seven shares were to go to Davenant 'for maintaining the
actresses of the company'.[17]

In 1660 Davenant certainly recruited six actresses: Hester Davenport, Mary Saunderson, Jane Long, Anne Gibbs, Mrs Jennings
and Mrs Norris. Four of these were boarded at his own premises
adjacent to his new theatre. Killigrew probably acquired at least four
actresses at the start: Katherine Corey, Anne Marshall, Mrs Eastland
and Mrs Weaver.[18] It is presumably one of these four who played
Desdemona in the King's Company's historic production of *Othello*
on 8 December 1660. Anne Marshall seems to be the most likely
candidate. Although Mrs Eastland's name appears on the prompter
John Downes' list of Killigrew's original actresses and there is no
reason to dispute this, her name appears on no dramatis personae
until 1669 and she only ever played minor parts. Mrs Weaver, also
known as Elizabeth Farley, played bigger roles than Mrs Eastland
later on, but never lead roles, and she usually performed in comedy.
Although in 1689 Katherine Corey described herself as 'the first and
is last of all the actresses that were constituted by King Charles the
Second at His Restoration' in a petition to the Lord Chamberlain,[19]
this simply means that she was the first woman sworn in as a servant
of the king, or that she was the first actress recruited by Killigrew. Her
casting as Desdemona is extremely unlikely: she was large and plain
and later specialised in ugly, comic parts. Anne Marshall, on the
other hand, was both talented and attractive; from 1661 she played
lead roles such as the Lady in Beaumont and Fletcher's *The Scornful
Lady* and she soon came to specialise in tragedy.

In his haste to get his actresses on the stage before those of his rival
Davenant, Killigrew may have had them perform in public before
they were ready. Only four weeks after *Othello*, Pepys complained
that a production of Middleton's *The Widow* by the King's Company
on 8 January 1661 was 'wronged' by the women not knowing their
lines. Four weeks of more rehearsal and the women seem to have
improved; when Pepys saw Killigrew's production of *The Scornful
Lady* on 12 February 'now done by a woman', this 'makes the play
appear much better than ever it did to me'.[20] Progress was rapid so
that by the middle of 1661 actresses were an established feature of the
English stage.

During the early months of the theatre's reopening, male actors continued to play women as well. On 18 August 1660 Edward Kynaston (who seems at the time to have been the most proficient and experienced performer of female roles in England) played the Duke's sister in *The Loyal Subject*, prompting Pepys to record delightedly that he made the most beautiful woman in the theatre, although his 'voice not very good'. However, Kynaston was already playing male as well as female parts. For instance, on 6 December he played Otto in *The Bloody Brother*, having played the heroine Arthiope in the same play only a few weeks before. On 7 January 1661, three days after he had seen a woman on the stage for the first time, Pepys saw Kynaston play Epicene in Jonson's comedy.

Kynaston had the good turn to appear in three shapes: I, as a poor woman in ordinary clothes to please Morose; then in fine clothes as a gallant, and in them was clearly the prettiest woman in the whole house – and lastly, as a man; and then likewise did appear the handsomest man in the house.[21]

The casting of Kynaston in this way implies a final effort to extract as much entertainment value as possible from his ability to impersonate women, now that actresses were beginning to supersede him and his kind. The transvestite convention, instead of being the accepted theatrical norm that it had been in the Renaissance, had become a curiosity. In his *Apology* Cibber relates how 'Kynaston, at that time was so beautiful a Youth, that the Ladies of Quality prided themselves in taking him with them in their Coaches, to Hyde-Park, in his Theatrical Habit, after the Play'[22] – Kynaston had become a theatrical freak. On 28 December 1661 he was still playing the eponymous heroine of John Suckling's *Aglaura*, but the 1661–2 season appears to have been the last in which he played female parts, although he remained a successful tragic actor for many years.

At the beginning of 1662 the casting of women in women's roles became not merely the popular choice but law. In a patent dated 25 April 1662 to Thomas Killigrew it was decreed that henceforth women should play women's parts:

And for as much as many plays formerly acted do contain several profane, obscene and scurrilous passages, and the women's parts therein have been acted by men in the habit of women, at which some have taken offence, for the preventing of these abuses for the future, we do hereby strictly command and enjoin that from henceforth ... we do ... permit and give leave that all the women's parts to be acted in either of the said two companies for the time to come may be performed by women, so long as their recreations, which by reason of the abuses aforesaid were scandalous and offensive, may by such reformation be esteemed not only harmless delight, but useful and instructive representations of human life.[23]

The mention of 'some' having 'taken offence' at the wearing of women's clothing by men refers to attacks on the stage by Puritans, like Prynne. Leo Hughes suggests that the Stuarts 'had had enough experience with puritans to insure their taking no chances',[24] and so the weighty language of the patent makes the introduction of women appear as some kind of social reform. In actual fact, of course, the use of female players had the opposite effect to the one specified in the patent – a good deal of the subsequent licentiousness of Restoration drama may be blamed on the sexual exploitation of the actresses. But in any case, whatever its consequences, the change was effected: woman had replaced boys forever in the English public theatre.

THE NEW PROFESSIONALS AND THEIR STATUS

The actresses apparently represent an exception to the general decline in professional opportunities for women after 1660.[25] The job of player was unusual in offering to women a prominent position in a public arena and it has been suggested that 'although the actresses were never as numerous or as well-paid as their male colleagues, they participated extensively in the life of the companies to which they belonged'.[26] However, the theatre was not as exceptional an employer as all that; the generally inferior status of women in the workplace and their exclusion from public power is reflected in the female situation within the companies. Although the number of actresses slowly increased during the two decades after the Restoration, men always outnumbered women by at least two to one. Only very occasionally did the companies apparently employ an unusually high number of women, as in the 1670–1 season when the King's Company contained seventeen players of each sex.[27]

For the first three decades of the period, in spite of the fact that the best actresses were among the most popular of all players, no woman was allowed to become a sharer in either company. After William Davenant's death in April 1668 his widow, Lady Davenant, did become manager of the Duke's Company, remaining in the position until June 1673 when her son Charles was old enough to take over. Lady Davenant seems to have been no token leader, but to have had all the powers of a working manager. John Downes declares that she had 'Rule and Dominion' over the company, while in a lawsuit of

1671 she stated that she 'had, used or exercised the sole Government of the said Theatres... & the appointment of Treasurers and Receivers, making Dividends and ordering of affairs'.[28] Lady Davenant may also have 'positively encouraged women writers and performers and positive images of women in plays',[29] but if she did so, her achievements for the actresses are not easily discernible. In her time, as before, the actresses had the status of hirelings, whose wages were paid along with other costs such as rent, scenery and costumes, before the box-office receipts were divided among the sharers. Married women in any case had their earnings controlled by their husbands – like all wives of the period. Thus an agreement between John and Susannah Verbruggen and the theatre manager Thomas Skipwith, dated 1695, states that 'John Verbruggen agrees that, for a payment of £75, his wife will act in the theatre'.[30] It is not surprising that the two actresses who eventually earned the most, Elizabeth Barry and Anne Bracegirdle, stayed single. (In dramatis personae all actresses were listed with the title 'Mrs', whether married or single.)

The women's wages were significantly lower than the men's. A good experienced actor was usually paid 50s. per week, an equivalent actress only 30s. Even Barry, the most popular of all, was only paid 50s. a week, while her co-star, Thomas Betterton, received £5. The only privilege that the women did receive after a time was liveries, elaborate scarlet cloaks with crimson capes to be worn on state occasions. These liveries made them recognised servants of the king and meant most usefully that they could not be sued or arrested for debt without the express permission of the Lord Chamberlain of the Household. On 30 June 1666, a warrant was issued granting the actresses Rebecca Marshall, Nell Gwyn and others 'foure yardes of bastard scarlet cloath and one quarter of a yard of velvett for their liveryes'[31] and later all actresses received the favour.

However, a very few exceptional actresses were also able to improve both their status and their earning power within the companies simply through their commercial success with theatre-goers, Barry being the prime example. As later chapters will show, Barry became the Duke's Company's main 'draw' and by the 1680s plays were being written around her. This popularity had financial consequences – sometime during the reign of James II, 'in Consideration of the extraordinary Applause, that had followed her Performance',[32] she was granted a benefit, a performance whose

profits went to her alone. Until the division of the United Company
in 1695, Barry remained the only individual player, male or female,
with such a privilege (stars of both sexes were periodically given
benefits after this date). One benefit could increase her yearly income
to more than Betterton's.[33] Barry's outstanding popularity at court
also brought her financial influence within the company. The usual
procedure for payment for performances at court was through a
warrant from the Lord Chamberlain. Barry's name appears on most
of these warrants because the money was assigned to her by the rest
of the players – warrants were often drawn to one member of the
company as assignee for the rest. As Eleanor Boswell says,

> the explanation seems to be...that she was persona grata to someone at
> Court who could secure prompt remittance...a warrant labelled 'Mrs
> Barry £5 for playing in ye Old Batchellr' is shown by the corresponding
> entry in the Accounts of the Treasurer of the Chamber to have been
> payments for the Company.[34]

Barry's popularity at court made her the person to whom performance fees were paid, giving her some authority over her fellow
players, as well as, presumably, a good share of the profits when the
payments were divided up.

While Barry's power within the company seems to have slowly
increased during the 1680s, the decisive moment for her rise in
authority came in 1695 when she took the lead, with Betterton, in the
split away from the United Company. Items on the players' petition
of complaint to the Lord Chamberlain show the individual interests
of Barry and two other leading actresses, Mrs Bracegirdle and Mrs
Verbruggen, represented very clearly. The very first clause, concerning the dubious dealings between Rich, Skipwith and Alexander
Davenant, mentions only one player by name – Barry. Although it
was ostensibly Alexander Davenant who bought his brother's share
in the company patent, it was in fact Rich and Skipwith who paid for
the share, simply making use of Davenant's name. His apparent
ownership of the patent gave Davenant credit among the actors and
'by means of the cheat he was advanced by Mrs Barry some £600 to
£800, and deceived others of the company in a like manner'.[35]
(Barry's financial success is implied by the fact that she was able to
lend Davenant so much!) Barry's other grievances are outlined in
clause 7 of the petition, before those of any of the other players. Her
protest, not surprisingly, is over her benefits: her agreement with the

sharers was for a wage of 50s. a week and a benefit each year. Later she made an agreement that if her profits from the benefit did not come to £70 then that amount should be made up to her. After this agreement had been carried out for a number of years, the patentees began not only to refuse to make up the £70, but also to demand one-third of the profits of her benefit. In clauses 12 and 13 Bracegirdle demanded an annual benefit (she had become as popular with the public as Barry by this time) and Verbruggen requested an extra 5s. per week. While the management did eventually offer some concessions in response to this petition, these came too late for the angry players. They broke away and in March 1695, after a hearing before the king, the three leaders, Betterton, Barry and Bracegirdle, secured a licence to form their own company. Four actresses, Barry, Bracegirdle, Mrs Bowman and Mrs Leigh gained shares in this new company.[36]

A dispute between the main shareholders of the rebel company and the actor John Verbruggen in the late 1690s reveals how great a part Barry and Bracegirdle played in the running of their company and its finances. Verbruggen had left Rich's troupe and joined its rival in 1696 when, according to articles dated 27 October between shareholders Betterton, Barry, Bracegirdle, Bowman, Underhill, Bright and Leigh on one side and Verbruggen on the other, Verbruggen was to get one share and 20s. a week. Around 1698 Verbruggen filed a petition of complaint. He accused Betterton, Barry and Bracegirdle of not allowing the books to be seen and of making huge profits. The preceding Michaelmas he had been told that the company's debts were about £800 and it was agreed that there should be no benefits at all and that all spare money should be used to pay off debts. During the ensuing winter receipts had been particularly large 'ever since the Italian woman hath sung'. However, Verbruggen protested, Betterton, Barry and Bracegirdle pretended that the debts were not yet settled and they stopped Verbruggen's 20s. a week. Betterton had also apparently ordered a benefit for himself with the popular Italian woman singing and she was to sing as well at benefits for Barry and Bracegirdle.[37] Verbruggen seems to have been mollified by concessions from Betterton and the rest soon after, since, in spite of his complaints, he continued to act for the company. The main interest of his petition lies in its attacks against the two actresses. Whether or not Verbruggen's accusations are true, the petition proves that Barry and Bracegirdle had truly acquired managerial status and were able to make the business work in their favour – in striking contrast to the situation of the actress at the beginning of the period.

Barry's remarkable achievement was not, however, without its price. By assuming a public 'masculine' role in theatrical affairs she, like the female playwrights, exposed herself to fierce public ridicule and condemnation. She was perhaps the most famous professional woman of her time in London, possessed of a strong and combative personality. (Her eighteenth-century biographer, Edmund Curll, for instance, relates how she stabbed another actress whom she disliked in a mock fight on stage so fiercely that she pierced the other woman's flesh with her dagger.[38]) Her combination of toughness and success made her the target for some of the most vicious and vituperative satire of the whole period. In lurid language Barry was pictured as a mercenary prostitute, unbounded in her lust for money, prepared to do anything for profit. With scant evidence that she actually *was* a prostitute, the attacks read convincingly as misogynist resentment of a woman who achieved popularity, power and, above all, material success in a public career. For example, the satirist Tom Brown's famous opinion, 'should you ley with her all Night, She would not know you the next Morning, unless you had another five Pound at her Service', often taken as evidence of Barry's licentious character, when read in context is not part of an account of Barry's personality or love affairs at all, but an attack on the power she and Betterton had in the theatre of the early 1690s.

Now for that Majestical Man and Woman there, stand off, there is no coming within a Hundred Yards of their High Mightinesses, they have revolted like the Dutch from their once Lords and Masters and are now set up for Sovereigns themselves. See what a defference is paid 'em by the rest of the Cringing Fraternity from Fifty down to ten Shillings a week; and you must needs have a more than Ordinary Opinion of their Abilities: Should you ley with her all Night, She would not know you the next Morning, unless you had another five Pound at her Service; or go to desire a piece of Courtesy of him, you must attend longer than at a Secretary's of State ... nor will her Celebrated Modesty suffer her, almost to speak to an Humble Servant, without a Piece or two to rub her Eyes with, and to conceal her Blushes, while She Sluggishly goes through a Vacation She might take more Pains in, did she not Grudge a Pennyworth for a Penny.

Significantly, Brown attacks Betterton's pride much less viciously than he does Barry's: the actor merely behaves like a king, *she* is portrayed as a whore. Barry was lampooned in similar terms by the anonymous author of a poem 'To the most Virtuous and most devoted Overkind, Notorious Madm Barry' (1689):

> Retyre thou Miser from thy Shop the Stage
> Retyrement will befit thy Sins and Age:
> The Vitious Treasure thy base ways have gain'd,
> Which for thy Daughters sake was still obtain'd,
> Give to some Pious Use, or thou'lt be damned.[39]

Some nine years earlier Barry had borne her lover the Earl of Rochester a daughter: this satire seems particularly cruel in view of the fact that it was probably written shortly after this child died in 1689.

Barry certainly had several affairs. Rochester was her most famous lover, but there is also evidence to suggest that Sir George Etherege, the Earl of Dorset and Sir Henry St John Bart were briefly his successors. In a letter to William Jephson dated 8 March 1688 the inveterate womaniser Etherege wrote that

Mrs. Barry bears up as well as I myself have done. My poor Lord Rochester could not weather the Cape and live under the line fatal... I am just now going to a Ball where there will be a great many and some pretty, young women, tho' to tell you the truth I have late liv'd as chaste as my Lady Etherege. The best fortune I have had here has been a player something handsomer, and as much a jilt, as Mrs. Barry.[40]

However, the evidence for Barry having a lucrative career as a prostitute or kept woman is nonexistent. Working as hard as she did as an actress, Barry would hardly have had time for a career on the streets as well, and any long-term keepers would surely have been publicised, as Rochester was. All documentary evidence suggests that her income was largely made through acting – hence her interest in carving her share from the company profits. The vicious satires against 'that mercenary Prostituted Dame'[41] represent, above all, a dislike of a remarkable female professional success.

Bracegirdle seems to have escaped a similar fate from the satirists for several reasons. Although also a highly popular star, she was perceived to possess far less power and influence in the theatre than Barry and she was paid significantly less. Her personality was also very different: contemporary accounts suggest a pleasant and charitable personality, retiring rather than aggressive.[42] Most important of all, perhaps, she was famed for chastity rather than love affairs. If she ever had lovers they have remained discreetly hidden, although contemporary speculation about them was rife.

Barry's and Bracegirdle's achievements shed light on both the workings of theatre between 1660 and 1700 and the limitations on working women in general at the time. As exceptions to the majority of actresses Barry and Bracegirdle suggest that in order to succeed in her profession a woman had to be not only outstandingly talented and successful in a sphere which affected male profits, but also persistent, hard-headed and unmarried. Even then there were limits to her power: the actors' republic at Lincoln's Inn Fields ended in 1700 when Betterton took over sole management. Whatever private influence Barry and Bracegirdle may still have possessed after that date, their official status as company managers came to an end after only five years.

THE ACTRESS AS PROSTITUTE

As we have seen, no 'respectable' woman became an actress. Society assumed that a woman who displayed herself on the public stage was probably a whore. Thomas Jordan's prologue 'to introduce the first Woman that came to Act on the Stage' implies that spectators' first reaction would be to wonder about the morals of a woman who allowed herself to pursue such a profession:

> Do you not twitter Gentlemen? I know
> You will be censuring, do't fairly though;
> 'Tis possible a vertuous woman may
> Abhor all sorts of looseness, and yet play;
> Play on the Stage, where all eyes are upon her,
> Shall we count that a crime France calls an honour?[43]

The assumption that the word 'actress' stood for 'prostitute' rapidly became a self-fulfilling prophecy. An unprotected woman would have found it impossible to avoid sexual advances if she worked in the theatre. Men were free to go behind the scenes and watch the actresses dressing: Pepys recorded a visit 'up into the Tireing-rooms and to the women's Shift where Nell [Gwyn] was dressing herself and was all unready; and is very pretty'.[44] On another occasion he encountered Rebecca Marshall and Nell Gwyn off stage just after they had been playing the saintly martyred Dorothea and her guardian angel in Dekker and Massinger's *The Virgin Martyr* and was shocked by the contrast between the stage roles of the two women and their behaviour in real life: 'but Lord, their confidence, and how many men do hover about them as soon as they come off the stage, and how confident they [are] in their talk'.[45]

The actresses had little protection from the men who approached them, for regulations against backstage visitors were ineffectual – males in the audience seem to have ignored such rules entirely. On 25 February 1664, for example, the king issued an order that 'no person of what quality soever do presume to enter at the door of the attiring house, but such as do belong to the company and are employed by them'.[46] Clearly, this order was flouted, as another part of an agreement drawn up between players and managers of the Theatre Royal in 1675 stated:

to avoyd the future inconveniency of strangers frequent Egresse and regresse when a play is done in ye House, it is thought fitt that some one or two be appoynted to stand at the Tyring house Dore till the House is discharged the persons appoynted are David Middleton and Brittaine.[47]

But again there is no evidence of a change in public behaviour as a result of such measures. The actress had no effective protection against male advances – as Tom Brown colourfully put it, "'tis as hard a matter for a pretty Woman to keep herself Honest in a Theatre, as 'tis for an Apothecary to keep his Treacle from the Flies in hot Weather; for every Libertine in the Audience will be buzzing about her Hony-Pot'.[48]

The difficulties of one actress, Rebecca Marshall, underline the vulnerability of the actresses' situation. When Marshall unwisely boasted that she had a 'gracious promise from his Maty [majesty] that shee should not be injured' by the courtier Sir Hugh Middleton, she was set upon on her way home from the theatre by a 'Ruffian' employed by Middleton who flung excrement in her face and hair and 'fled away'.[49] On another occasion Marshall appealed to the king for protection from one Mark Trevor who had 'assaulted her violently in a Coach' and 'pursu'd her with his Sword in his hand', but her attacker appears to have escaped without punishment.[50] Society in general seems to have considered the actress fair game.

Of the eighty or so actresses we know by name on the Restoration stage between 1660 and 1689, apparently about a mere one-quarter of this number led what were considered to be respectable lives. These, like Mary Betterton or Elinor Leigh, were usually married to fellow actors who could presumably protect them to some degree from harassment at the theatre. The remainder, whether they sustained a stage career for a substantial period, or merely trod the boards until a suitable keeper presented himself, were all seen as some form of kept woman. The companies in fact exploited the sexual availability of their women as a means of attracting audiences. As the epilogue to Shadwell's *The Libertine* (1676) put it:

> Item, you shall appear behind our Scenes,
> And there make love with the sweet chink of Guinnies
> The unresisted Eloquence of Ninnies.
> Some of our Women will be kind to you,
> And promise free ingress and egress too.

Whether or not she exploited it off stage, the actress's sexuality – her potential availability to men – became the central feature of her professional identity as a player. It has been observed that contemporary critics and satirists discuss the actress's private life and lovers as 'an extension of her histrionic function'.[51] Thus Colley Cibber's account of Bracegirdle's acting career in his autobiography includes the tribute, 'her Youth, and lively aspect, threw out such a Glow of Health, and Chearfulness, that, on the stage, few Spectators that were not past it, could behold her without Desire'.[52] In his *Roscius Anglicanus* John Downes cannot resist reminding readers of Moll Davis's involvement with Charles II after her performance as Celia in Davenant's *The Rivals*:

And all the Womens Parts admirably Acted; chiefly Celia, a Shepherdess being Mad for Love; especially in Singing several Wild and Mad Songs. *My Lodging it is on the Cold Ground*, etc. She perform'd that so Charmingly, that not long after, it Rais'd her from her Bed on the Cold Ground, to a Bed Royal.

Similarly, in the anonymous critical work *A Comparison Between Two Stages*, a discussion on Barry's performance as Cleopatra includes a passing reference to her off-stage reputation:

SULLEN: Age and Intemperance are the fatal Enemies of Beauty; she's guilty of both, she has been a Riotter in her time, but the edge of her Appetite is long ago taken off.[53]

This preoccupation with the actresses' sexual activities is also highlighted if we compare their treatment in contemporary satire with that of their male colleagues. Partly, no doubt, because Restoration satirists followed misogynist tradition and reserved their most vituperative abuse for women, theatrical satires in general refer in far greater detail to the sexual liaisons of the actresses than to those of actors. For example, Edward Kynaston, Charles Hart and Cardell Goodman were all 'kept' by aristocratic ladies at some stage in their careers, but there is comparatively little contemporary comment on their situation. By contrast, court satires of the period are full of the sexual exploits of the actresses. 'The Session of Ladies' (April 1688) is actually set in a playhouse where, among a variety of lecherous ladies known to the court, Boutell, Cox and Barry compete for the favour of Adonis, the actor Cardell Goodman, who is enthroned upon the stage. The three women players are described thus:

> There was chestnut-maned Boutell, whom all the Town fucks,
> Lord Lumley's cast player, the famed Mrs. Cox,
> And chaste Mrs. Barry, i'th'midst of a flux
> To make him a present of chancre and pox.

Although the poem is centred on female competition for the sexual services of Goodman (the winner being his notorious mistress, the Duchess of Cleveland), it is the women who compete whose sexual habits are luridly described. Similarly 'Lampoons' describes how the actress Mrs Johnson passed through the hands of more than one keeper,

> From Duke and from Lord pritty Johnson is fled
> Thus kindly embraceing her Godfrey she said,
> If plenty of money my dearest had more
> I should not be Counted so Arrant a Whore
> If thou would'st maintaine me I'de not goe astray
> Nor ever receive more rings from Tho: Gray,

and 'Satyr on both Whigs and Toryes. 1683' mentions in passing a liaison between Rebecca Marshall and the famous fop Sir George Hewett, 'With whom as much as our Satyr strives in Vain / As Love, to wound his heart, since Marshal's Reign'.[54]

Even if an actress's private life seemed exemplary, writers focused on her sexuality rather than on her acting ability. Anne Bracegirdle was famed as much, in fact more, for her chastity than for her considerable talent in both tragic and comic roles. As the authors of the *Biographical Dictionary* of players of the period ruefully put it, 'though some critical comments on Anne's acting were made, none, unfortunately, are as extensive as the numerous examinations into her virtue or lack of it'.[55] Tom Brown summed up the attitude of contemporaries when he wrote, in the form of a letter from Aphra Behn to Bracegirdle, that 'The Roman Empress Messalina was never half so famous for her Lust, as you are for your Chastity'. The speakers in *A Comparison Between Two Stages* typically speculate about her personal character:

SULLEN: But does that Romantick Virgin still keep up her great Reputation?
CRITIC: D'ye mean her Reputation for Acting?
SULLEN: I mean her Reputation for not acting: you understand me – [56]

Significantly, Bracegirdle's ability to act professionally as a player is deliberately confused with her 'acting' in the sense of responding to sexual advances. The latter is of more interest than the former.

This constant, even obsessive, emphasis on the actress's sexuality effectively diffused the threat to male society of having women speaking, acting and creating characters on the public stage. As a sexual object she was no danger to the patriarchal system, but rather its toy. As one critic comments bitterly, 'What better place for an aristocrat to exhibit his most recent acquisition than in a public theatre, framed excellently by the proscenium?'[57]

CHAPTER 2

Sex and violence

As performers, the first English actresses were used, above all, as sexual objects, confirming, rather than challenging, the attitudes to gender of their society. 'In practical terms', says Harold Weber, 'the freedom women gained to play themselves on stage was to a large extent the freedom to play the whore.'[1] In this chapter I explore a number of ways in which the sexuality of the actress was exploited by dramatists who wrote for her. In general, such exploitation resulted in a strengthening in the drama of traditional literary representations of women, such as the virtuous woman whose virtue is equated with chastity, passivity and silent suffering, the transvestite heroine who gladly sheds her male disguise to 'dwindle into a wife' at the end of a play and the highly sexual, demonic female who trespasses in some way onto male territory and is soundly punished for her transgression. However, the presence of women in the theatre did not only result in stage pornography and an easy reinforcement of popular female stereotypes. In the outstanding plays of the period the sexual realism provided by the actress helped to promote a fresh, sensitive, and occasionally even a radical consideration of female roles and relations between the sexes. It is important to understand the varied, often ingenious ways in which the actresses' bodies were exploited in the bulk of the drama before we can see how playwrights utilised the sexuality of the female player in a more challenging and exciting way. Because the means of exploitation within the contrasting constraints of the more domestic comedy and high-flown mode of tragedy differ, it is useful to separate the two genres.

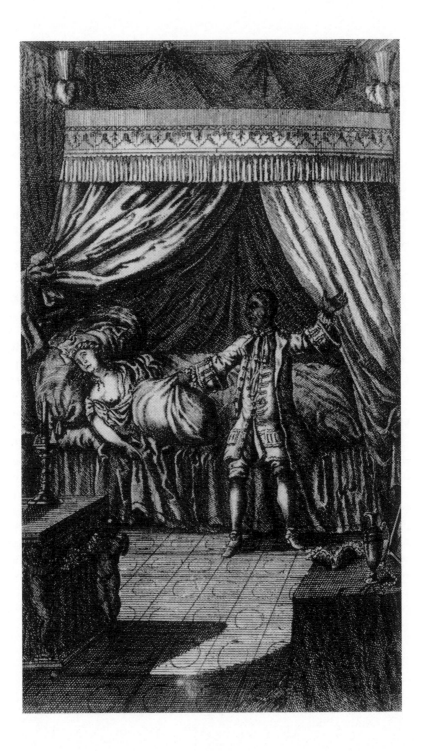

THE ACTRESS AND HER BODY IN TRAGEDY

From the beginning, the conventions that Restoration tragic dramatists chose to follow in respect of their virtuous female characters
tended to emphasise the women's sexuality, passivity and inarticu-
lacy. It is not surprising that the first part known to have been taken
by a woman in tragedy was that of Desdemona. Desdemona is a part
well suited to an alluring emphasis on an actress's femininity: she is
gentle, passive and vulnerable, she is suspected of being a whore and
she is ultimately the victim of horrific bedroom violence. Significantly, the frontispiece illustration to *Othello* in Nicholas Rowe's 1709
edition of the works of Shakespeare shows a bare-breasted Desdemona sprawled across a bed, Othello moving towards her with a
pillow (see plate 2).

A variety of types of Restoration play belong in the large category
of 'tragedy'. In the early years so-called heroic drama predomi-
nated; plays, often in rhyming couplets, focused on an exalted male
figure pursuing glory, love and self-aggrandisement against a
background of war and politics. During the 1670s this type was
slowly superseded by what has come to be termed pathetic, affective
drama – plays seeking to arouse a pitying, involved response, even
tears, in spectators. By the 1680s a whole sub-genre of 'she-tragedy'
had developed from this, centred on a virtuous, suffering female
protagonist (to be discussed in chapter 5). At the same time other
diverse forms were produced throughout the period, such as high
tragedy (like *Othello*), operatic spectaculars, sensational and gory
melodramas and tragicomedy. Many tragedies, of course, share
features of several of these categories.[2] But whatever the type of play,
the heroine's important quality was her beauty. Actresses were
frequently required to do no more than pose, like pictures or statues,
to be gazed upon and desired by male characters in the play and,
presumably, by male spectators. This, for example, was the function
of what I have called 'couch scenes' in plays throughout the period.
Here female characters were directed to lie at a distance, asleep on a
couch, bed or grassy bank where, attractively defenceless and
probably enticingly *déshabillée*, their beauty unwittingly aroused

---

2 Frontispiece engraving to *Othello*, possibly from a Restoration production, in vol.
v, Rowe's *Works of Shakespeare* (1709).

burning passion in the hero or villain who stumbled upon it. A typical use of the device is in John Crowne's *The History of Charles the Eighth of France* (1671) when the hero Charles comes upon the heroine Julia asleep and falls in love with her, to the accompaniment of a passionate love-song performed in the background:

> Yet Oh Ye Powers! I'd dye to gain
> But one poor parting Kiss!
> And yet I'de be on Wracks of pain,
> 'Ere I'd one Thought or Wish retain,
> Which Honour thinks amiss.[3]

In the same year a minor dramatist named Samuel Pordage used the pose to excess in his melodramatic *Herod and Mariamne*, a lurid portrayal of the excesses of that biblical tyrant. In the first act Mariamne, the wife of Herod, is '*discover'd lying on a Couch*' while her desperate lover, Tyridates, declares his passion for her. In Act IV, more sensationally, she appears at first '*lying on a Couch sleeping*' and being watched lasciviously by Herod, and then in a horrible reversal of this reappears on the same couch soon after, beheaded.[4]

The couch scene was not of course an invention of the Restoration playwrights, but a comparison between its use in a play of Southerne called *The Fate of Capua* (1700) and its use in Shakespeare's *Cymbeline* highlights how far the later dramatist converted the device into voyeurism. In *The Fate of Capua* the heroine, a wife named Favonia, is presented '*asleep on a Couch in an undress*', while her husband's friend Junius, who has fallen hopelessly in love with her, stares hungrily:

> – let me fix here –
> Stretch wide the Gates of sight to take her in,
> In the full triumph of her conquering charms.
> My eager Eyes devour her Beauties up,
> Insatiable, and hungring still for more.
> O! the rich Glutton, that enjoys this store!

In *Cymbeline* the villain Iachimo breaks into Imogen's bedroom and watches her sleeping but there is no direct expression of lust

---

3 Frontispiece engraving to *Cymbeline*, possibly from a Restoration production, in vol. VI, Rowe's *Works of Shakespeare*.

comparable to that of Junius for Favonia. Iachimo's most erotic lines
when actually contemplating Imogen are,

Cytherea,
How bravely thou becom'st thy bed! fresh lily,
And whiter than the sheets! That I might touch!
But kiss; one kiss,[5]

and significantly his most sensual lines about his experience – his
account of kissing the mole beneath Imogen's breast – are spoken
afterwards, to her husband Posthumus, *and* he is lying. The erotic
image here is an imaginary one, whereas the Restoration tragedy
staged male lust being directly aroused by a real female body.

Another striking example of female exploitation in tragedy was the
genre's salacious spectacles of blood and violence involving women.[6]
The actresses were indirectly responsible for a wealth of gruesome
suffering right through the period. John Dryden's *Tyrannick Love*
(1669) offered an especially memorable spectacle of female suffering
in its final act. The tyrant Maximin threatens St Catherine with an
appalling death for her mother if she refuses his love. At the climax of
his menaces, '*the Scene opens and shows the Wheel*'. Maximin's
commands gruesomely emphasise the impact of this terrible machine
on the mother Felicia's vulnerable flesh, with particular reference to
her breasts:

> Go bind her hand and foot beneath that Wheel:
> Four of you turn the dreadful Engine round:
> Four others hold her fast'ned to the ground:
> That by degrees her tender breasts may feel
> First the rough razings of the pointed steel:
> Her Paps then let the bearded Tenters stake,
> And on each hook a gory Gibbet take;
> Till th'upper flesh by piecemeal torn away,
> Her beating heart shall to the Sun display.[7]

The account is part of a long and flourishing tradition of sadistic
female martyrdom that began with saints' legends, but in this case
the presence of the victim and the wheel adds a sensational visual
dimension. With real women and elaborate scenery at its disposal,
the Restoration theatre could attach visual detail to a suggestive
description. In this case, at the climactic moment when guards have
seized St Catherine and her mother and are about to strap them to
the wheel, their guardian angel, Amoriel, suddenly descends and
shatters the wheel with his flaming sword. In other dramas women

were not so fortunate. Stabbing was very popular, offering as it did the striking image of a naked bosom spattered with blood. Elkanah Settle's *The Empress of Morocco* (1673) concludes with the empress, Laula, running amok with a dagger before stabbing herself. At the close of Dryden and Lee's *Oedipus* (1678), the mad Jocasta murders her children and the stage directions dictate: '*Scene draws and discovers Jocasta held by her women, and stabb'd in many places of her bosom, her hair dishevel'd, her Children slain upon the Bed.*' Significantly, madness in the drama of the period is almost entirely confined to female characters and is presented as a state in which the victim is rendered helpless, incapable of rational thought. Such madness was a convenient means of forcing female characters to commit entertaining violence against themselves, as in Robert Gould's *The Rival Sisters* (1695) in which Alphanta is brought out '*mad, stab'd in many places*'[8] with stage directions to tear her wounds wider – presumably by tearing her clothes open to reveal more bloody flesh.

Restoration audiences would, of course, be more accustomed to spectacles of naked women suffering violence because of public floggings and pillories. It has been suggested that such experiences, combined with 'inattention and dim lights' must have made blood-covered heroines seem far less shocking than they seem when abstracted by the modern reader.[9] Nevertheless, however shocking these spectacles may or may not have been, the advent of actresses certainly encouraged a great deal of stage violence which was clearly intended to provide a sexual thrill for spectators.

RAPE

The most striking manifestation of sexual exploitation in tragedy is its portrayal of rape. The actresses caused rape to become for the first time a major feature of English tragedy. From 1594–1612, for instance, there are only four plays in which rape actually occurs, and there are only five between 1612 and 1625.[10] However, after 1660, beginning with Thomas Porter's *The Villain* in 1662, rapes occur regularly in plays right into the eighteenth century.[11] Anne Brace-girdle actually specialised in having her virgin innocence brutally taken from her.

Rape became a way of giving the purest, most virginal heroine a sexual quality. It allowed dramatists to create women of such 'greatness' and 'perfect honour'[12] as was felt to be appropriate to

tragedy and heroic drama, but at the same time to exploit sexually the new female presence in the theatre. The contemporary critic and dramatist John Dennis even chauvinistically suggests that the fact that rape involved women being enjoyed against their will made it acceptable not only to lustful males in the audience, but also to those hypocritical lady spectators who would censure sex scenes in comedy:

I would fain know from you...for what Reason the Women, who will sit as quietly and passively at the Relation of a Rape in a Tragedy, as if they thought that Ravishing gave them a Pleasure, for which they have a just Apology, will start and flinch...at the least approach of Rem to Re in Comedy...'tis not the luscious Matter which disturbs them in Comedy, but the secret implicite Satire upon the Sex...a Rape in Tragedy is a Paneygyrick upon the Sex: For there the Woman...is suppos'd to remain innocent, and to be pleas'd without her Consent.[13]

Rape rapidly proved a most effective means of exposing naked female flesh. Dryden's potboiler *Amboyna* (1673) has the heroine, Ysabinda, dragged off stage and raped before being revealed, bound to a tree, her clothes torn, her breasts exposed (her lover comments as he unties her, 'Your Breast is white, and cold as falling snow'[14]). An illustration to the 1735 works of Dryden shows most of her body displayed in this scene (see plate 4).[15] As the device came to be used more frequently it had to be milked to satisfy an audience who had watched so many similar scenes before. Thus by 1696 we find that Mary Pix, in *Ibrahim, The Thirteenth Emperour of the Turks*, has to offer first of all a suspenseful build-up to the rape as the villainous Ibrahim (who has already taken his pick from twenty virgins lined up for his delectation and deflowered her) marches off stage with the resolution, 'I'll rush thro' all and seize the trembling prey', then the appearance of the victim '*her Hair down and much disorder'd in her dress*', and finally an explicit account of the experience related by her father to her lover:

> – suppose
> Her prayers, her tears, her cryes,
> Her wounding supplications all in vain,
> Her dear hands in the Conflict cut and mangled,
> Dying her white Arms in Crimson Gore,
> The savage Ravisher twisting his
> In the lovely Tresses of her hair,

---

4 Frontispiece engraving to *Amboyna* from John Dryden's *Dramatick Works of... 1735*, showing Ysabinda being untied just after her rape.

> Tearing it by the smarting Root,
> Fixing her, by that upon the ground:
> Then – (horrour on horrour!)
> On her breathless body perpetrate the fact.[16]

To illustrate his account, '*The Scene draws and discovers Morena upon the ground disorder'd as before*'. (Interestingly rape was never actually simulated on stage; dramatists extracted more titillation by avoiding a staging of the gruesome details.) Here, as frequently occurred, the novelty of moving scenes, or shutters, in the theatre was combined with the image of a female body in order to provide a thrilling spectacle. Having expressed her wretchedness and raised her bloody hands for justice, the scene finally shuts upon Morena. Such use of the moving scene enhances the sense of the actress's body being offered to the audience as a piece of erotic entertainment – a kind of pornographic painting brought to life.

Even in their adaptations of Shakespeare, Restoration dramatists added gratuitous rapes. In Nahum Tate's notorious version of *King Lear* (1680) Cordelia is seized by lustful ruffians before being rescued by Edgar. The last act of Tate's adaptation of *Coriolanus*, called *The Ingratitude of a Commonwealth* (1681), offers a totally new sequence of sadistic events, including a scene in which Virgilia, the wife of Coriolanus, pleads for mercy from her husband's enemy Aufidius, thereby inflaming him with lust. Aufidius imagines the joys of possessing Virgilia, conjuring up a picture of these for spectators:

> To Lock the tender Beauty in my Arms;
> Blushing, yet Granting; Trembling, and yet Embracing,
> I shall go Mad with the Imagination.[17]

In fact this rape does not take place, but Virgilia is '*brought in wounded*' to bid her husband an agonised farewell. When adapting *Cymbeline* into *The Injured Princess* (1682), Thomas Durfey replaced the very minor part of Helen with a confidante for Eugenia (Imogen) and daughter for Pisanio, named Clarona, in order to provide a new rape sub-plot. When Eugenia escapes from the court, Clarona is blamed and Cloten orders that she be raped and then hanged. Jachimo (a new character, Durfey having renamed Shakespeare's Iachimo 'Shatillion') volunteers to do the deed and drags her out. As with Aufidius, his desire is increased by the victim's pleas for mercy. When Clarona's father appears Jachimo, undaunted, prepares to ravish her in front of him. Both Tate and Durfey used the idea of a rape taking place before the eyes of a loved one to produce an additional thrill.

Again, a comparison between a Renaissance treatment of a device and a Restoration one is instructive in highlighting the move towards voyeurism in the late seventeenth-century theatre's use of actresses. The contrast between Fletcher's *Valentinian* (*c.* 1610) and its typically explicit adaptation by the famous courtier and poet John Wilmot, Earl of Rochester, staged in 1685, vividly illustrates how Restoration drama used rape to promote an image of women as little more than a source of male gratification. Both plays deal with the rape of the virtuous wife Lucina by the Emperor Valentinian, but Fletcher's heroine is a much more vigorous and positive character than Rochester's. Her personality is captured in the first scene of the earlier play when one of the emperor's servants tells how he asked her what she would do if the emperor did rape her and she simply

> pointed to a Lucrece, that hung by,
> And with an angry looke, that from her eyes
> Shot Vestall fire against me, she departed.[18]

When, in the next scene, panders try to tempt her to the emperor's bed, the earlier Lucina resists with similar robustness, 'I charge ye in the name of Chastity, / Tempt me no more' (I.ii.43–4). Rochester, on the other hand, portrays Lucina as much weaker and more passive, as well as paying greater attention to her sexual attractions and Valentinian's lust. His original second scene presents a direct confrontation between the emperor and his victim in which Valentinian dwells at length on his passion for her: 'I in Her Arms such Blessings shou'd obtain, / For which th'unenvy'd Gods might wish in vain.'[19] At the climax of his wooing he '*lays hold on her*' and her defence seems mild, even coy, in comparison with her predecessor's response to the panders: 'Hold, Sir, for Mercy's sake – / Love will abhor whatever Force can take' (p. 8). Fletcher's Lucina shows no interest in 'Love' at all.

Rochester also added a new scene to the third act in which his heroine wanders apprehensively in a '*Grove and Forest*' for no other reason than to ponder anxiously upon her vulnerable state:

> 'tis my wonder how the Pow'rs above,
> Those wise and careful Guardians of the Good,
> Have trusted such a force of tempting Charms
> To Enemies declar'd of Innocence! (p. 28)

With the phrase 'force of tempting Charms' Lucina is made to point up her own seductive attraction, in order to create additional excitement over the coming rape. She also dwells briefly but suggestively on her own pleasure when she imagines it is her husband Maximus who embraces her:

> My longing Arms of th'Embrace they covet:
> Forgive me, Heav'n! if when I these enjoy,
> So perfect is the Happiness I find
> That my Soul satisfi'd feels no Ambition
> To change these humble Roofs and sit above. (p. 28)

Rochester's changes to the climactic rape scene are small but significant. Fletcher's Lucina roundly condemns the words of the obscene songs played at her at the emperor's court as 'lascivious' and 'over-light for Ladies' (II.v.51–2). Rochester's heroine hears the same songs but declares coyly, 'the words, I thank my Gods, / I did not understand' (p. 43). The fact that she is able to 'thank the Gods' implies, of course, that she perfectly understands the obscenity of the lines but is too modest and delicately feminine to show that she understands them. The pimp Chylax comically assures her that the emperor will soon teach her what they mean. Then Rochester added a new stage direction, '*Enter Emperor drawing in Lucina*' and some new, explicitly sensual lines for him:

> For what you are, I am fill'd with such Amaze,
> So far transported with Desire and Love,
> My slippery Soul flows to you while I speak. (p. 44)

Then, after Lucina is led out, the Restoration Valentinian arranges for some dancing to take place while the rape is being committed. He warns his servant Lycinus, 'And if by chance odd noises should be heard, / As Women's Shrieks, or so, say, 'tis a Play / Is practising within.' Lycinus responds aptly, 'The Rape of Lucrece, / Or some such merry Prank – It shall be done Sir' (p. 46). At last Valentinian retires to do the deed, assuring himself 'I'll plunge into a Sea of my Desires'. The 'scene' then opened to disclose '*5 or 6 Dancing-masters practising*' (p. 46), the audiences highly conscious, as they watched the dance, of the rape taking place off stage. With the dramatic lines from one of the emperor's servants (as in the original), ''Tis done', another backdrop at the back of the stage was removed and '*discovers th' Emperour's Chamber. Lucina newly unbound by th' Emperour*' (p. 48).

Rochester's version of the rape places more emphasis on Valentinian's lust (as a point of identification for male spectators?) and more emphasis on his victim's helplessness. Lucina is '*drawn off*', raped and then '*unbound*'. By contrast, the Fletcher rape is achieved swiftly and without sensationalism – interest is focused more on her bitter lamentation and heroic suicide afterwards. Ironically, the fact that the later version was able to cast a woman as Lucina did not result in greater insight into her feelings, but rendered her more of an object.

SEXUAL RHETORIC

While rape is the most graphic illustration of the exploitation of the actress's sexuality, it comes as no surprise to find that the language used towards and about women in tragedy was also highly erotic. For example, with none of the risk that Shakespeare and his contemporaries ran of a comic disparity between what an audience saw and what it heard, Restoration love scenes were enhanced by strikingly explicit avowals of desire and torrents of sensual language about the female character in question. In Dryden's *Aureng-Zebe* (1675) the hero, reunited with his love, Indamora, after their enforced separation, declares his passion for her thus:

> Oh I could stifle you with eager haste!
> Devour your kisses with my hungry taste!
> Rush on you! Eat you! Wander o'er each part,
> Raving with pleasure, snatch you to my heart!
> Then hold you off and gaze! Then, with new rage
> Invade you, till my conscious limbs presage
> Torrents of joy which all their banks o'erflow![20]

To similar effect precise details of a female character's appearance were sometimes outlined in erotic detail, presumably corresponding to the looks of the actress who took the role. In Nathaniel Lee's *Caesar Borgia* (1679) the actress Mary Lee (no relation) is recreated for us in the Cardinal's sensual celebration of the charms of her character, Bellamira:

> Oh such a skin full of alluring flesh!
> Ah, such a ruddy, moist, and pouting Lip;
> Such Dimples, and such Eyes! such melting Eyes,
> Blacker than Sloes, and yet they sparkl'd fire.[21]

So too the picture of Florimell in Dryden's *Secret Love* (1667): 'such an Ovall face, clear skin, hazle eyes, thick brown Eye-browes, and Hair',[22] we know from portraits to be a description of Nell Gwyn, the actress who played Florimell. The sexual quality of such female descriptions is heightened if they are compared with a description of female beauty in earlier tragedy. The metaphorical account of the

beauty of Amidea in Caroline playwright James Shirley's *The Traitor*
(1631) is wholly abstract:

> Is she not fair,
> Exceeding Beautiful, and tempting, Florio?
> Look on her well. Methinks I could turn poet,
> And make her a more excellent piece than heaven.
> Let not fond men hereafter commend what
> They most admire by fetching from the stars
> Or flowers their glory of similitude,
> But from thyself the rule to know all beauty.
> And he that shall arrive at so much boldness
> To say his mistress' eyes, or voice, or breath
> Are half so bright, so clear, so sweet as thine
> Hath told the world enough of miracle.
> These are the duke's own raptures, Amidea,
> His own poetic flames, an argument
> He loves my sister.[23]

The Duke's raptures are not only generalised, but are here expressed
ironically through another person. Amidea is simply an 'excellent
piece', representing a higher standard of beauty than stars or flowers.
Shirley did not attempt to help the audience visualise the beauty in
physical terms and there is nothing sensual in his chosen adjectives,
'clear', 'sweet' and 'bright'. In contrast, the account of Bellamira is
notably sensual.

   In all the examples so far discussed, the actress's role essentially
resembles that of Indamora – she plays the passive object of male
desire. In time, however, as skilled and popular actresses emerged in
both companies, dramatists began to create more vocal roles for
women in tragedy, roles in which they were allowed to express their
own sexual feelings in detail, rather than merely eliciting such
feelings in the men around them. One of the most extreme instances
of this is the outrageous Homais in Delariviere Manley's *The Royal
Mischief* (1696). Homais is the frustrated wife of the elderly and
impotent Prince of Libardian, consumed with desire for Levan,
Prince of Colchis. Her eunuch paves the way for Levan's seduction by
supplying him with a description of his mistress which is outstandingly explicit, even by Restoration standards:

> How often have I see this lovely Venus,
> Naked, extended, in the gaudy Bed,
> Her snowy breast all panting with desire,
> With gazing, melting eyes, survey your form,
> And wish in vain 't had life to fill her arms.[24]

Homais plans to charm the prince to her bed, although she burns
with so much excitement at the very thought that she fears she will
not properly be able to enjoy herself fully when sexual intercourse
finally takes place. Having succeeded in getting the prince to her
bedchamber, she has herself brought to him, veiled, he kisses her, she
swoons. The shutters are closed as they retire to bed, only to open
again a scene later, to reveal the couple in an appropriately blissful
state. Homais is intoxicated by the experience:

> I've embrac'd a god.
> No mortal sense can guess his excellence,
> Where the divine impress has been
> A pleasing trickling cools through all my veins,
> And tempers into love, what else would be
> Distraction. (p. 239)

Later, she explicitly describes how she took the lead in their sexual
encounter, 'rais'd his longings to their utmost height' and brought
them to 'joys which dye upon my breath unutterable' (p. 240).

Taking the active rather than the traditionally passive female role
in this way (and enjoying sex) gives the impression of Homais having
achieved a new female freedom. Homais has been seen as a
'sympathetically studied femme fatale', whose bloody end (Homais
belongs to the tradition of the lustful villainess who is always
punished by death) is still a triumph: 'it seems her death results more
from sheer excess of energy than from any stab of moral retribution'.[25]
However, this impression of female freedom is surely largely illusory.
Homais dies frustrated in her attempt to strangle Levan (so that she
can take him with her) and her husband is given the last word:
'What mischief two fair guilty eyes have wrought. / Let lovers all
look here, and shun the dotage' (p. 261). Homais' lovemaking seems
ultimately to bring her nothing but failure and death, and the play's
final lines certainly seem to suggest some kind of 'moral retribution'.
If there is a 'feminist' message in this play it is one that can easily be
ignored. Presumably male spectators just relished the erotic spectacle
of Homais' promiscuity – she and her kind can easily be seen as no
more than another variation on the actress as sex object.

VENICE PRESERVED

There are, nevertheless, occasional outstanding exceptions to the
familiar range of limited female sexual stereotypes in tragedy. The
finest tragic drama of the age, Thomas Otway's *Venice Preserved*

(1682), offers Belvidera, a passionate yet virtuous wife whose powerful sexuality is accorded the same attention and the same complexity as that of her husband Jaffeir. Instead of focusing on male desire, with the woman merely existing as its object, Otway realises the feelings of both lovers equally. Belvidera's main role is still to exert her sexual attraction over the men around her, but she does not do so passively and is allowed to articulate fully her own sensual feelings. Unlike Homais, however, Belvidera's sensuality does not brand her a villainess — to the end she is portrayed as a heroine who is stronger and more virtuous than her husband.

Swayed by his best friend, Pierre, Jaffeir becomes involved in a plot to overthrow the Senate of Venice and uses his wife as a hostage with which to prove his sincerity to his fellow rebels; he offers to stab her if he betrays them. A bewildered Belvidera demands an explanation and when she discovers the facts vigorously exerts her erotic power over her husband to make him report the conspiracy to the authorities (her father is a Senator). Divided in his loyalties, Jaffeir is eventually persuaded by his wife's passionate arguments — particularly her account of the attempt of the rebel leader, Renault, to rape her. Although threatened by rape like so many other Restoration heroines, Belvidera turns this to her advantage — the sexual jealousy that the rape engenders in Jaffeir sways him like nothing else. The image of Renault's visit to his wife in her bed haunts him:

> Yes faith, in virgin sheets
> White as her bosom, Pierre, dished neatly up,
> Might tempt a weaker appetite to taste.
> Oh how the old fox stunk, I warrant thee,
> When the rank fit was on him.[26]

Finally he is precipitated into reporting the rebellion by the irresistible effect of Belvidera's caresses:

> Methinks when in thy arms
> Thus leaning on thy breast, one minute's more
> Than a long thousand years of vulgar hours
> ...
>   come, lead me forward now like a tame lamb
> To sacrifice.   (IV.i.82–4, 87–8)

However, Belvidera's own sexual desires are as intense and complex as her husband's. While he alternately holds a dagger to her breast and collapses in her arms, she dominates him and yet also enjoys the role of victim in their relationship, playing masochist to his sadist. When, for example, Jaffeir discovers, after his betrayal of the rebellion, that the lives of the conspirators are not to be spared, and he again draws his dagger on his wife, Belvidera shrinks but then offers her breast to the knife:

> Now then kill me.
> (*Leaps upon his neck and kisses him*)
> While thus I cling about thy cruel neck,
> Kiss thy revengeful lips and die in joys
> Greater than any I can guess hereafter. (IV.ii.409–12)

The play's crude sub-plot further emphasises the sexuality in such exchanges between husband and wife. There is a sordid parallel to Jaffeir's threats of violence as the courtesan Aquilina also draws a dagger on her client, the old masochist Antonio, and kicks him to the ground. The senator's cry as he reaches sexual climax recalls the 'death' that Belvidera craved earlier: 'Ohhh, yet more! Nay then die, I die – I am dead already (*Stretches himself out*)' (V.ii.91–2).

Belvidera is now swayed by Jaffeir and she forcefully begs her father, Priuli, to intercede and save the lives of the rebels. He agrees but his attempts come too late, and at the news of the conspirators' execution Belvidera invites Jaffeir to take her life, making still more explicit the earlier link between his threats to kill her and a masochistic form of lovemaking:

> Yes, and when thy hands,
> Charged with my fate, come trembling to the deed,
> As thou hast done a thousand thousand dear times
> To this poor breast, when kinder rage has brought thee,
> When our stinged hearts have leaped to meet each other,
> And melting kisses sealed our lips together,
> When joys have left me gasping in thy arms,
> So let my death come now, and I'll not shrink from't. (V.ii.117–24)

This time, however, Jaffeir remains firm and is determined to end the relationship, although, as she throws her arms around his neck, he does for a moment play their old game and draw his dagger. As he walks away she begs him to at least leave her the weapon ' Leave thy dagger with me. / Bequeath me something' (V.ii.206–7) – but he refuses. The dagger, symbolic of their whole twisted relationship, is withheld.

However, having joined his friend and fellow conspirator on the scaffold and stabbed himself with the fateful weapon, Jaffeir expresses his abiding love for his wife by a dying request that the bloody knife be sent to her – 'A token that with my dying breath I blessed her' (V.iii.107). Belvidera, meanwhile, goes insane and dies, imagining that her husband and his friend are dragging her with them into the earth. Her penultimate line, 'They have hold on me and drag me to the bottom' (V.iv.28), grimly echoes her earlier vow of love to Jaffeir:

> And may no fatal minute ever part us,
> Till, reverend grown, for age and love, we go
> Down to one grave, as our last bed, together,
> There sleep in peace till an eternal morning.   (V.ii.149–52)

The images of dagger and grave brilliantly symbolise the doom and destruction inherent in the bond between husband and wife based, as it is, not on mutual understanding and respect, but on a mixture of mutual desire and a violent struggle for power and domination. *Venice Preserved* skilfully develops the themes of desire and sexual violence that appear so often in Restoration tragedy. Instead of merely exploiting these themes for crude thrills, Otway probes some of the disturbing implications behind his contemporaries' glib, sensationalistic portrayal of sexual relationships – above all by giving the woman a fully active role. Whereas most Restoration tragedy is centred on a traditional feminine type – frail, passive and victimised – Otway's tragedy offers us a heroine who actively participates in her own terrible destiny. The fact that her destiny is so terrible, her marriage doomed, painfully highlights how limited are sexual relationships in tragedy throughout the period.

COMIC OBJECTS OF DESIRE

'When a Poet flags in writing Lusciously, a pretty Girl can move Lasciviously, and have the same good consequences for the author' – thus noted a cynical Richard Steele, in *The Spectator*.[27] This was certainly true by the time that the so-called 'sex comedy' boom of the late 1670s and early 1680s swept the stage[28] and bedroom scenes involving adulterous wives in a provocative state of semi-nudity abounded. Edward Ravenscroft's highly successful *The London Cuckolds* (1681) offers a delightfully suggestive bedroom scene in which a wife, Arabella, clad only in her nightgown, puts up an attractive token resistance to the advances of her lover Ramble and then hurries off stage to prepare herself for their ensuing romp. Ramble has appeared unexpectedly in her bedchamber and, after announcing that he is going to seduce her, adds, 'Madam, come, your night-dress becomes you so well, and you look so very tempting – I can hardly forbear you a minute longer.' Arabella refuses him in such a way as to encourage him as much as possible, declaring,

Take notice then, thou desperate resolute man, that I now go to my chamber, where I'll undress me, go into my bed, and if you dare to follow me, kiss or come to bed to me; if all the strength and passion a provoked woman has can do't, I'll lay thee breathless and panting, and so maul thee, thou shalt ever after be afraid to look at a woman in the face.

As she exits her maid assures Ramble, 'I'll go and help her to bed, she has nothing but her night-gown to slip off.'[29]

Restoration adaptations of earlier comedies show very clearly the way in which the opportunity for such explicit sex scenes was seized after 1660. Although her plays often assert the rights of women in a patriarchal society, Aphra Behn had no qualms about exploiting her sex in this way and seems to have been especially fond of inserting bedroom scenes and characters in an 'undress' into earlier dramas. For *The Debauchee* (1677),[30] for instance, she extended the original bedroom scene in Act III of Richard Brome's *A Mad Couple Well Match'd* (c. 1637). While Brome simply had '*the Bed put forth, Alicia in it*', Behn directed, '*A Bed-Chamber, Alicia sitting in her Nightgown at a Table undressing her.*' At the end of the scene she had Alicia's husband Saleware lead his wife to bed while Brome had to be content with the cryptic stage direction, '*puts in the bed*', which presumably symbolises some future coupling.[31] A similar alteration was made to Middleton's *No Wit No Help Like a Woman's* (c. 1617), in *The Counterfeit Bridegroom* (1677), again probably by Aphra Behn. In both plays the transvestite heroine substitutes her brother for herself as lover of the passionate widow. However, the final act of the later version offers a new scene in which the widow is '*discover'd sitting on a Bed, in a Nightgown, Noble in Bed, holding her by the Gown*'.[32] He tries to rape her, they struggle and she breaks free. In Middleton's play the couple are never seen in bed together – they simply '*enter confusedly*' after the door to the bedroom is broken down.

BREECHES ROLES

The state of undress was an easy way to entertain audiences, common to both tragedy and comedy. A state of dress could be equally erotic, however, when Restoration playwrights reversed the popular transvestite convention of early seventeenth-century drama and had women dressed as boys. Breeches roles seem to have been designed to show off the female body – there was no question of the actress truly impersonating a man. As the critic Pat Rogers rightly says, 'it was central to the effect that the actress's femininity showed through'.[33] The breeches role titillated both by the mere fact of a woman's being boldly and indecorously dressed in male costume and, of course, by the costume suggestively outlining the actress's hips, buttocks and legs, usually concealed by a skirt. In addition, the revelation of a disguised woman's true sex offered a useful opportunity to show off more of the actress's physique. For example, in Act IV of the sex comedy *Tom Essence* (1677) by Thomas Rawlins, Mrs Monylove is seen '*dressing herself at a Table, having Night-cloaths on her head, in her half Shirt, and her Breeches on*'; while the villainous Vernish feels Fidelia's breasts to discover her identity in one of the best-known comedies of the period, Wycherley's *The Plain Dealer* (1676). In Aphra Behn's tragicomedy *The Younger Brother* (1696), when the disguised page, Olivia, is accused of courting her mistress, Mirtilla '*Opens Olivia's Bosom, shews her Breasts*' to prove her innocence.[34]

Dryden's use of the breeches role in *The Rival Ladies* (1664) is typical. Two women disguised as pages pursue, in competition with each other, the man they love. In the play's first act one of them is discovered bound to a tree and about to be stripped by robbers before he/she is rescued just before her true sex is revealed. On arriving at an inn, both disguised girls make a great fuss about not wishing to spend the night with men and at the end, as they prepare to fight each other, each unbuttons her doublet. One exclaims, 'Two swelling Breasts! a Woman, and my Rival', before tearing open her costume to reveal a similar sight.[35] Prologues and epilogues, direct addresses to the audience given by a popular player at the beginning or end of a performance, pointed up the erotic effect of the transvestite convention used with real women. In the prologue to a hugely successful adaptation of Shakespeare's *The Tempest* (1667) by Dryden and William Davenant, the actress Jane Long, who played the male character Hippolito throughout, warned the audience about this beforehand and added coyly, 'Or if your fancy will be farther led / To find her Woman, it must be abed.' Similarly, the epilogue to the tragicomedy *The Generous Enemies* (1671) by John Corye was spoken by a popular actress with a notorious reputation, Elizabeth Boutell. In spite of the fact that she often played pure heroines Boutell is portrayed in contemporary satire as 'chestnut-maned Boutell, whom all the Town fucks'.[36] Having spent most of the play disguised as a man, Boutell then reminded the audience of what they had thus gained: ''Tis worth Money that such Legs appear, / These are not to be seen so cheap elsewhere.' The last line obviously hints that Boutell's sexual favours might be purchased off stage for a sufficiently generous price.

Breeches roles proved enormously popular with audiences. It has been calculated that of some 375 plays produced on the public stage in London during the period from 1660 to 1700, including alterations of pre-Restoration plays, eighty-nine – that is, nearly a quarter – contained one or more roles for actresses in male clothes. In at least fourteen more plays actresses were required to don male costumes to play roles originally intended for men. This practice does not seem to have been tied to a particular actress, nor to a part of the period. In 1671 Jane Long appeared as Osiris in Settle's *Cambyses*, while as late as 1696 the leading comedienne Susannah Verbruggen appeared as Achmet, a eunuch, in Mary Pix's *Ibrahim, The Thirteenth Emperour of the Turks* (1696), and a minor actress called Mary Kent played Young Fashion in Vanbrugh's popular comedy *The Relapse*. In addition, there were many revivals of older plays with breeches parts originally played by boys, such as Beaumont and Fletcher's *Philaster*. Almost every actress appeared at some time or other in a breeches role.[37] It is hardly surprising to find breeches roles inserted quite gratuitously into a production. For example, John Crowne's adaptation of Shakespeare's *Henry VI Parts II and III, The Misery of Civil-War* (1680), contains a new and entirely unnecessary mistress for Henry's son Edward, the Lady Elianor Butler. who pursues him to the battlefield and eventually '*appears in man's habit, challenges Edward and falls*'. At the end of the performance of *The English Princess* by John Caryll, Moll Davis was sent on stage to dance a jig and announce the next day's play. As Pepys put it, 'it came in by force only to please the company to see her dance in boy's clothes'.[38]

Taking the popularity of female breeches roles to an extreme, three plays were apparently produced with all-female casts during June

1672: Killigrew's *The Parson's Wedding*, Dryden's *Secret Love* and Beaumont and Fletcher's *Philaster*. (According to *The London Stage*, Killigrew also prepared his *Thomaso* for an all-female production in the autumn of 1664, for which the intended cast list survives. We have no evidence that this production was actually staged.[39]) The prologues and epilogues to the three plays furnish ample evidence of the provocative intention behind the all-female casting. The prologue to *Secret Love*, another spoken by Boutell, states:

> Accept us these bad times in any dress.
> You'l find the sweet on't, now old Pantaloons,
> Will go as far, as formerly new gowns,
> And from your own cast Wigs, expect no frowns.
> The ladies we shall not so easily please.
> They'l say what impudent bold things are these,
> That dare provoke, yet cannot do us right.

The most openly obscene is the epilogue to *The Parson's Wedding*, which suggests, jokingly, that the boy-actors sold their sexual favours to homosexuals:

> When boys play'd women's parts, you'd think the Stage
> Was innocent in that tempting Age.
> No: for your amorous Fathers then, like you,
> Amongst those Boys had Play-house Misses too:
> They set those bearded Beauties on their laps,
> Men gave 'em Kisses, and the Ladies Claps.
> But they, poor hearts, could not supply our room:
> While we, in kindness to ourselves, and you,
> Can hold our Women to our Lodgings too.

The actresses, the audience is assured, can be far more effective whores. The epilogue then discusses why women cannot always replace men in male roles and decides it must be because the women in the audience would be unable to find lovers:

> The Madams in disguise would steal no more
> To th'young Actors Chambers in mask'd Faces,
> To leave Love off'rings of Points and Laces.
> Nor can we Act their Parts: Alas! too soon
> You'd find the cheat in th'empty Pantaloon.
> Well; though we are not Women's-Men, at least
> We hope to have your Gallants constant Guests.

The epilogue concludes with an offer to set up another theatre and to turn the present one into a brothel for the benefit of the gentlemen:

> We will return your kindnesses this way:
> We'll build up a new Theatre to gain you,
> And turn this to a House to entertain you.[40]

Critical opinion is divided as to how subversive, both before and after 1660, transvestite roles in comedy might be. While one critic, for instance, argues that 'transvestite disguise in Shakespeare does not blur the distinction between the sexes but heightens it', another sees male disguise as attacking 'narrow' stereotypes.[41] After 1660 it has been suggested that breeches roles became more subversive – because 'the female transvestite role is played by a female performer, and the play too may be written by a woman' so 'mockery of male behaviour is now likely to be prominent, and the balance of power is significantly altered'.[42] However, the weight of evidence for this period points, as I have shown, to a minimal shift in the balance of power: breeches roles became little more than yet another means of displaying the actress as a sexual object. Even in those plays where the device does not blatantly exploit the actress's physical attractions, transvestite roles rarely seem to have been written in a way which might disturb male spectators. In most cases a woman dons male disguise as an unnatural action caused by some obstacle to her marrying her lover or otherwise getting her own way. Once her wishes are met she almost invariably returns, like her Renaissance predecessor, to a conventional female role at the end of the play. While a number of heroines are frankly uneasy in men's clothes (see, for instance, Fidelia in Wycherley's *The Plain Dealer*), even characters who thoroughly enjoy impersonating men (such as Florella in William Mountfort's *Greenwich Park* of 1691 or Annabella of George Powell's *A Very Good Wife* of 1693) return to some kind of wifely subservience at the end of their dramas.[43]

An unwillingness to seriously challenge the male status quo is even perceptible in the most potentially 'feminist' transvestite role of the period – that of Lucia in Southerne's remarkable comedy *Sir Anthony Love* of 1690 (this play most obviously supports arguments in favour of the subversiveness of Restoration breeches roles). In this highly successful play Southerne exploited the idea of woman as man more fully than any of his contemporaries. In male garb Lucia, or Sir Anthony Love as she calls herself, proves a sharper wit, a better intriguer and a more skilful seducer than the gallants she makes her companions. She organises all the action in the play and, except for the act of sex itself of course, can do everything men do in society and do it better. In her disguise she also satirises male behaviour, showing, for instance, that as a man she need never show real courage, but merely swagger about seeming brave, while avoiding actual fighting wherever possible:

Why 'tis only the Fashion of the World, that gives your Sex a better Title than we have, to the wearing a Sword; my Constant Exercise with my Fencing Master, and Conversation among men, who make little of the matter, have at last not only made me adroit, but despise the Danger of a quarrel too.[44]

Similarly, she mocks the male habit of boasting of one's sexual conquests without any genuine seductions to back up the claims. She is one of those

who beat about more for Company, than the pleasure of the Sport; and if they do start any thing, are better pleas'd with the accidents of the Chase, the Hedges, and Ditches, than the close pursuit of the Game; and these are sure never to come into the Quarry. (I.i.34–9)

Most important of all, unlike all other Restoration transvestite heroines, she has no interest in marrying her lover, Valentine, ultimately. At the end of the play she gives him to another woman, Floriante, for a husband, herself preferring to remain his mistress – a position in which she ironically considers she has a better chance of retaining his love, as well as keeping her own independence. Her protests against marriage are not a cautious female defence against man's inconstancy, they are genuine: 'I am for Universal Empire, and wou'd not be stinted to one Province; I wou'd be fear'd, as well as lov'd: As famous for my Action with the Men, as for my Passion for the Women' (I.i.11–14). Instead of wedding Valentine in the final scene, she tricks her old keeper, Sir Gentle Golding, into marrying her and, when he realises his mistake, she gains £500 a year from him for a separation.

However, for all her radicalism, Sir Anthony offers no real threat to the established social order. Her decision to remain single is carefully contrasted with four conventional marriages at the end; she is a freak rather than the norm. The comedy is set in remote and exotic 'Mompelier', not Restoration London, which also suggests an element of fantasy. In any case Sir Anthony is, it must be admitted, not so much a 'feminist hero' as an amoral trickster and prostitute, exploiting the corruptions and deceptions of society in her favour.[45] The character she most resembles in the play is the Pilgrim, its greatest rogue, who lives permanently in his pious disguise for profit. Sir Anthony recognises him as a professional cheat like herself: 'Tho' you pass upon the Abbé, and other Fools, I expected you wou'd have open'd your self to me: I profess my self, what I thought you were under your habit, a Rogue: We might have been of use to one another' (III.i.50–3). Palmer, the Pilgrim, significantly treats Sir Anthony as one of his own kind, 'I am errant a Rogue as you can be; a shifter of Shapes and Names; have travell'd through every Profession, and cheated in all' (III.i.98–100). Although Sir Anthony is neither passive nor conventional, she is no advertisement for her sex either.

A lack of subversion in the play appears more than anywhere else in the epilogue, a suggestive address by Charlotte Butler, the actress who played Floriante (the comedy's conventional heroine who finally marries Valentine). In addition to a 'sweet ton'd Voice' and a 'manner of blending her assuasive Softness, even with the Gay, the Lively, and the Alluring', Butler also had, according to contemporary satires, a reputation for loose morals:

> Fam'd Butler's Wiles are now so common grown
> That by each Feather'd Cully she is known
> So that at last to save her Tott'ring Fame
> At Music Club she strives to get a Name
> But mony is the Syren's cheifest Aym.
> At Treats her sqeamish Stomach cannot bear
> What Amorous Spark Provides with Cost and Care,
> But if She's hungry, faith I must be blunt
> Sh'l for a Dish of Cutlets shew her C--t.[46]

Butler's epilogue cheerfully reinforces the familiar image of the actress as sexual object. Sir Anthony, it reassures spectators, simply constituted another chance to see a good pair of women's legs,

> You'l hear with Patience a dull Scene, to see,
> In a contented lazy waggery,
> The Female Mountford bare above the knee.
>
> (Epilogue, 14–16)

The lines suggest, ironically, that the fact that a woman, rather than a boy, played Sir Anthony could make the character not more, but far less, disturbing. Men could ignore, or laugh indulgently at Lucia's prowess, while relishing the spectacle of Mountfort 'bare above the knee'. The epilogue continues by making a joke of Sir Anthony:

> She's all for Womankind, and aws the Town,
> As if her Husband's Breeches were her own.
> She's been to Night our Hero, tho' a Female,
> Show me but such a Whoremaster, tho' a Male.
>
> (Epilogue, 19–22)

Butler then mocked old men in the audience who professed to be great ladykillers, but were in fact all talk and no action, finally promising that she and her kind (presumably other actresses) would conceal such men's impotency so long as they paid well:

> Supply our Wants, and we'll conceal all yours.
> No matter what you can, or cannot do,
> You shall cheat others still, if we cheat you:
> Keep us but rich, and fine, and we shall find
> Young Lovers, always able to be kind.   (Epilogue, 34–8)

The image here is once again that of the actress as prostitute, and this was the image spectators were finally left with at the end of their evening's entertainment.

Significantly, the play proved highly popular with both sexes. Although in the play's dedication Southerne acknowledges the ladies' support for the play in particular, 'I am gratefully sensible of the general good Nature of the Town, to me…But I must make my boast…of the Favours from the Fair Sex…in so visibly promoting my Interest, on those days chiefly (the Third and the Sixth) when I had the tenderest relation to the welfare of my Play [i.e. his benefits]' (Epistle Dedicatory, 32–9), other contemporary comments make it clear that everyone liked the comedy. Langbaine writes that *Sir Anthony Love* 'was acted with extraordinary Applause', while the *Gentleman's Journal*, when it reviewed Southerne's next comedy, *The Wives' Excuse*, identified its author as 'Mr. Southerne, who made that call'd *Sir Anthony Love* which you and all the Town have lik'd so well'.[47] Men clearly enjoyed the play as much as women.

THE ACTRESSES AND COMIC CHANGE

The drama's exploitation of the actresses' sexuality played an important part in determining the nature of comedy between 1660 and 1700. The decline in the popularity of Shakespearian comedy and the cynical focus on adultery, inconstancy and conflict in

Restoration comedy can partly be attributed to the provocative use of the actress and society's view of her as whorish, fickle and sexually available.

In her comparison between Shakespeare's *The Tempest* and the Dryden–Davenant version of 1667, Katherine Maus pinpoints a major cause of the decline in support for Shakespeare's style of romantic comedy after 1660. The massive social and political changes between the beginning of the seventeenth century and its end meant that the magical sense of wonder and harmony on which Shakespearian comedy is often based was no longer possible: these things were the product of a confident acceptance of a relatively stable social and political order. Although such order was questioned, to varying degrees, by Shakespeare and his contemporaries, their scepticism cannot be compared with the profoundly traumatic disruption created by the English Civil War and the new terms on which the monarchical system of government after 1660 was based. Thus, for instance, Maus points out that all sense of a possible Arcadian ideal in Shakespeare's *Tempest* was ruthlessly removed in the more political and highly cynical Restoration version: 'while the original Prospero dreams of a world in which repression is unnecessary, the Restoration Prospero, entirely devoid of the Arcadian impulse, dreams instead of a world in which repression is merely unproblematic'.[48]

However, the cynicism and lack of harmony in the Dryden–Davenant *Tempest* is particularly evident in its presentation of women and of relations between the sexes, and this is best explained by its use of actresses rather than boys. Here, played by an actress whom the audience perceived as sexually experienced and available,[49] Miranda's purity and ignorance of the male sex become a huge suggestive joke, her naiveté merely an opportunity for innuendo. Dryden and Davenant gave her an equally naive sister, Dorinda, in order to increase the possibilities for such innuendo – the two discuss the strange creature, man, and display a comically smutty ignorance of the facts of life. In a new scene in Act I Miranda declares to Dorinda of the male phenomenon, 'I know no more than you: but I have heard / My father say we Women were made for Him.' Similarly, the two girls speculate on the mystery of how they came into being: 'I think he found us when both were little, and grew within the ground.'[50]

The adapters also added Hippolito, a lover for Dorinda who has never seen a woman before and therefore furnishes fresh scope for 'innocently' salacious sex talk, and Sycorax, the mother of Caliban. Trinculo courts Sycorax and she makes grotesque advances to him, promising to produce him children. Sycorax is as ignorant as Hippolito of conventional morality and would like to marry and copulate with three other sailors as well as Trinculo. As Hippolito and Ferdinand quarrel over Miranda, Stephano and Trinculo fight for possession of Sycorax.

Contemporary attitudes to the actress in a sense demanded that the female characters in *The Tempest* be portrayed, not as Shakespeare's Miranda is, as a chaste ideal, but with a cynical recognition of the nature of the real women who would be playing them. Whereas Shakespeare's Prospero preaches pre-marital chastity to his daughter, Miranda and Dorinda are advised to exercise the same caution in their treatment of men as the heroines of Restoration social comedy. Dorinda, for example, should not allow Hippolito to touch her naked hand: 'It is the way to make him love you more; / He will despise you if you grow too kind' (III.i.136–7). Similarly, Prospero preaches to Hippolito the contemporary belief, reflected in both poetry and drama, that love once consummated never lasts – when Hippolito grows older he will no longer care for Dorinda. It is not surprising that Davenant's Miranda, unlike her predecessor, is full of anxiety over whether or not Ferdinand will be faithful: 'for I will dye when you are false' (IV.i.42). On his part, Ferdinand is suspicious that Miranda is at heart a Restoration coquette:

> It is too plain: like most of her frail Sex, she's false
> But has not learnt the art to hide it;
> Nature has done her part, she loves variety:
> Why did I think any Women could be innocent.   (IV.i.105–8)

The Dryden–Davenant *Tempest* highlights the kind of impact that the actress had on comic drama – an impact which has been defined as 'a persistent element of cynicism both in writing and performance that surpassed anything that had gone before'.[51] The negative consequences of this impact are obvious. As in tragedy, women in comedy were reduced at times to being no more than the objects of male desire – 'many comedies ... allow their female characters hardly any inner lives, presenting them simply as prizes the men must win: this is especially true of the most sexually explicit plays'.[52]

However, the satiric, unromantic presentation of love relationships encouraged by the new female players also had positive results. Restoration comedy's forceful scrutiny of social problems concerning women, such as arranged marriage, the double standard and divorce is not solely a consequence of a change in political and philosophical climate; it is also a consequence of a changed approach to female characterisation that the sexual exploitation of the actress made necessary. As the Dryden–Davenant *Tempest* shows, society's view of the actress discouraged an idealised presentation of true love moving smoothly to an unequivocal happy ending, fostering instead, in the best writers, a harsh, yet subtle appraisal of the complexity of relations between the sexes. The finest comedies of the age – Wycherley's *The Country Wife*, George Etherege's *The Man of Mode*, Aphra Behn's *The Rover*, Southerne's *The Wives' Excuse*, Vanbrugh's *The Provok'd Wife*, William Congreve's *The Way of the World* – all offer sensitive explorations of sexual conflict and are a product of the new theatrical climate, cynical, critical, socially acute. 'The new actresses' may not have brought 'a feminine delicacy or compassion to the relationships between characters', as one critic puts it,[53] but in some cases they brought a satiric honesty which was just as good.

CHAPTER 3

The actress, the dramatist and comedy

The Restoration theatre has been called an 'actors' theatre'.[1] As we have seen, almost all dramatists wrote their plays for one specific company, tailoring roles in accordance with the 'lines' of the players within that company. Casting was something that happened before, rather than after, a play was written, and so the presence, and the disappearance, of popular and talented actresses changed and shaped the course of the drama to a degree which has gone unrecognised. The close relationship between drama and actress is vividly illustrated if we survey the writing of female roles in comedy between 1660 and 1700 in terms of the women who came and went in each company during those years.

NELL GWYN AND THE CREATION OF THE GAY COUPLE

The creation of the so-called 'gay couple' has been called 'the most distinctive new contribution to comedy of the 1660s, the first new change in the comic form in the Restoration'.[2] The typical 'gay couple' consists of a pair of lively, witty lovers whose love contains an element of antagonism – each desires the other but is wary of commitment. The male, who is generally a rakish gallant, dislikes the notion of marriage because it entails a loss of freedom; the lady appears to distrust marriage for the same reason, but is usually using her apparent dislike of the commitment to keep her lover at bay until she is sure that his motives are honest. This mutual antagonism is expressed through a battle of wits and repartee by which they test one another's affection. Whilst the concept of the 'gay couple' did not originate in the Restoration – its roots have been traced from Shakespeare's *Much Ado About Nothing* through Shirley, Brome and Davenant[3] – the phenomenon only became a recurring element of comedy in this period. What is remarkable about the gay couple's

66

success in the Restoration is that it stemmed directly from the talent and popularity of a single actress, Nell Gwyn.

Born in a London slum and practically illiterate when she joined the theatre, Nell Gwyn rose to become the most famous Restoration actress of all time, possessed of an extraordinary comic talent. She was apparently warm-hearted, impudent, witty and determined, all qualities which came to influence the roles she created. She began, as has become legendary, selling oranges (and probably herself as well) in the theatre before becoming the mistress of the star actor Charles Hart, who subsequently introduced her to his profession. In May 1665 the two played their first gay couple for the King's Company as the anti-platonic lovers Philidor and Mirida in James Howard's *All Mistaken*. Philidor and Mirida are each pursued by a flock of other lovers and, although they are immediately attracted to each other, they make an agreement very early on that neither is to feel committed to the other and 'we will be both as mad / As we please'.[4] Even when they come together at the end of the play, both reject marriage, emphasising that they hate the idea of being chained together. Thus the play contains the fundamental ingredients of what was to become the characteristic Restoration 'gay couple' mode. Hart and Nell Gwyn performed brilliantly together: 'Nells and Hearts [*sic*] mad parts are most excellently done, but especially hers', Pepys said of a later production.[5] After this the lovers went on to perform opposite each other in earlier plays with some kind of 'gay couple': another play of Howard's called *The English Mounsieur* and Richard Rhodes' *Flora's Vagaries*, both of which had had only limited success when first performed, but which now gained a new lease of life.

The success of Hart and Gwyn then seems to have led George Villiers, Duke of Buckingham, to adapt Fletcher's *The Chances* in order to provide another 'gay couple' for them to play in 1667.[6] For Nell Gwyn, Buckingham enlarged and transformed the part of the Second Constancia who had only a small, non-speaking part in the original. Fletcher's Second Constancia is a drunken whore who appears on stage only once to arouse the lust of the play's hero, Don John: 'a stout whore, / I love such stirring ware'.[7] In Buckingham's version Constancia is changed into the kind of attractive, witty heroine that Gwyn specialised in. She is not, it seems, a virgin, but her murky past is ignored, or made a joke of, and she is presented as a kind of free spirit who engages in bouts of wit with the hero and wins

5 Nell Gwyn – studio of Sir Peter Lely.

him in the end. She and Don John are equally lively and independent and both distrust marriage – 'that charme', says Constancia, in Buckingham's new section in Act V, 'seldom proves fortunate'. At the end of Buckingham's *The Chances*, as in *All Mistaken*, the lovers jestingly reject marriage:

6 Nell Gwyn as Venus, with Cupid, by Sir Peter Lely, painted for Charles II's personal enjoyment. Pepys mentions seeing the picture at the back of a large press in James II's apartments.

DON JOHN: And shall we consummate our Joys?
CONSTANCIA: Never; We'll find out ways to make 'em last for ever.
DON JOHN: Now see the odds 'twixt marry'd Folks and Friends: Our Love
   begins just where their Passion ends.[8]

The link to Nell Gwyn's previous roles is clear.

A month or so after *The Chances* came Hart and Gwyn's greatest success together – John Dryden's *Secret Love*, in which they played the 'gay couple' Celadon and Florimell. As has been pointed out, Dryden definitely wrote the part of Florimell specifically for Nell Gwyn because the description of the character in the text of the play is also a description of the actress herself.[9] Although the whole production proved enormously popular, Nell Gwyn was more popular, it seems, than anything else. Pepys wrote,

the truth is, there is a comical part done by Nell, which is Florimell, that I never can hope ever to see the like done again by man or woman…so great performance of a comical part was never, I believe, in the world before as Nell doth this.[10]

After this, almost every performance of comedy by the King's Company during that season and the next was designed to make use of Hart and Gwyn as a gay couple. We know of at least six more performances of *Secret Love*, four of Robert Howard's *The Surprizal* with Nell as its bold heroine, and two each of James Howard's *All Mistaken* and *The English Mounsieur* and Rhodes' *Flora's Vagaries*. There were also revivals of plays by Beaumont and Fletcher with suitable pairs of lovers – *Philaster* in November 1667 with Nell as Bellario and Hart as Philaster and *The Wild Goose Chase* early in 1668, in which Nell probably played the heroine Oriana and Hart her lover Mirabell. Significantly, Nell and Hart became so identified with their roles in *Philaster* that they are mentioned in the prologue to another revival of the play a quarter of a century later:

> That good old play Philaster ne'er can fail,
> But we young actors, how shall we prevail?
> Philaster and Bellario, let me tell ye.
> For these bold parts we have no Hart, no Nelly,
> Those darlings of the stage that charmed you there.[11]

The lines suggest how great was the impact of the couple at this time.

Secret Love became a major influence on subsequent comedies, and to a degree all subsequent gay couples were based on the characters of Celadon and Florimell. In this respect, the most important way in which Florimell and Celadon differ from their counterparts in *All*

Mistaken and *The Chances* lies in their attitude to marriage. At the end of the earlier comedies both partners apparently reject marriage in favour of freedom. Florimell, however, is resolved that Celadon shall be her husband and she wins him finally by disguising herself as a man and charming her rivals, Orinda and Sabina, from him. At the end, although in a jesting way, the lovers agree to marry, their mutual acceptance expressed in terms of a proviso-scene in which, in a lighthearted manner, each lays down conditions with a view to escaping the conventional horrors of matrimony. Such scenes and such an attitude to marriage were to become a major feature of future portrayals of the gay couple. The idea of a comic marriage bargain was not new; there are proviso-scenes, of a kind, in several pre-Restoration plays as well as in Dryden's *The Wild Gallant* (1663).[12] However, such scenes usually consist of shrewish females commanding extravagant conditions intended to assure them of absolute sovereignty in marriage. *Secret Love* is the first Restoration comedy in which both partners mutually recognise the difficulties of marriage and, through a battle of wits, make some balanced attempt to safeguard both their own freedoms and the bond between them. They agree, for instance, never to be jealous, to love as long as possible and when they no longer do, to admit it. They also decide not to be called husband and wife but 'Mistress' and 'Gallant'. If Florimell breaks any of the conditions she will suffer a month of fasting nights: if Celadon breaks the agreements his wife will make him a cuckold. Although the exchange is a joke, this is still a significant recognition of the dangers and difficulties of matrimony. Dryden's innovation represents an important advance in the treatment of love and marriage in comedy. The Hart–Gwyn style of lovers are in a new sense equals, each fighting to maintain his or her independence and to form an alliance which will not constrict and so stifle their love. The dramatist conceived the innovation, but the inspiration of his assertive heroine was Nell Gwyn and thus, albeit indirectly, she brought a new approach to comic love relationships between the sexes.

Not surprisingly, the next new comedy the King's Company produced, *The Mulberry Garden* (May 1668), by the aristocrat Sir Charles Sedley, contained another gay couple, Wildish and Olivia, for Hart and Gwyn.[13] *The Mulberry Garden* concludes with another lighthearted proviso-scene between the lovers in which each discusses what he or she sees as the pitfalls of marriage. The scene is noteworthy for the way in which it picks up and develops what had presumably been a popular feature of *Secret Love*. Here, instead of laying down conditions, the lovers jokingly describe the disadvantages they feel they will suffer once they lose their freedom. The play ends with an idea lifted directly from *Secret Love* – Olivia, like Florimell, threatens her future husband with cuckoldry if he displeases her. A sense of the difficulties besetting love after marriage would now seem to have become an intrinsic part of the gay couple formula.

A month later, the King's Company produced *An Evening's Love*, another play by Dryden created as a vehicle for the talents of Hart and Gwyn, who played the hero and heroine Wildblood and Donna Jacintha. Although the plot of this comedy is partly based upon Molière's *Le Dépit Amoureux*, its real source lies in its performers' previous successes together. Not surprisingly, the play also contains another variation on the proviso-scene – in this case taking the form of a duet sung by Jacintha and Wildblood in Act V which is a competition between husband and wife as to who shall dominate. The character of Donna Jacintha seems particularly closely related to the personality and talents of Nell Gwyn. Not only do Jacintha's wit, resourcefulness and ability to play-act reflect what we know of the actress herself, but one of the character's speeches actually implies a direct reference to Nell's own life. When Wildblood asks Jacintha 'Then what is a gentleman to hope from you?', she answers,

To be admitted to pass my time with, while a better comes: to be the lowest step in my Staircase, for a Knight to mount upon him, and a Lord upon him, and a Marquess upon him, and a Duke upon him, till I get as high as I can climb.[14]

Nell, of course, began as the lover of Hart and from him became the mistress of Charles, Lord Buckhurst (in the summer of 1668) and was the following year to become the mistress of the king, her 'Charles III' – 'as high as I can climb'. This was a bold, even a dangerous speech, with the king among the spectators!

The success of Hart and Gwyn in *Secret Love* may be seen as a catalyst which established their particular kind of anti-platonic lovers as the most popular type of protagonists in comedy. After Dryden's success for the King's Company, its rival the Duke's Company quickly followed suit. George Etherege's fine comedy *She Would If She Could* (February 1668) contains two pairs of such lovers, the cousins Ariana and Gatty and their gallants, Courtall and Freeman. Like Florimell, Ariana and Gatty (played by Mrs Jennings and Moll Davis) are lively and independent, they hold their own in battles of wit with their lovers and test their constancy. Florimell gave Celadon a year to prove his constancy: at the end of Etherege's play the girls give their suitors a trial period of a month in which to keep their resolution to marry them.

Moll Davis, the actress who created the part of Gatty, seems to have been the Duke's Company's attempt to provide an equivalent to Nell Gwyn. Said to be the illegitimate daughter of Colonel Thomas Howard, later Earl of Berkshire, Mary or Moll Davis, 'the pretty girl' as Pepys called her,[15] joined the Duke's Company as a child in 1662. She soon became renowned for her singing and dancing and it seems likely that originally Nell Gwyn was promoted by the King's Company as a rival attraction to her. Like Moll Davis, Nell Gwyn was trained as a dancer and, although Pepys did not think her dancing anything like as good as her rival's, she too became famous for her jigs. Similarly, in *All Mistaken*, Nell Gwyn sang an obvious parody of the celebrated song 'My Love is on the Cold Ground', which Moll Davis performed in Davenant's *The Rivals*.[16] After Gwyn's success opposite Hart, however, Davis had to imitate *her*, instead of vice versa, and the Duke's Company gave her a similar madcap role as Gatty.

Unfortunately for the Duke's Company, by the end of May 1668 Moll Davis had left the stage to become one of Charles II's mistresses. (Here too she bears a remarkable resemblance to Nell Gwyn, who also became a mistress of the king a year later.) The prolific playwright Thomas Shadwell's first comedy, *The Sullen Lovers*, produced in that month, reflects the company's lack of a leading comedienne equivalent to Gwyn to carry the play. Shadwell's 'gay couple', Carolina and Lovel, are significantly less prominent as well as more restrained than the gay couples created by Dryden and Sedley. (We have no cast list for this play, so the actress who played Carolina is unknown.) Shadwell's attack, in the preface to his comedy, on the kind of gay couple produced by the King's Company – 'the two chief persons are most commonly a Swearing, Drinking, Whoring Ruffian for a Lover, and an impudent, ill-bred tomrig for a Mistress, and these are the fine people of the Play' – may well have been no more than an effort to make the best of a bad job. Certainly it is interesting to find that a later comedy by Shadwell, *Epsom Wells* (1672), contains two pairs of witty, impudent lovers, Rains and Carolina and Lucia and Bevil, who are very much the kind of 'gay couple' that he complained about in 1668.

Moll Davis's replacement was Winifred Gosnell, who was apparently less talented both as a comedienne and as a singer. Seeing Gosnell in a revival of Dryden and Davenant's *The Tempest* in 1669, Pepys wrote that 'it [presumably the role of Ariel] is but ill done, by Gosnell in lieu of Mall [*sic*] Davis'.[17] Lack of a suitable comic actress seems to have affected all the new comedies produced by the Duke's Company in the late 1660s and early 1670s. The only new comedies of 1669 were farces with only minor parts for women. Aphra Behn's tragicomedy *The Forc'd Marriage* the following year does include the light-hearted Aminta (played by Mrs Wright who only appeared on the stage in that year), a Gwyn-type character who flirts skilfully with her lover Alcander and is pursued by a fool, Falatius (as Gwyn's character was also pursued by a fool in *All Mistaken*). However, Aminta is only a supporting role and the grave Alcander is not at all the Charles Hart type of lover. The main female role in the play is definitely Erminia, a part which is rather tragic than comic. Erminia is an honourable bride, strangled by her jealous husband, and she was played by Mary Betterton, wife of Thomas, one of the Company's leading tragic actresses and famous for her ability to play noble heroines of all kinds.

COMIC HEROINES 1670–8

Some time after playing Valeria in Dryden's tragedy *Tyrannick Love* in June 1669 Nell Gwyn became the mistress of Charles II. She acted on a few occasions after that, but in 1671 she left the stage for good. There were, naturally, attempts to replace her. In Wycherley's *Love in a Wood* (1671), Hart was partnered with the actress Elizabeth Cox and they played the gay couple Lydia and Ranger who end the play with a typically light-hearted exchange on marriage. But Cox was no substitute for Nell Gwyn. No comment on her performance as Lydia survives, but thereafter she played only romantic parts, so she cannot have been particularly successful. Interestingly, when Shadwell adapted Molière's *L'Avare* (probably 1672), he made the principal couple, Theodore and Isabella, more serious than the French originals.

Drury Lane's Nell-substitute in Dryden's successful *Marriage à la Mode* (*c.* 1672) was Elizabeth Boutell who, though skilled, popular and adept at delivering suggestive prologues and epilogues, was not the obvious choice for an assertive heroine. Although she had 'very agreeable Features' and 'a good Complexion' her prettiness had a

'Childish Look' and her voice was 'weak, tho' very mellow'.[18] The nature of her part and the fact that she was cast opposite Hart suggests that the character was probably originally written for Nell Gwyn rather than for her. The play's recent editor, Mark Auburn, argues that 'if Dryden had written Melantha for Betty Boutell (and we may be sure he knew the capacities of his company), we would expect more naiveté and innocence'.[19] This makes sense, for Boutell had taken only romantic and serious parts up to that date. Melantha has a wonderful comic monologue of her own in which she practises her French words and makes expressions in her mirror which one imagines Nell Gwyn would have performed superbly. Boutell was a better actress than Cox, however, and presumably proved more capable as a gay heroine, for she was cast in another lively role as Laura in Dryden's *The Assignation* (1672) shortly after – so Dryden at least was impressed by her comic acting. However, this play failed and, with one notable exception, after 1672 Boutell's speciality was playing tragic heroines (see chapter 5). The exception was her role as Margery Pinchwife in what has remained the most famous comedy of the age, William Wycherley's *The Country Wife* (1675). Wycherley skilfully capitalised on his actress's demure and childish appearance and her famous ability to portray innocence and purity. Margery is an innocent when she is married off to middle-aged, savagely jealous Mr Pinchwife, but she quickly learns the sexual ways of the world when she is brought to London. At the end of the play she is learning to deceive her old spouse while maintaining an appearance of artless naïveté – just as Boutell would convincingly play a pure young heroine in a tragedy, before stepping forward to deliver a knowing and provocative epilogue.

While the King's Company continued to suffer for lack of a brilliant comedienne, the situation of the Duke's Company improved slightly in this respect through the comic success of one of its most long-standing female members, Jane Long. Long joined the Duke's Company at its inception in 1660, but did not make her mark until 1667 when breeches roles became her speciality. As we have seen, she played Hippolito in the Dryden–Davenant *Tempest* and she also played Dulcino in Shirley's *The Grateful Servant* (c. 1667) – the prompter John Downes noting that this was 'the first time she appear'd in Man's Habit'. Then, around 1670 and to great acclaim, Long played the title role in Betterton's *The Woman Made a Justice*. 'Mrs Long, Acting the Justice so Charmingly; and the Comedy being perfect and justly Acted, so well pleas'd the Audience, it continu'd

Acting 14 Days together.'[20] Frustratingly, this play was never printed, but from the title, the nature of Long's parts in *The Grateful Servant* and *The Tempest* and Downes' review, we can deduce that the actress played a bold, resourceful heroine who disguised herself as a judge. Betterton probably wrote the play with Long's talent for breeches roles in mind.

About this time Betterton seems to have written another leading role for Long as Mrs Brittle in his cynical comedy *The Amorous Widow* (*c.* 1670). As an attractive wanton wife who deceives her old spouse in various inventive ways, Mrs Brittle gave Long another opportunity to deceive and outwit other characters 'charmingly'. She played the wife 'so well', says Downes, 'that none Equall'd her but Mrs Bracegirdle' (who presumably played the role some years later).[21] Mrs Brittle and her lover, the rake Lovemore, are no gay couple; they do not really love each other and are solely bent on enjoying themselves. When Mrs Brittle gets the opportunity to be free of her husband entirely – 'I'll give a Sum of Money to be rid of her', he says – she realises that her lover is only a philanderer and that she is better off as she is: 'I'm glad I know it in time, whilst I have power to make my Retreat. I had like to have been finely caught.'[22]

Jane Long was popular and talented, but she never seems to have become a comedienne of Nell Gwyn's standard. For Edward Revet's *The Town-Shifts* (1671) she created the role of Fickle, another bold and lively heroine, but the play significantly gives first place to its serious couple, Leticia (played by Mary Betterton) and her lover, rather than to its witty couple, Fickle and Friendly. The Duke's Company still had no actress to rival Nell Gwyn. During the early 1670s surviving cast lists record a variety of different actresses taking the lead roles in new comedies (most new plays came from the Duke's Company at this time since, quite apart from the loss of Nell Gwyn, the King's Company was now in serious financial trouble). As the casting of *The Town-Shifts* suggests, the most important actresses remained those who specialised in tragedy, Mary Betterton and Mary Lee.

In the mid-1670s Mary Lee, later Lady Slingsby, was at the height of her success, having played a variety of passionate lead roles in tragedy, both heroines and villainesses (see chapter 5). Her popularity, combined with the lack of good comediennes, had the interesting result that the only comedy of this period obviously centred on a women – Thomas Durfey's *Madam Fickle* (1676) – was written for her, with her tragic skills in mind. In the character of Madam Fickle Durfey seems to have deliberately recalled Mrs Lee's part two years before as Nigrello in Elkanah Settle's tragedy *Love and Revenge*; in both plays the actress created a heroine who ruthlessly seeks revenge after being ill-used by a man. When her plots succeed, like Nigrello Madam Fickle exults in her success in a verse soliloquy: 'and Hell shall laugh to see a woman's wit'.[23] In both plays the soliloquies come at the end of Act IV.

More tragic skills were required in the deception of Fickle's suitors. A modern editor of the play has noted that 'one unusual feature of the dialogue is the occasional use of blank verse, especially in the amorous interviews that Fickle conducts with her various lovers'.[24] This 'unusual feature' was surely a further means of using Lee's tragic experience. To charm her suitors, Madam Fickle deliberately assumes the poses and rhetoric of a tragic heroine: 'Now to my posture – This book – Languishing eyes – So – And necessary handkerchief to wipe imaginary tears off' (II.ii.155–7). When an admirer suspects her of being unfaithful, she regains his trust with a pretence of tears which later, in private, she scorns, 'Thus with the snowy veil of innocence, / Contriving women cover their pretence' (III.ii.320–1). Madam Fickle finally dresses as a man and in this disguise offers to fight all her suitors at once, a possible reference to another of Lee's roles that year, Amavanga in Settle's *The Conquest of China*. (Amavanga is a vigorous female warrior who, by a quirk of fate, engages her lover in single combat.) For her challenge to the men Durfey gave Lee a melodramatic *tour de force* which forms the climax of the play's parody of tragic rhetoric:

I'll bathe my lips in gore, kiss bleeding wounds, cleave helmets, stand a breach, and dare a cannon, divide a heart in two, hah! Hah! – 'Tis done. Soul of Belona, I'll exhaust a flood, turn Earth to chaos, oceans into blood. Consume your timorous cringing amorists, that would possess their Heav'n, but dare not bleed for't. Blood is my province; therefore with you all am I resolv'd to fight. (V.iii.153–60)

This speech offered the actress a marvellous opportunity to display her histrionic talents and probably earned her a special round of applause from spectators. Madam Fickle is then deterred from actually fighting by the husband who had deserted her. He reveals her true identity to the others before removing his own disguise and effecting a reconciliation with his wife. In *Madam Fickle* Durfey produced an entertaining parody of Lee's roles in tragedy and a type of comic heroine eminently suited to her talents in both genres. The play is a remarkable instance of a dramatist adapting his comedy to the best, but not necessarily the most suitable, actress available.

ELIZABETH CURRER AS WHORE 1675–9

During the second half of the 1670s we need to take account of another comic actress who had her own individual impact on the drama. Prostitutes and mistresses are a persistent feature of Restoration comedy, but in plays produced by the Duke's Company in the late 1670s one particular type predominates – the tough, calculating, successful professional mistress. The popularity of this type may be partly attributable to social factors; in time a substantial number of women (several of them actresses) had become successful kept mistresses with an accepted place in the London social scene. The most famous of these, from the point of view of the playhouse, was of course Nell Gwyn. But this development was undoubtedly aided by the fact that the skilled comedienne Elizabeth Currer began to specialise in such roles.

Apparently from Ireland, Elizabeth Currer probably became a member of the Duke's Company in 1674 and had her first whore role in comedy soon after playing Betty Frisque, who resourcefully deceives her keeper Drybone, in Crowne's *The Countrey Wit* (1675?). This robust and cunning manipulator was to become typical of the kind of prostitute Currer portrayed. Inconstant Betty retains the upper hand by alternately upbraiding her old lord and showing extravagant fondness. She is excessively mercenary – Drybone complains plaintively that he has to pay 'Forty pound a Dimple'. Betty flirts with the rake hero, Ramble, but is finally reconciled with Drybone on condition that he gives her a settlement of £500 a year in case they quarrel again. This secured, she promises, 'I am yours in the new-fashion'd Matrimony for ever.'[25]

Currer probably played a similar whore a year later in Aphra Behn's *The Town Fopp* (1676). The cunning Betty Flauntit strongly resembles Betty Frisque and must have been created by the same actress. Betty Flauntit skilfully controls her unpleasant keeper, Sir Timothy and, even when he is tricked into marriage to another woman at the end, she manages to organise matters in her favour. Although the play's most important female character is the heroine, Celinda, the last lines of the play belong to Betty:

BETTY: What am I like to lose my Timy? Canst thou have the heart to leave
me for ever? I who have been true and constant to you.

SIR T: Alas! now do I melt again, by Fortune – thou art a Fool, dost think
I wou'd have had her, but for her Fortune; which shall only serve to
make thee out-flaunt all the Cracks in Town – go – go home and
expect me, thou'lt have me all to thy self within this day or two.[26]

Interestingly, Currer was a 'Betty' herself and the repetition of this
Christian name in Behn's play surely makes the possibility that she
played Flauntit more likely. She probably also created Mrs Tricksy
in Dryden's *The Kind Keeper* (1678) – an extreme version of Betty
Frisque, ruthlessly managing her keeper, Limberham, with a
combination of ranting fury and extravagant affection. Tricksy, like
Betty Flauntit, also unsuccessfully pursues the comedy's hero and
gains a good settlement from her besotted lover at the end. He
declares that 'to give good example to all Christian Keepers', he 'will
take thee to my wedded Wife: And thy four hundred a year shall be
settled upon thee, for separate maintenance'.[27] Currer certainly
played the similarly deceitful, mercenary Madam Tricklove in
Durfey's *Squire Oldsapp* in the same year. Triumphing in her schemes,
Tricklove has the last word in the play: 'But to forge plots in
extremity, / Let every Mistress henceforth learn from me.'[28]
Madam Tricklove is at least as important a character in the play as
the two pure heroines, the wife Christina, played by a certain Mrs
Price, and her niece Sophia, played by Elizabeth Barry. In the first
printed edition (1679) Currer's name is placed first in the female cast
list (whereas normally one would expect the virginal heroine's name,
not the whore's, to come first) and she spoke the highly entertaining
epilogue in which Madam Tricklove pokes fun at her foolish old
keeper:

> Yet, Gallants if you please, you may be kind,
> Prove so – or may this Curse your Fortune be;
> May you all live, till y'are as dull as he;
> *(points to Oldsapp)*
> And all your darling Misses prove like me.

This and the number of other prologues and epilogues that she was
called upon to speak during these years suggest that Currer was then
at the height of her popularity – which explains why her type of kept
mistress, bold, deceitful, unscrupulous and triumphant, predomi-
nated in the late 1670s.

ELIZABETH BARRY AS COMEDIENNE 1676–81

In the meantime, from 1676 another actress in the Duke's Company gradually took over most of its female lead roles in comedy. Elizabeth Barry's later career will be discussed in detail in subsequent chapters; in this account it is necessary only to note that at the beginning of her long and illustrious career, aged 23 (she was recruited to the Duke's Company in 1675), she became her company's main creator of witty comic heroines. In 1676 Barry was allowed to play serious heroines: Elvira in Ravenscroft's *The Wrangling Lovers* and Theodocia in Rawlins' *Tom Essence*. Soon after this she took the livelier part of Constanta in *Madam Fickle* and is listed by Downes in *Roscius Anglicanus* as playing Mrs Loveit in *The Man of Mode*. However, in view of the comic roles that she created immediately before and after this play, it is far more likely that Barry had the *lead* as the intelligent heroine Harriet opposite Betterton's reformed libertine, Dorimant. Although Downes names most of the comedy's female cast, he most surprisingly omits all mention of Harriet. Betterton and Barry were paired together in similar lead roles a few months later in Aphra Behn's *The Rover*. In no comedy of this period did Barry play a discarded mistress; she was invariably cast as virgin or wife. It would seem to have been far more natural for Mary Lee to play Mrs Loveit, especially since Downes lists Mary Betterton as playing Dorimant's other discarded mistress, Belinda. How appropriate to have these two, the most important actresses in the Company at that time, ousted in favour of the rising young star, Barry, as was to occur in real life. The melodramatic histrionics of Mrs Loveit's part seem very well suited to Lee's style of acting. In listing Barry for Mrs Loveit Downes may have been thinking of a production later on, for she did take this role in revivals many years later.[29]

At all events, Barry certainly then went on to create the most attractive heroine of the decade apart from Etherege's Harriet, Hellena in Aphra Behn's best comedy *The Rover*. *The Rover* was adapted from Thomas Killigrew's *Thomaso* (written in 1654 and published a decade later) and Behn's most important addition was the character of Hellena as an appropriate match for the rake hero Willmore.[30] In these two figures the type of gay couple popularised by Hart and Gwyn made its most effective reappearance to date. Like Florimell, Hellena holds her own against the womaniser Willmore and assumes male disguise to successfully court her rival, the courtesan Angellica Bianca. Finally she tames the rake, threatening 'to find out all your haunts, to rail at you to all that love you, till I have made you love only me in your own defense, because nobody else will love you'.[31] However, Hellena is openly in favour of marriage and instead of a proviso-scene she gives a comically bleak picture of what will become of her if she becomes a mistress: 'what shall I get? A cradle full of noise and mischief, with a pack of repentance at my back?'[32]

After playing Hellena Barry remained the company's leading comic actress for ten years, the number of prologues and epilogues she spoke at this time conveying how popular she had become. She began to play adulterous wives as well as ingenues: Emilia in Durfey's *A Fond Husband* (1677) for example, and Mrs Goodvile in Otway's exceptionally bitter satire *Friendship in Fashion* (1678).[33] Outstandingly versatile (no other actress played anything like such a range of different character types), her comic speciality was to be neither of these, but the fallen woman, a figure she did not begin to play until the 1680s and one which is strongly linked to the kind of heroine she played in tragedy at that time. Tragedy in fact was where Barry truly excelled and while she played both witty heroines and wives successfully, she does not seem to have made either type especially her own. It would seem that during the late 1670s and early 1680s comic dramatists produced lead roles in a popular style (like that of the gay couple) and then Barry was automatically cast in them as the company's best actress, rather than that she directly inspired her roles, as she did in tragedy after 1680 (see chapter 5).

And what of the King's Company at this time? It continued to produce fewer new comedies than the Duke's Company and its lack of talented comediennes is aptly illustrated by the best of its comedies from this period, Wycherley's *The Plain Dealer* (1676), whose two main female roles, Olivia and Fidelia, were clearly designed for and played by actresses better suited to tragedy – Rebecca Marshall and Elizabeth Boutell. Olivia plots, rants and raves like a tragic villainess, while Fidelia faithfully serves her lover in the guise of his page and even speaks in verse. Then, in 1682, the company finally collapsed, the United Company was created and the consequent lack of competition led to very few new comedies being produced at all for the remainder of the decade. Hume notes that the years 1683–8 produced only four new plays per annum on average.[34]

With the theatre's revival in the early 1690s, the actresses began again to make their presence felt in comedy. The two most influential comediennes of this decade were Anne Bracegirdle and Susannah Mountfort (or Susannah Percival as she was called before her marriage to William Mountfort in 1686, or Susannah Verbruggen as she was known after her second marriage to the actor John Verbruggen in 1694). Having first appeared on the stage at the age of 14 in 1681, by the end of the decade Susannah Mountfort had established herself as the United Company's leading comedienne, skilled in the performance of both witty breeches roles and grotesque characters. *A Comparison Between Two Stages* calls the actress 'a Miracle' and in the preface to *The Female Wits* (1696), the anonymous author mourns her as one 'whose Loss we must ever regret, as the Chief Actress in her Kind, who never had anyone that exceeded her'.[35]

Although her father, Thomas Percival, was a minor actor in the Duke's Company, Susannah joined the King's Company in 1681. Her first role, at the age of 14, was the minor one of Welsh Winifred in Durfey's comedy, *Sir Barnaby Whigg*. Her first leading role was the robust Nell in *The Devil of a Wife* (1686) by the actor Thomas Jevon. She also spoke the epilogue to this successful comedy with Jevon (who played her husband in the play) so by this time the company had begun to recognise her talents. Soon after this she married the rising young actor and playwright William Mountfort and the two of them frequently played together thereafter in the style of Gwyn and Hart, until the murder of Mountfort by Captain Hill on 10 December 1692. Thus for a few years the Mountforts encouraged the 'gay couple' to flourish in such comedies as Carlile's *The Fortune-Hunters* (1689), Shadwell's *Bury Fair* (1689), Dryden's *Don Sebastian* (1689) and Mountfort's own *Greenwich Park* (1691).[36] Husband and wife spoke the epilogue together to *Don Sebastian*, with a humorous exchange between their characters Antonio and Morayma which was clearly written to take advantage of the performers' real-life relationship. Antonio suggests that they first enjoy a night of passionate love and then marry, but Morayma insists on marriage first, and she adds, 'First wed and, if you find that life a fetter, / Die when you please; the sooner, sir, the better.' These lines would obviously be much funnier with the knowledge that they were actually directed at a man by his wife, just as the Mountforts' real relationship must have added piquancy to all their witty quarrels in the comedies themselves.

After her husband's death Mountfort continued to specialise in gay resourceful heroines, inspiring several comedies centred on such a character. Cibber mentioned that she was extremely good in breeches roles, 'a more adroit pretty Fellow than is usually seen upon the Stage', and that 'people were so fond of seeing her as a Man, that when the Part of Bays in the *Rehearsal*, had, for some time, lain dormant, she was desired to take it up'.[37] This ability certainly led Southerne to create for her the title role in his successful comedy *Sir Anthony Love* (1690) for he stated as much when commending her acting of the part in the dedicatory epistle:

since I have this occasion of mentioning Mrs Montford, I am pleased, by way of Thanks, to do her that publick Justice in Print, which some of the best Judges of these Performances, have, in her Praise, already done her, in publick places... as I made every Line for her, she has mended every Word for me; and by a Gaiety and Air, particularl to her Action, turn'd every thing into the Genius of the Character.[38]

Southerne's lively heroine masterminds all the plots in the play and proves that a woman can do everything a man can do in society and do it better – all of which gave Mountfort the opportunity of fully employing her talents as a male impersonator.

The success of his wife as Sir Anthony presumably inspired Mountfort to write another major breeches part for her as Florella in *Greenwich Park* the following year. Florella's relish for playing a man recalls Lucia's: 'there's such an Air and Freedom belongs to the Breeches, to what our Dull and dragging Petticoats allow of, that adsheartlikins I fancy my self of the Masculine Gender, and am for ravishing the first woman I meet'.[39] Two years later, George Powell (who played opposite Susannah Mountfort on several occasions) wrote another leading breeches role for the actress as Annabella in *A Very Good Wife*. Mountfort played the wife of the title who courts a rich widow dressed as a man in order to help her impoverished husband, Courtwit. Like Aphra Behn's *The Counterfeit Bridegroom* fifteen years earlier, the play was based upon Middleton's *No Wit No Help Like a Woman's*. One imagines that the achievements of Mountfort at this time were what prompted Powell to use the Jacobean play again.

Susannah Mountfort stands out among her fellow comediennes for her ability to play not only charming heroines but also ugly, foolish and low-life characters. She played grotesques with as much relish as she played women of wit. Cibber noted that she

was so fond of Humour, in what low Part soever to be found, that she would make no scruple of defacing her fair Form, to come heartily into it; for when she was eminent in several desirable Characters of Wit, and Humour, in higher Life, she would be, in as much Fancy, when descending into the antiquated Abigail, of Fletcher, as when triumphing in all the Airs and vain Graces of a fine Lady; a Merit, that few Actresses care for.

She was 'Mistress of more variety of Humour, than I knew in any one Woman Actress'[40] and this other talent also had its impact upon the repertory. She soon developed a line, for instance, in uncouth country girls, such as Winifred in Durfey's *Sir Barnaby Whigg* (1681) and Nell in *The Devil of a Wife* (1686). For Southerne's *The Maid's Last Prayer* (1693) she created the old maid of the title, Lady Susan Malepert – 'that Youthful Virgin of five and forty, with a swelling Rump, bow Leggs, a shining Face, and colly'd Eyebrows...sure she's an Original'.[41] The eye-brows are false, a source of considerable anxiety to their owner. Lady Susan's speech is also full of comic potential, her lines continually punctuated with squawked exclamations, 'O law!', 'O Jesu!', 'O Crimine!', and so on. Mountfort's success in the role is implied by the fact that she played a very similar role a few months later as Catchat, a 'stale Virgin' who fancies that every man is in love with her, in Thomas Wright's *The Female Vertuoso's*. Still in character, she spoke also the epilogue to this play:

> I try'd to leave you, Gentlemen, in vain,
> The rest are gone, but I'm return'd again;
> And that you're pleas'd, my Vanity discovers,
> I'll set you all down in my List of Lovers.

Thomas Durfey was particularly strongly influenced by Mountfort's (now Verbruggen) talent for the grotesque. In his adaptation of *Don Quixote* for the stage he added for her the part of the vulgar, extremely funny Mary the Buxom, whose success extended itself over two more plays after this and culminated in her marriage. In the preface to *The Second Part of the Comical History of Don Quixote* (1694) Durfey wrote,

Then I must tell my severe Censurers...that I deserve some acknowledgement for drawing the Character of Mary the Buxom, which was entirely my own, and which I was not obliged to the History at all for...by making the Character humorous, and by the extraordinary well acting of Mrs Verbruggen, it is by the best Judges allowed to be a Masterpiece of Humour.[42]

The epilogue to this was clearly designed to further exploit the actress's success. In a parody of the many female epilogues in which the speaker offers her sexual favours to spectators, her father urges Mary to 'serve 'em in some other way / Provided they'll be civil to the Play'. Mary replied in her usual crude vigorous style,

> What other way Zooks can I serve 'em in,
> Unless they have any Lockram Smocks to spin;
> Will these, dee think, prefer a Country Tool
> In Serge and Dowlas – Vather you're a Fool:
> For ought I see amongst this longnos'd Crew,
> They'd rather wear out Smocks, than pay to make me.

Not surprisingly, *The Third Part of The Comical History* is advertised as being with the attraction of 'the Marriage of Mary the Buxom'.

Durfey went on to create a similar role for Verbruggen as Gillian Homebread in *The Bath* (1701). Verbruggen more than matched Durfey's conception of the part – her 'incomparable performance answering my design, has rais'd it, if not to her Master-piece, yet at least second to any'. Cibber was equally impressed by Verbruggen as Gillian.

In a Play of D'urfey's, now forgotten, call'd *The Western Lass*, which Part she acted, she transform'd her whole Being, Body, Shape, Voice, Language, Look, and Features, into almost another Animal; with a strong Devonshire Dialect, a broad laughing Voice, a poking Head, round Shoulders, an unconceiving Eye, and the most be-diz'ning dowdy Dress that ever cover'd the untrain'd Limbs of a Joan Trot. To have seen her here, you would have thought it impossible the same Creature could ever have been recovered, to what was as easy to her, the Gay, the Lively, and the Desirable.[43]

Both Mary and Gillian, like Lady Susan, require a skilled rendering of peculiarities of speech to make them funny, so Verbruggen must have been adept at capturing such peculiarities.

At the same as Susannah Mountfort inspired lively breeches roles and comic grotesques, her fellow comedienne Anne Bracegirdle created a series of somewhat different comic heroines. Bracegirdle was born around 1663, the daughter of Justinian and Martha Bracegirdle of Northamptonshire. According to Anthony Aston, it was commonly believed that her father was a coachman, coachmaker or coach-renter of Northampton. Curll relates that the family fell on

7 Anne Bracegirdle, probably by Thomas Bradwell.

hard times and were obliged to place Anne with Thomas and Mary Betterton. Presumably through their influence she chose a stage career. Her name first appears in documents pertaining to the Duke's Company during the 1679–80 season and Curll believes that her first

8 Anne Bracegirdle as Semernia, the Indian Queen, in Aphra Behn's
The Widow Ranter.

role was the page Cordelio in *The Orphan* in 1680 (the actress who
took the role is referred to in the dramatis personae as 'The Little
Girl'). However, he also says that she was less than six years old when
she took the role, which is clearly impossible. The '6' may be a scribal
error for '16', about the right age for Bracegirdle in 1680. She first
appears in the Lord Chamberlain's accounts as a member of the
United Company on 12 January 1688 and her name does not appear

in any cast lists until that year.[44] In 1691, having hitherto played only supporting comic roles, Bracegirdle played the first of her most characteristic type of comic lead, the orphan Mirtilla, 'witty, modest, virtuous' and an heiress, in Durfey's *Love for Money*. After this she inspired a special kind of witty heroine, the irresistible heiress who is pursued by admirers but who finds it difficult to be sure of the man who loves her. Millamant in Congreve's *The Way of the World* is the greatest of these parts. When she created this role Cibber recalls that 'all the Faults, Follies, and Affectation of that agreeable Tyrant, were venially melted down into so many Charms, and Attractions of a conscious Beauty'.[45] In fact, Bracegirdle's involvement with Congreve – the greatest comic dramatist of the age – must have contributed to her success. As Barry's relation to Otway, the greatest tragic dramatist of the age, seems to have helped generate a particular kind of female protagonist to dominate tragedy, so it appears that Congreve's passion for Bracegirdle enriched his appreciation for her acting skills and so impelled him to create for her a range of especially bewitching and memorable heroines: Araminta, Cynthia, Angelica and Millamant.

Here it is illuminating to compare Bracegirdle's comic roles with those of Mountfort. The typical Mountfort witty heroine is cunning, resourceful, frequently assumes a breeches disguise and is very active. Sir Anthony and Annabella (the heroine of Powell's *A Very Good Wife*) initiate and carry out plots for financial gain, they are pursuers rather than pursued. It was, on the other hand, comparatively unusual for Bracegirdle to disguise herself as a man; her characters have wealth and they are usually pursued rather than pursuing. The typical Bracegirdle heroine is passive; her task is to protect her reputation and discern if her lover is worthy of her, not to initiate action.[46] In Southerne's *The Wive's Excuse* (1692), for instance, Mountfort played Mrs Witwoud, an arch plotter on other people's behalf as well as her own, while Bracegirdle played Mrs Sightly, the innocent victim of Witwoud's plots. Mountfort also, of course, played a variety of comic caricatures while Bracegirdle consistently played young and attractive females. One can even discern a trace of this contrast in typecasting in Congreve's *The Old Bachelor* in which Mountfort was called upon to create the affectations of Belinda, and Bracegirdle the steadiness and good sense of Araminta.

The other main difference between the roles of the two actresses lies in their degree of seriousness. Mountfort's roles are predominantly light-hearted, be they breeches roles like Sir Anthony, or 'character' parts such as Gillian and Mary the Buxom (her role in *The Wives' Excuse* is an exception, but this is an exceptionally serious comedy). Bracegirdle's heroines, however, tend to be more serious, both in terms of their personalities and their thematic functions. The fact that the Bracegirdle character is often wealthy and therefore the prey of fortune-hunters renders her particularly wary, cynical and suspicious of men. In Durfey's *The Richmond Heiress* (1693), for example, when Fulvia discovers that her lover Frederick is only interested in her fortune, she becomes embittered and scorns marriage entirely: 'the Race of Men are all Deceivers'.[47] Mrs Sightly, in *The Wives' Excuse*, similarly rejects marriage because the suitor is unworthy. It is not until Congreve's *Love for Love* (1695) that the Bracegirdle heiress finally gains a lover who is worthy of her. Valentine proves the depth of his affection for Angellica and she, echoing Fulvia, tells another of her admirers:

You would all have the Reward of Love; but few have the Constancy to stay 'till it becomes your due. Men are generally Hypocrites and Infidels, they pretend to Worship, but have neither Zeal nor Faith: How few, like Valentine, would persevere even to Martyrdom, and sacrifice their Interest to their Constancy![48]

Millamant embodies a similar problem. She loves Mirabell but is wary of showing her affection too freely. Nevertheless, we are allowed glimpses of the depth of her feelings behind her mask of wit and raillery, as when she admits to Mrs Fainall, 'Well, If Mirabell should not make a good Husband, I am a lost thing; – for I find I love him violently' (p. 470). Millamant too is an heiress, pursued by worthless suitors, and Mirabell is a rake who has already seduced one mistress – Mrs Fainall – and married her off. Millamant's charm and wit, which would be the whole essence of a Mountfort witty heroine, are partly a protection of more serious feelings. None of the characters created by Mountfort have the subtlety and grave overtones of Fulvia, Slightly or Millamant and here it may be significant that Bracegirdle was also a leading tragedienne while Mountfort rarely performed in tragedy (she did take the breeches role of Achmet the eunuch in Pix's *Ibrahim*, in 1696 – presumably as an entertaining variation on her breeches roles in comedy). Here we have two very different kinds of actress, each leaving her own highly individual mark on comedy between 1690 and 1700.

Thus comic drama throughout the period was constantly affected by the actresses for whom it was written. As subsequent chapters will show, similarly influential lines of female casting may also be found in tragedy, although at the beginning of the period the actresses had less impact here because the genre then contained fewer leading parts for women than comedy. My account of comedy is not, of course, an exhaustive one. There were a number of other comedies written apart from those I have mentioned, and a number of other actresses. However, my discussion includes most of the major comedies and all the major developments in female comic characterisation during the period. An account of this kind highlights the fact that the history of Restoration drama must be seen as partly the history of its female players. Such drama can never be properly understood unless we take account of which actresses were available at each and every stage of its development.

CHAPTER 4

Life overwhelming fiction

Restoration audiences were accustomed to enjoying a drama on two
levels for much of the time – that is, they enjoyed the spectacle of the
characters and their adventures in the play, but they were also
particularly strongly conscious of the personalities of the players
behind the fiction. In the twentieth century we acquire our
knowledge of actors and actresses from newspapers, magazines and
chat-shows. Restoration spectators gained theirs more directly from
gossip, from satires and from knowing members of the two companies
personally. They also took a special interest in the private lives of
actresses. As we have seen, the women's sexual exploits were discussed
in satires and dramatic criticism as their male counterparts' were not,
while some theatre-goers actually arranged liaisons with female
players. This chapter examines the exceptionally personal relationship between actresses and their public and the effects of this
relationship on the roles the women played.

PROLOGUES AND EPILOGUES

Prologues and epilogues increased audience awareness of the real
woman behind the actress's role. Restoration theatre developed a
new brand of highly familiar, highly personalised prologue and
epilogue and these forged a new link between player and spectator.
Prologues and epilogues existed sporadically in both medieval and
Renaissance theatre, but in the Restoration the content of such
addresses changed and they became an integral part of almost every
production. Nearly every play in print had its prologue and epilogue
printed along with it and a huge new range of possibilities in the form
were realised. Restoration prologues and epilogues were not limited,
as most earlier examples of the genre were, to pleas for a good
reception of a particular drama. They constituted spicy and intimate

pieces of theatrical gossip, freely discussing personalities, politics, the rival company, current scandal and the latest improvements in scenery. They were generally more scurrilous, more satirical and more wittily polished than their Renaissance predecessors and, most important of all, they were often tailored to the personality of the player who was to deliver them and could only be spoken by that player. Thus the new prologues and epilogues created theatrical moments when the players apparently abandoned their roles and stepped forward as 'themselves' to address spectators.

The personal nature of the Restoration prologue is highlighted if we compare a typical example, the actor Charles Hart's lively prologue to Wycherley's *The Country Wife* (1675), with a prologue to a well-known Jacobean play, Jonson's prologue to *Volpone* (1606). Jonson's prologue, beginning 'Now, luck yet send us, and a little wit / Will serve, to make our play hit', typically pleads a good reception for the play; its central argument is to praise and defend the playwright and his work. It promises to 'mix profit with your pleasure', to avoid 'monstrous, and forced action' and plagiarisms, and to adhere to the three unities of time, place and action.[1] It could have been spoken by anyone, not necessarily an actor in *Volpone*. (A number of prologues in Jonson's time were not spoken at all, but merely appeared in the printed text.) Wycherley's prologue, on the other hand, was clearly designed to be spoken by Hart,[2] the star of the play who created the role of Horner, and it is an intimate communication between actor and audience from which the playwright is jestingly excluded. Hart does not go so far as to poke fun at the play itself, as the speakers of many Restoration prologues and epilogues did, but he separates himself immediately from the dramatist, who is described as a 'baffled scribbler' who 'stands trembling' in the wings.[3] The very first lines, in fact, make fun of all playwrights: they are like 'cudgelled bullies', always beaten, as their plays fail, yet never giving up, 'but will provoke you still, and ne'er have done / Till you are weary first with laying on' (1, 3–4). This playwright, Hart goes on, typically hopes to bludgeon his way into his audience's favour, but he, as a player, will have nothing to do with this, and will do only what the audience would like:

> Well, let the vain rash fop, by huffing so,
> Think to obtain the better terms of you;
> But we, the actors, humbly will submit,
> Now, and at any time, to a full pit;

> Nay, often we anticipate your rage,
> And murder poets for you on our stage. (19–24)

In fact, Hart adds, often we, the players, go further and 'murder', that is ruin, a playwright's work for you as we perform it. Appropriately, Hart's final comment:

> We set no guards upon our tiring-room,
> But when with flying colours there you come,
> We patiently, you see, give up to you
> Our poets, virgins, nay, our matrons too (25–8)

is an invitation to the public to go behind the scenes and join the actors, and more particularly, the actresses. Occasionally, prologues and epilogues from the first half of the seventeenth century point up the performer's real self – as, for instance, in the epilogue to Shakespeare's *As You Like It* (1600) – but never with such outrageous assaults on the plays they begin and end. In the Restoration, however, such assaults became the norm. Wycherley's prologue shows that by the mid-1670s prologues and epilogues had become a familiar and direct communication between player and spectator.

It is interesting to find the moralist Jeremy Collier attacking Restoration prologues and epilogues for precisely this reason. Although he felt them to be no more coarse or indecent than play dialogue, the words were put into the mouths of real people, not of imaginary characters:

Now here properly speaking the Actors quit the Stage, and remove from Fiction into Life. Here they converse with the Boxes, and Pit, and address directly to the Audience... But here we have Lewdness without Shame or Example: Here the Poet exceeds himself... And to make it the more agreeable, Women are Commonly pick'd out for this Service.[4]

Collier's criticism contains two points worthy of note. First, he felt that through prologues and epilogues the actors moved 'from Fiction into Life'. This being so, spectators would presumably become more aware of the performance as a fiction and the actors as themselves, merely playing fictional characters. Secondly, Collier was particularly disgusted to see that it was women who were usually chosen to deliver the prologues and epilogues. It was the actresses, therefore, who entered most of all into this personal relationship with theatre-goers.

From the start, both the King's and Duke's Companies were quick to use the charms of their female members to put their audiences into a receptive and benevolent mood at the beginning and the end of a performance. In 1691 the epilogue to Durfey's *Bussy D'Ambois* was to make this point:

> Writers sometimes may Interest want,
> But something's in a Female supplicant,
> The Learned tell us, that can never fail
> To move the Kindly Nature of the Male.

The actresses undoubtedly proved very successful at coaxing their audience into good humour. Pepys was presumably not alone in finding an indifferent evening's entertainment offset by a good female address at the end: a visit to a revival of Shirley's *Hyde Park* with an epilogue newly attached elicited the diary entry, 'it is but a very moderate play, only an excellent Epilogue spoke by Becke Marshall'.[5] Their success brought the women more and more prologues and epilogues to speak. Whereas before 1660 such addresses were hardly ever performed by a transvestite female speaker – as Rosalind puts it at the end of Shakespeare's *As You Like It*, 'it is not the fashion to see the lady the epilogue' – during the period 1660–1710 at least a hundred were spoken by a particular named actress, in addition to some simply designed to be delivered by any female speaker. It has been calculated that of the eighty or so women who became actresses before 1689, at least twenty-six were entrusted with one or more prologues and epilogues; this was far in excess of the number of named male players so entrusted.[6] The only male speakers who figure with equal prominence were the leading comedians of the two companies – James Nokes, Anthony Leigh, Cave Underhill, John Lacy and, most popular of all, Joseph Haines. But even Haines could not compete with the two greatest and most popular actresses – Bracegirdle had at least nine prologues and twenty-two epilogues, Barry six prologues and twenty-one epilogues. These statistics suggest, incidentally, that epilogues were much more important than prologues. The final impression counted most in creating the mood spectators took home with them and in perhaps obliterating the effects of a bad play.

By the end of the 1670s leading actresses were being given strikingly personalised prologues and epilogues, tailored much more closely than the men's to their stage roles and public reputations. The intimate, personal nature of their speeches is vividly illustrated in two of the epilogues given by Charlotte Butler who, as already mentioned, was famed for her lovers as well as for her acting, singing and dancing. Her epilogue at the end of Behn's *The City Heiress* (1682) reflects this dubious reputation. Having played the pure heroine and 'city heiress' of the title, Charlot (or Charlotte, her own name), Butler stepped out of her fictional role and addressed the audience as 'herself', as the 'Syren' and 'Strumpet-Termagant' Butler portrayed in the satires. Her epilogue began with a joking fear that very few spectators would have believed in her as a virtuous heiress: 'My Part, I fear, will take with but a few [spectators] / A rich young Heiress to her first Love true!' Butler then affected to complain of male spectators' preference for aristocratic women as mistresses, rather than actresses like herself,

> What is't you see in Quality we want?
> What can they give you which we cannot grant?
> We have their Pride, their Frolicks, and their Paint
> We feel the same Youth dancing in our Blood;
> Our dress is gay... All underneath as good.

The last suggestive line was delivered, presumably, with a wink. The whole epilogue suggests a degree of intimacy that no actor could achieve. In his prologue Hart allied himself with the audience against the playwright, but his subject was the play, not himself. Butler's address, on the other hand, is entirely based on her individual personality.

Personality is the subject of another highly entertaining epilogue – this time a duologue between Butler and fellow actor William Mountfort at the end of Durfey's *Love for Money* (1691). In this play Butler took a role closer to her public image – that of the 'cunning, singing, weeping, wheedling, toying, chattering, mercenary Town jilt' Betty Jiltall.[7] The play done, Mountfort and Butler returned to the stage and discussed her part:

BUTLER: D'ye hear me Mr. Mountford, pray come back,
D'ye know what I've done here?
MOUNTFORT: Yes, play'd a Crack. [whore]
BUTLER: A Crack, what's that?
MOUNTFORT: Pisk leave your bant'ring stuff,
I'm sure you know what th'word means well enough.

Here Butler affected an ignorance that everyone knew she did not possess. She and Mountfort called each other names until she finally flounced off the stage:

The Key to the Rehearsal.

BUTLER: 'Faith Monford thou'rt a Coxcomb.
MOUNTFORT: You're a Jilt.
BUTLER: Made so here only by a Poet's pen;
Send him his part, I'll never play't agen.

(*Throws away the part and exit*)

Again the epilogue plays on the difference between actress and role, but in this case the implication is that the two are very similar. When Butler had made her exit, Mountfort turned to the audience and assured them, 'This is a Trick, and done, or I'm a Chouse, / To get a greater pension from the House.' Butler's behaviour was just an elaborate trick to seem ill-used and so get higher wages.

Like Butler, Barry had a reputation in contemporary satire for being mercenary in her sexual dealings (see chapter 1), and this was played on in epilogues in a way which stressed the actress's 'real' personality as opposed to her part in the play. In Durfey's *The Intrigues at Versailles* (1697) Barry played the 'jilt' of the title, a bad-tempered mistress named Madame de Vendosme. The comedy finished, the actress re-entered as 'herself' in angry mood, '*as in a fret*', complaining,

How long, and oft, have I, in well wrought Scenes,
Dazled like Glittering Empresses and Queens,
Acted all passions, love, grief, joy and shame,
The Great Court Lady, and the City Dame.[8]
And if sometimes, a wanton subject came
Yee Poets Characters, decent were, and civil,
But ours... Curse on't here, makes me act the Devil.

However, the actress found consolation in the idea of the money she would be able to earn from the part:

The Play by Judges, has commended been,
And if it bring but the new Money in:
Money's a certain Medicine for my Spleen.

She concluded that although 'my part, I own, I hate to a degree', she would 'set a good face, and play't agen tomorrow', for the sake of the cash.

---

9 Nell Gwyn rising from the dead to speak the epilogue to *Tyrannick Love*, from *The Key to the Rehearsal*, in Buckingham's *Works* (1715), vol. II.

Nell Gwyn's famous epilogue at the end of Dryden's tragedy *Tyrannick Love* (1669), when having 'died' in her character during the play's last act she suddenly came to life at the end and berated those trying to carry her 'corpse' off the stage, works, of course, on a similar premise. Having played the virtuous heroine Valeria in the tragedy, Nell Gwyn reminded audiences how much such a role was at odds with her true personality and talents:

> To tell you true, I walk because I dye
> Out of my calling, in a Tragedy.
> O Poet, damn'd dull Poet, who could prove
> So senseless! to make Nelly dye for Love.

It really was 'senseless' because in real life, as mistress of the king and others, 'Nelly' did not die, but lived by love.

In speaking these epilogues, Butler, Barry and Gwyn lightheartedly reinforced the idea of themselves as whores, corroborating, as it were, what the satirists and the gossips said about them. Whether or not their public images represented the truth about their private lives, the women accepted and sustained on stage the personae they were given, and these personae became stronger and more significant in the eyes of the public than any of the roles they played. In this way a 'star system' was born, in which the scandalous, glamorous personal reputation of the performer, rather than the role she played, held people's attention.

THE RELATION BETWEEN ACTRESS, PERSONA AND STAGE ROLES

Anne Bracegirdle

How far did the audience's awareness of the actresses' 'real' selves impinge on the drama that was written for the women to act in? Certainly in many cases it impinged a great deal, for playwrights began to base the roles they wrote for an actress around her public persona – as presumably occurred in the case of Charlotte Butler's role as Betty Jiltall. A similarity between persona and roles is especially marked in the case of Anne Bracegirdle, the actress who spoke most prologues and epilogues and who seems to have been the greatest favourite with spectators. As we have seen, the most striking feature of Bracegirdle's public image was her reputation for chastity, which was played on suggestively again and again in her prologues and epilogues as well as in satires. In the epilogue to Dryden's *Cleomenes* (1692), for example, the actress declared,

> This Day, the Poet, bloodily inclin'd,
> Has made me die, full sore against my Mind!
> Some of you naughty Men I fear, will cry
> Poor rogue! would I might teach thee how to die!
> Thanks for your Love: but I sincerely say,
> I never mean to die, your wicked Way.

The popular pun on 'die', of course, involved the experience of sexual orgasm. Similarly when, in Durfey's *The Marriage-Hater Match'd* (1692), Bracegirdle took a breeches role – such exposure of her legs being not what one would expect from an actress of spotless reputation – she complained in the prologue (dressed in her '*Boy's Cloaths*'),

> Would the Play were Damn'd:
> I shall ne'er wish the Poet good Success:
> For putting me into this nauseous Dress;
> A Dress, which of all other things I hate.

She then proclaimed her chastity, 'Men, nor their Garbs, did e'er my Credit wrong', to which Mountfort responded, 'That's much, faith, having known the Stage so long, / Well, we'll allow your Modesty is Fam'd.'

Bracegirdle's parts in both comedy and tragedy are strikingly in line with her chaste image. In tragedy she generally played the virtuous heroine, loved by both hero and villain, sometimes raped but always pure. Typical roles in this vein include Antelina in Mountfort's *The Injur'd Lovers* (1688), Urania in Powell's *Alphonso, King of Naples* (1690) and Camilla in Charles Hopkins' *Boadicea, Queen of Britain* (1697). In comedy, as we saw in chapter 3, she was most often cast as an attractive young heroine, dogged by numerous importunate suitors but resolutely refusing them all, though usually finally united with the man of her choice.[9] In *The Way of the World* Congreve went so far as to deliberately echo a particular feature of two of Bracegirdle's epilogues in the behaviour of her character, Millamant. In the epilogue to Dryden's *King Arthur* (1691), Bracegirdle walked on to the stage at the end of the drama flourishing a handful of love-letters which she proceeded to read out loud for spectators' benefit:

> Here's one desires my Ladiship to meet
> At the kind Couch above in Bridges-Street.
> Oh Sharping Knave! That wou'd have, you know what,
> For a Poor Sneaking Treat of chocolat.

She read several more, mocking the authors in each case, before strengthening her popular chaste image by the conclusion, 'My wisest way will be to keep the Stage, / And trust to the Good Nature of the Age.' The joke was repeated in the epilogue to Peter Motteux's *Beauty in Distress* (1698) when Bracegirdle produced what she apparently thought was a petition from the dramatist to the spectators and exclaimed, 'H'as sent me a Petition here for you. / That's it – Cry Mercy! That's a Billet-Doux.' She seemed about to read yet another love-letter. However, in this case, affecting surprise, she put it away, '*in haste*', and pulled out the proper petition. In *The Way of the World* Millamant would seem to be deliberately recalling this epilogue stage business with the *billets-doux* when she complains, in her pose as a heartless coquette, of all the love-letters she receives,

O ay, Letters – I had letters – I am persecuted with Letters – I hate Letters – No Body knows how to write Letters; and yet one has 'em, one does not know why – They serve one to pin up one's hair.[10]

Durfey may also be presumed to have been playing on Bracegirdle's well-known habit of teasing and rejecting her followers when he inserted a coquette role for her into the first and second parts of his three-part version of Cervantes' story *The Comical History of Don Quixote* (1694, 1695). In the first part her character, Marcella, hardheartedly rejects all who love her, as Bracegirdle did, but in the second part Durfey punished her for this by making her fall unrequitedly in love. As he explained,

I think I have given some additional Diversion in the continuance of the Character of Marcella; which is wholly new in This Part, and my own Invention; the Design finishing with more pleasure to Audience, by punishing that coy Creature by an extravagant Passion here, that was so inexorable and cruel in the First Part, and ending with a Song so incomparably well sung, and acted by Mrs. Bracegirdle, that the most Envious do allow, as well as the most Ingenious affirm, that 'tis the best of that kind ever done before.[11]

Durfey had supplied what the public were clearly delighted to see –

their favourite in love for once, instead of being loved. Delariviere Manley pandered to popular taste in an opposite way in her tragedy *Almyna* (1706) by finally giving Almyna/Bracegirdle the man she loved. Unusually in this tragedy Bracegirdle was cast not as a rape victim but as an unrequited lover driven mad by the frustration of being rejected. Having observed that at no time in her career had Bracegirdle ever acted better in a tragedy, Manley explained in the preface to the printed edition that 'she so far Acted herself into the kind Wishes of the Town, that in Compliment to their better Opinion, the Author has thought fit to make her happy in her Lover'. *Almyna* furnishes a particularly vivid example of the way in which an actress's popularity could affect the writing of drama. But the mass of examples shows that every dramatist, more or less, had the public's view of Bracegirdle in mind when he or she produced roles for her.

Elizabeth Currer

The case of Currer affords another striking instance of a cor-respondence between stage role and the persona derived from prologue and epilogue – although the persona in this case is somewhat different. In tragedy as well as comedy of the 1670s and 1680s Currer specialised in playing mistresses and whores and she frequently displayed her legs in breeches roles.[12] Her most famous part in a tragedy was as Aquilina the courtesan in the comic sub-plot of Otway's *Venice Preserved*, kicking the old senator Antonio about the stage to satisfy his masochistic lusts. Antonio was played by the brilliant and popular comedian Anthony Leigh and, according to Thomas Davies, 'when Leigh and Mrs. Currer performed the parts of doting cully and rampant courtezan, the applause was as loud as the triumphant tories, for so they were at that time, could bestow'.[13] Nahum Tate cashed in on their success in *Venice Preserved*: in his adaptation of Cokain's *Trappolin Suppos'd a Prince* called *A Duke and No Duke* (1684), Tate had Leigh as Trappolin gaze lustfully at Currer as the Duchess in her nightgown and chase her lasciviously at every opportunity. As Sir Patient Fancy and his wife in Behn's *Sir Patient Fancy* (1678), Leigh and Currer represented another comic case of thwarted desire. Currer also played the passionate mistress whom Crowne added for Edward in his adaptation of Shakespeare's *Henry VI Parts II and III*, *The Misery of Civil-War* (1680), the Lady Elianor Butler who pursues her lover to the battlefield and begs to share his struggles. At this, Edward immediately seeks a cottage where they can bed together and although she puts up a token protest, 'Fye, Fye, such thoughts as these at such a time?', she is easily persuaded, 'Well – since I must.'[14]

These roles reflect Currer's 'real' personality as given in satire and in her personalised prologues and epilogues. The one satire that survives about her, a few lines in 'A Satyr on the Players', urges her rudely, as a prostitute, to leave London and go back to Ireland:

> Currer 'tis time thou wert to Ireland gone
> Thy utmost Rate is here but half a Crown
> Ask Turner if thou art not fulsom grown.[15]

Turner was presumably a lover who discovered that she had become 'fulsom', that is, promiscuous. In the prologue to Ravenscroft's *Dame Dobson* (1693) Currer began by declaring, 'Gallants, I vow I am quite out of heart, / I've not one smutty Jest in all my part.' Two years earlier, in Tate's *The Loyal General*, Currer played a villainous queen who ended up in a nunnery after which, in her epilogue, she impudently told her audience,

> I'faith I've broke my Prison Walls to see ye;
> Must I be cloyster'd up? Dull Poet stay,
> I hate Confinement tho' but in a Play,
> Doom me to a Nun's Life?...A Nun! Oh Heart!
> The Name's so dreadful, that it makes me start!
> No! Tell the Scribbling Fool [the playwright] I'm just as fit
> To make a Nun as he to make a Wit.

Again, typically, the credibility of the play is destroyed cheerfully by the intimate relationship between actress as herself and her audience.

The actress in general

It has been suggested that Restoration playwrights were severely limited in the characters they could create because of the audience's intrusive awareness of the actress's own personality:

Shakespeare's women were the creations of a teeming imagination; his poetic pen gave to airy nothing a local habitation and a name, and its only limitation was the number of competent, well-trained boys available at a given time...But the Restoration playwright, working in an age when the speaker had become more important than the word, confined by the necessity of writing not just for actresses but for a specific Nell, Anne, or

Betty... had to suit his roles to their abilities, their types and, worst of all, to their personal reputations.[16]

The Restoration critic and playwright John Dennis would have agreed with this. In 1711 he observes:

For it has been a Complaint of Two thousand Years standing, that Poets have been us'd to violate their Subjects, and to force their Characters out of complaisance to their Actors, that is, to their Interest. Most of the Writers for the Stage in my time, have not only adapted their Characters to their Actors, but those Actors have as it were sate for them.[17]

Colley Cibber seems to lend support to this view when he notes that

the private Character of an Actor, will always, more or less, affect his Publick Performance... I have seen the most tender Sentiment of Love, in Tragedy, create Laughter, instead of Compassion, when it has been applicable to the real Engagements of the Person, that utter'd it. I have known good Parts thrown up, from an humble Consciousness, that something in them, might put an Audience in mind of – what was rather wish'd might be forgotten.

Significantly his example of such an embarrassing clash is of a woman's role: 'those remarkable Words of Evadne, in *The Maid's Tragedy* – A Maidenhead, Amintor, at my Years? – have sometimes been a much stronger Jest, for being a true one.'[18] This was one problem that can certainly never have arisen when *The Maid's Tragedy* was performed by boy-actors. The critic William Chetwood also relates a sorry tale concerning women: how Barry received a 'Horse-laugh' from the audience when, as Cordelia in Tate's *Lear*, she delivered the line 'Arm'd in my Virgin Innocence I'll fly', her lack of such innocence being all too well known. This 'turn'd to Ridicule' a scene 'of generous Pity and Compassion'. Bracegirdle, on the other hand, apparently gained a round of applause when she spoke the line, 'more as a Reward for her reputable Character, than, perhaps, her Acting claim'd'.[19]

However, it would be most inaccurate to say, as Dennis and Cibber imply, that an actress of dubious reputation could never take a serious part without provoking laughter. This was certainly not true, for instance, in the case of Jane Rogers during the 1690s. After various immoral exploits, this actress eventually went to live with the actor Wilks. This did not prevent her from being cast as the pure and suffering wife Amanda in Cibber's *Love's Last Shift*(1695), and in its sequel, Vanbrugh's *The Relapse* (1696). She also played the

Bracegirdle equivalent in tragedy for Rich's company = the suffering, noble, virginal young heroine. In Abel Boyer's *Achilles* (1699) she played Iphigenia, in Catherine Trotter's *The Unhappy Penitent* (1701) she played Margarite of Flanders, in Bevill Higgons' *The Generous Conqueror* (1701) she played the pure Armida. The difference between these roles and her real-life character is highlighted in an amusing anecdote by Cibber. He relates how Rogers hoped that, since she was playing a chaste heroine in an anonymous tragedy called *The Triumphs of Virtue* (1697), she might be able to play such a character in real life:

Her Fondness for Virtue on the Stage she began to think might perswade the World that it had made an Impression on her private Life; and the Appearances of it actually went so far that, in an Epilogue to an obscure Play, the Profits of which were given to her, and wherein she acted a Part of impregnable Chastity, she bespoke the Favour of the Ladies by a Protestation that in Honour of their Goodness and Virtue she would dedicate her unblemish'd Life to their Example.

The epilogue in question included the lines:

> I'll pay this duteous gratitude; I'll do
> That which the play has done – I'll copy you.
> At your own virtue's shrine my vows I'll pay,
> Study to live the character I play.

But shortly afterwards she apparently agreed to live with fellow actor Wilks. Cibber laments mockingly, 'But alas! how weak are the Strongest Works of Art when Nature besieges it?'[20]

Rogers is not the only example of such an anomaly. As we have seen, the 'jilt' Butler played the naive, virginal heroine Charlot in *The City Heiress* and Elizabeth Boutell, 'whom all the Town fucks', 'generally acted the young, innocent Lady whom all the Heroes are mad in Love with'.[21] For instance, Boutell played the most chaste and innocent of all comic heroines, Fidelia, in Wycherley's *The Plain-Dealer* (1676). The anomaly could work the other way as well. Mary Betterton, faithful wife of Thomas, never appeared in any satire and never spoke a suggestive prologue in her life, yet on occasion she did play a lustful villainess, notably the Empress of Morocco in Settle's play of that title in 1673 (although she did specialise, it must be admitted, in pure heroines).

A correspondence between an actress's persona and her roles is generally less pronounced in tragedy than it is in comedy (as might be expected in a drama that tended to be further removed from real and contemporary life than comedy was). For example, by the 1680s Barry, who was known to have had several lovers and was portrayed in lampoons as a mercenary prostitute, usually played mistresses and unfaithful wives in comedy, but in tragedy she played a large number of virtuous heroines. Her three most famous parts were the honourable wives Monimia, Belvidera and Southerne's Isabella. It has been suggested that in tragedy, where events and characters were so incredible anyway, 'it made little difference whether the players were saints or sinners, so long as the writer avoided those unfortunate lines which could suddenly expose the incongruity between stage character and actor character and arouse a "Horse-laugh"'.[22] However, the creative process with regard to Barry, at least, is more complex than this. It is interesting to note that in almost all her parts, from Monimia in 1680 onwards, however honourably her characters behave they are generally in some way sexually experienced. Even though she is cruelly deceived, Monimia does sleep with Polidor. The heroines Belvidera, Isabella, Anna Bullen or Fulvia (in Crowne's *Regulus* of 1692) are all wives, who can thus behave virtuously without actually possessing 'virgin innocence'. This feature is highlighted when Barry's tragic roles are compared with those of Bracegirdle, her opposite in so many serious dramas. Right through the period from 1688 to 1706, while her foil Barry performed a range of parts from virtuous wife to lustful villainess, Bracegirdle's parts in tragedy remained comparatively constant: every one a variation on the innocent virgin. In the tragedies in which she did play a wife rather than a virgin her characters were still markedly pure in comparison with those of Barry. In *Cleomenes* (1692), for example, she played the meek and helpless Cleora, while Barry played the jealous, passionate Cassandra. In Rowe's *The Fair Penitent* Bracegirdle's role as Lavinia, the idealised, obedient wife of Horatio, was designed to highlight the tragic weakness of the Barry heroine, Calista, who is a magnificently repentant 'fallen woman'.

However, for a variety of reasons, an actress's public image might not be in accord with her stage role. In some cases, a dramatist must not have been able to obtain the actress he wanted, or else have deliberately refused to limit his female cast to the reputations of the female players available. We need also to take account of those subtle instances in which a dramatist might create a role for an actress that was purposely at variance with her public persona to make a particular point, of which perhaps the most striking example was Southerne's taking the extreme step of casting Bracegirdle as a sin-hardened, unfaithful wife in his bitter satire *The Maid's Last Prayer* (1693) to emphasise the degraded type of libertine society he had chosen to portray. In one sense, of course, this technique reinforces Dennis's point that dramatists had to rely on what was known of their performers' private characters. But it also negates the criticism that a player's 'sitting' for his or her part had a limiting effect on the drama. The common correlation between persona and role gave the Restoration playwright a very effective weapon. He could cheat audience expectations and make thematic and satiric points by producing an unexpected part for an actress that was at odds with her usual behaviour both on stage and off.

The crucial fact to be aware of is that, by the late 1670s, the actresses' own public personae had intervened somehow in the creative process behind every play in which they appeared, and in this way the women had become more important than the roles they played. The unfortunate experience of Dryden's protégé George Granville offers a final, illuminating cautionary tale of what could happen if a dramatist failed to take into account the special relationship between a leading actress and her public when giving her a role in his play. In the preface to his first tragedy, *Heroick Love* (1698), the young Granville explains why he decided to make Bracegirdle's role, most unusually for a tragedy, one of a vain coquette and supporting character, rather than that of the virtuous heroine:

Had he form'd her a moving Character, should he have brought her in lamenting her Misfortune and attracting Compassion, this would have prejudic'd the Chief Hero of the Play; for all the Pity which she had excited, must necessarily have rais'd so much Indignation against him. The Author thus was under a Necessity to represent her in such a manner, that no Body might be concern'd, or take any part in her Misfortune.

But Granville underestimated both Bracegirdle's talent for playing coquettes (much exercised in comedy) and her popularity with audiences. His aim was to divert attention and sympathy onto the hero, but so charmingly did Bracegirdle perform her role that the teasing Briseis actually turned out to be the part 'which in the Representation meets the loudest Applause', as Granville puts it elsewhere in the preface. As her prologues and epilogues and roles like Millamant show, theatre-goers loved to see Bracegirdle captivating and then frustrating her languishing admirers – when she played a coquette this character became enormously attractive. Granville's plan failed because the bond between actress and public was strong enough to outweigh the dramatic impact of the lines he had written for her. One cannot write a supporting role in a scene for a star.

CHAPTER 5

Elizabeth Barry and the development of Restoration tragedy

The influence of the actresses on the development of Restoration tragedy has been surprisingly neglected by historians and critics. No full critical investigation of this topic has ever been made and yet, while the leading tragic styles of drama during the 1660s were all male-dominated, the 1670s and 1680s saw a major shift from heroic to pathetic tragedy, and by the end of the century a highly popular genre known as 'she-tragedy'[1] had emerged, focused on pure and suffering women. The factors behind the evolution of pathetic and 'she' tragedy are several and complex but, oddly, the importance of the actresses as a cause of the changes has gone almost unrecognised. So far only a handful of scholars have made even a brief mention of any actress's contribution to Restoration tragic form. In a few lines, Rothstein and Hume comment on the way in which typecasting of Barry and Bracegirdle helped to determine the form of tragedies during the 1680s and 1690s; Nicoll mentions in passing, as he discusses Barry's 'debased' and 'licentious' private life, that she also helped to make affective tragedy popular. Most recently, Jocelyn Powell claims that Barry was the 'key figure' in the shift from heroic to pathetic drama because she pioneered a new acting style designed to 'stir rather than penetrate human nature' and that tragic actors like Betterton then followed her lead. It is difficult either to support or refute this suggestion, since acting is an all-too-ephemeral art. While clearly Barry's affective acting was remarkable, pathetic drama began to develop from the early 1670s, some years before Barry created her great pathetic roles.[2]

In the first two decades of the period, within a gradual overall movement towards larger roles for women and towards more scenes of love and pathos in tragedy, various actresses made their own individual, not always 'pathetic', contributions. Then in 1680 Elizabeth Barry triumphantly created the pathetic role of Monimia in Otway's *The Orphan* and her success in the part clinched the movement away from heroic drama and started the establishment of 'she-tragedy' as a popular genre. 'In the Art of exciting Pity', exclaims Cibber, 'she had a Power beyond all the Actresses I have yet seen, or what your Imagination can conceive.'[3]

THE ACTRESSES AND THE DECLINE OF HEROIC DRAMA
1670–80

While the typical heroic drama is focused on the pursuit of ideals by a powerful, aggressively masculine hero through both his public career as ruler and conqueror and his private life as lover, the heart of pathetic drama is love and its concerns are primarily domestic, even though its main characters may be rulers and leaders. Obviously one genre blends into the other, many plays combine characteristics of both types and it is only by surveying twenty years' development that the shift from one style to the other becomes apparent. Still, by the 1680s heroic dramas, though sometimes written and performed, had gone out of style. A number of reasons have been suggested for this change in fashion. The restoration of the monarchy was followed by a period of bitter political disillusionment and several critics relate the rejection of heroic drama to a growing sense of the non-viability of the old absolutist, aristocratic ideology.[4] This loss of faith in old masculine ideals of behaviour may have been accompanied by a new desire to use women as social models. The suffering victim who maintains her honour in spite of her frailty in a domestic sphere, emphatically separate from the newly differentiated public world of state power, law and politics, represented a vital image for a society in which 'aristocratic protagonists are replaced with protagonists who have less and less access to individual power'.[5] The appearance of 'she-tragedy' also coincided with other female developments: a popular sovereign, Queen Mary, ruled alone while her husband campaigned abroad, a number of pamphlets were published extolling the rights of women, and the first English periodical conceived solely for women was produced.[6]

Some literary and theatrical causes of the heroic decline have also been suggested, such as a general denunciation of the style of rhyming couplets, in which many heroic dramas were written, a shift from a largely aristocratic to a largely bourgeois audience and an increase in the number and influence of the 'ladies' in the audience who preferred pathos to heroics.[7] The effects of the last two factors are particularly hard to prove. Recent research has shown that there is little evidence to support the suggestion that the class composition of the Restoration audience changed appreciably during the 1670s and 1680s,[8] while the extent of female spectators' influence is difficult to ascertain conclusively, the main evidence being prologues and epilogues of the 1670s and 1680s advertising scenes of love and occasions for pity as a special attraction for the women in the audience. Such advertisements may well have been the effect, rather than the cause, of a shift from heroic to pathetic drama, designed merely to please the women and so ensure a good reception for the chosen dramatic style.

There is, however, another reason for the shift in tragic style. By the 1670s, some leading tragic actresses had emerged whose popularity and talent must have made it necessary for dramatists to modify existing models of drama in order to accommodate them. Being rooted in the honour and glory to be won in war and politics, heroic plays could never offer women more than subordinate roles. It is no coincidence that at the same time as love, pathos and female characters were becoming more prominent in tragedy,[9] actresses were proving themselves in a variety of serious roles. Pepys' diary shows that two leading actresses had made their presence felt by the end of the 1660s. As early as 1662 he began to praise Mary Betterton, or 'Ianthe' as he called her, after her success playing that character in Davenant's opera about a battle between Christians and Turks, *The Siege of Rhodes* (1661). In a revival of Massinger's *The Bondman* in 1664, 'Batterton [Betterton] and my poor Ianthe out-do all the world', while Mary Betterton's part in Orrery's *The History of Henry the Fifth* (1664) was 'most incomparably wrote and done'.[10] Pepys' early admiration for Rebecca Marshall is still more striking. Her talent apparently first struck him when she played Evadne in a 1666 revival of Beaumont and Fletcher's *The Maid's Tragedy*: 'the younger Marshall is become a pretty good actor'. Of her role as the Queen of Sicily in Dryden's *Secret Love* (1667) Pepys wrote enthusiastically, 'it being impossible, I think, ever to have the Queen's part, which is very good and passionate...ever done better then...by young Marshall'.[11] A revival of Shirley's *The Cardinal* in the same year occasioned the remark 'wherewith I am mightily pleased; but above all with Becke Marshall', while *Secret Love* in 1668 brought 'certainly the best acted of anything ever that House did, and perticularly, Becke

Marshall, to admiration'.[12] A revival of *The Virgin Martyr*, also in 1668, was redeemed by Marshall, 'it is mighty pleasant; not that the play is worth much, but it is finely Acted by Becke Marshall'.[13]

By the early 1670s two more tragic actresses had emerged with the talent to attract the attention of dramatists and spectators. One was Elizabeth Boutell, who joined the King's Company in 1670 and promptly created the leading roles of Aurelia in William Joyner's *The Roman Empress* (1670), Benzayda in Dryden's *The Conquest of Granada* (1670, 1671) and Cyara in Nathaniel Lee's *Nero* (1673). In his preface to *The Roman Empress* Joyner singled out Boutell, with Marshall, for praise. Marshall's part 'was incomparably acted', while Aurelia, 'though a great, various, and difficult part, was excellently perform'd'. By the mid-seventies Boutell had begun to specialise very successfully in gentle, timorous heroines such as Rosalinda in Lee's *Sophonisba* (1675), Cleopatra in Dryden's *All For Love* (1677) and Clarona in Crowne's two-part *Destruction of Jerusalem by Titus Vespasian* (1677). During the same period, acting for the Duke's Company, Mary Lee had emerged as a leading tragedienne, taking the central role in three out of four of Elkanah Settle's bloody melodramas of the early 1670s. The extravagantly produced *Empress of Morocco* (1673) had Betterton unusually cast as the play's lustful, ranting namesake and Lee as her opposite, the noble Mariamne. The gory *Love and Revenge* (1674), adapted from William Hemings' *The Fatal Contract*, had its action controlled by Lee disguised as a man. Settle transformed Hemings' Eunuch, who appears to be a sinister, obscene and utterly blackhearted manipulator of events until the very end, into Nigrello, played by Lee, who in the first act reveals to the audience that she is the ravished Chlotilda, bent on revenge. Thus the later version is much more obviously dominated by a woman.

Settle's next drama, *The Conquest of China* (1675), exploited still further the idea of giving Lee overall control by putting her into man's dress. Here the actress created the role of Amavanga, a brave Chinese queen, who disguises herself as a soldier and by adhering to a ridiculous code of honour persuades herself to propose a duel with the man she loves. The two fight and Amavanga falls, revealing her true identity to her unfortunate lover in her dying speech. However, at the end of the play Settle has her miraculously resurrected and all is happily resolved. Amavanga is not, of course, a pathetic heroine. *The Conquest of China* shows the ingenious lengths a dramatist had to

go in order to place a woman at the heart of a tragedy preoccupied with the honour code and victory in battle. All three of Settle's plays show an effort to make the actress predominant within the more heroic styles of tragedy. Of course, a logical next step would be for dramatists to write tragedy which centred on a woman behaving in a more conventional fashion – suffering, pleading, weeping – or, in other words, for dramatists to write pathetic 'she-tragedy'. Although their exact influence cannot be determined, it is impossible to separate the emergence of successful tragediennes from the evolution of affective tragedy.

THOMAS OTWAY AND ELIZABETH BARRY

Although by the end of the 1670s the pathetic style of tragedy had superseded the heroic, plays were still usually focused on a hero rather than a heroine. With a few notable exceptions, successful as actresses such as Marshall and Lee were, the leading actors Betterton, Smith, Harris and Hart continued to play the majority of star roles in tragedy. It took the association of the master of pathos Thomas Otway with Elizabeth Barry to shift the focus of such drama decisively from hero to heroine.

In Otway's plays of the 1670s love and pathos soon became central. Although his first play, *Alcibiades* (1675), follows popular heroic conventions and centres on a warrior hero, the main action of his second tragedy, *Don Carlos, Prince of Spain* (1676), consists almost entirely of the doomed love affair between the royal prince Don Carlos and his stepmother the Queen (played by Mary Lee). The play represented a significant advance for the pathetic style of tragedy. As Otway's editor J. C. Ghosh points out, the play's source is a French historical romance by César Vischard, from which Otway omitted all the political elements and retained only the love story.[14] Every scene involving the lovers is designed to inspire pity as they attempt to part for ever and yet are unable to bear the separation. Significantly, in its time *Don Carlos* was apparently more successful than any other tragedy. Downes states that 'all the Parts being

---

10 Frontispiece engraving to *Antony and Cleopatra*, in vol. VI of Rowe's *Works of Shakespeare*. The setting and especially the posture of the dying Cleopatra, however, suggests that the illustration is more likely to have been taken from a production of Dryden's *All for Love*.

admirably Acted, it lasted successively 10 Days; it got more Money than any preceding Modern tragedy'.[15]

Elizabeth Barry was born in 1658, the daughter of the distinguished barrister and Royalist soldier Robert Barry. When the family apparently lost all its wealth and sank into obscurity, Elizabeth was taken up and educated by the Davenants who had been friends of her father. Otway and Barry were certainly acquainted by 1675 because in that year the actress played the small supporting role of the maid Draxilla in *Alcibiades*, apparently her first stage role. Unfortunately she played the part so badly that she was dismissed from the company at the end of the season.[16] However, around the same time she became mistress of the Earl of Rochester and, possibly for a wager, he coached her for a successful return to the stage.[17] Rochester appears to have done more than simply train his protégée in the mechanical aspects of her profession. Her eighteenth-century biographer, Edmund Curll, describes how he also made her enter into the 'Nature of each Sentiment',

perfectly changing herself, as it were, into the Person, not merely by the proper Stress or Sounding of the Voice, but feeling really, and being in the Humour, the Person she represented, was supposed to be in.[18]

Barry returned to the stage and instantly had a triumphant success playing Isabella the Hungarian Queen in Orrery's *Mustapha*. Curll's account of her performance is worth quoting in full:

The first Night she played the Hungarian Queen...The very Air she appeared with, in that distressed Character, moved them with Pity, preparing the Mind to greater Expectations, but when she spoke these Words to the insulting Cardinal,

> My Lord, my Sorrow seeks not your Relief;
> You are not fit to judge a Mother's Grief:
> You have no Child for an untimely Grave,
> Nor can you lose what I desire to save.

Here, Majesty distressed by the hostile Foe, the Widow Queen forlorn, insulted by her Subjects, feeling all an afflicted Mother could suffer by a stern Counsellor's forcing her to yield her only Son to be sacrificed to the Enemy to save themselves and the City, these Passions were so finely expressed by her, that the whole Theatre resounded with Applauses...that little Speech of

> What means my giving Subjects?

was spoken with such a Grace and Emphasis as was never before, or since, to be imitated; her Performance giving the Audience an Idea of that Princess in many important Passages of her Life.[19]

11 Elizabeth Barry, after Godfrey Kneller.

Barry seems to have excelled in the tragic technique of harmonising suitable expressions, tones of voice and emotions. She was 'mistress of all the passions of the mind: love, joy, grief, rage, tenderness, and jealousy, were all represented by her with equal skill and equal effect'. In his 'Supplement' to Colley Cibber's account of the leading players of the Restoration stage Anthony Aston describes how her face 'somewhat preceded her Action, as the latter did her Words, her Face ever expressing the Passions'. In praising her as Sakia in his play *Liberty Asserted* (1704), John Dennis describes Barry as 'that incomparable Actress changing like Nature which she represents, from Passion to Passion, from Extream to Extream, with piercing Force, and with easie Grace, changes the Hearts of all who see her with irresistible Pleasure'. Gildon himself seems particularly struck by the way in which Barry continued to act appropriately even when not speaking, changing her expression in line with the speeches of others (the majority of players apparently only bothered to act when they had to speak). 'This', he exclaims, 'is to know her Part, this is to express the Passions in Countenance and Gesture.'[20]

Barry's success in moving audiences was all the greater in that she was in real life a plain woman. Surviving portraits suggest intelligence, but heavy features and a large Roman nose. One critic mentions a lop-sided mouth, 'op'ning most on the Right Side', and her figure in later life was certainly not one to be displayed – a letter from the playwright Thomas Shadwell to the Earl of Dorset in January 1692 states that he would have Nicholas Brady's *The Rape* 'acted in Roman habits and then w'th a Mantle to have covered her hips Mrs Barry would have acted ye part'.[21] But her acting talent was such as to enable spectators to forget her looks. As *A Comparison Between Two Stages* puts it, she was 'the finest Woman in the World upon the Stage', even though she was 'the ugliest Woman off on't'.[22]

With her success in the minor role of Isabella, Barry proved her tragic ability and soon after came her crucial association with Otway. Her influence on him was two-fold. On a personal level, the dramatist is known to have nursed an intense, unrequited passion for her for years,[23] a fact which presumably encouraged him to place her at the centre of his tragedy and which must have helped to invest it with its peculiarly overpowering emotional and sexual intensity. More importantly, on a professional level, he undoubtedly recognised and utilised her outstanding talent for performing emotional scenes. Remarkably, in the roles he wrote for Barry Otway seems to have been able to unite his subjective involvement and his objective appreciation.

Otway was the author of Barry's second known leading role in a tragedy (her first was as Polyxena in John Banks' *The Destruction of Troy* in 1678). She played the heroine, Lavinia, in the play he wrote after *Don Carlos*, *The History and Fall of Caius Marius* (1679). This play was a melodramatic combination of Shakespeare's *Romeo and Juliet* and the history of Marius from Plutarch and Lucan. The latter is more important, the play's main plot being the political career of Caius Marius (played by Betterton) as he gains and then loses rule over Rome. His son Marius (Romeo) falls in love with Lavinia (Juliet), the daughter of a family enemy. Otway made fashionable alterations to the original, wrenching the last drop of pathos and sensation from the tragedy by having Lavinia awake just in time to bid farewell to the dying Marius in the final act. Juliet's comparatively restrained lines were replaced with sensational, extravagant rhetoric for Lavinia. For instance, Juliet's brief pleas to her parents, to spare her marriage with Paris, are expanded into bombast:

> Will you then quite cast off your poor Lavinia?
> And turn me like a Vagrant out of Doors,
> To wander up and down the streets of Rome,
> And beg my bread with sorrow? Can I bear
> The proud and hard Revilings of a Slave,
> Fat with his Master's plenty, when I ask
> A little Pity for my pinching wants?
> Shall I endure the cold, wet, windy Night,
> To seek a shelter under dropping Eves,
> A Porch my Bed, a Threshold for my Pillow,
> Shiv'ring with my sighs, and almost choak'd with Tears?

The sight of dead Romeo prompts Juliet almost immediately to suicide, but Lavinia rants:

> What shall I doe? how will the Gods dispose me?
> Oh! I could rend these Walls with Lamentation,
> Tear up the Dead from their corrupted Graves,
> And dawb the face of Earth with her own Bowels.[24]

In other words, Otway would seem to have altered the language of Skakespeare's heroine so as to provide Barry with the kind of affecting speeches he realised she would be adept at delivering.

Less than a year after *Caius Marius*, Otway produced *The Orphan* and transformed Barry into a star. This tragedy is based ˌlely, as the preceding Shakespearian adaptation was not, on love and a distressed heroine. The plot marks a significant break away from heroic tradition – it is centred on a private family as opposed to royalty, and the setting is the pastoral retreat of Acasto, a retired courtier who is determined to turn his back on the corruptions of court life. The tragedy is focused entirely on sexual love relationships rather than the heroic goals of glory and power. At its centre is Monimia (Barry's role), the orphan of the title who innocently precipitates the catastrophe by being desired by both 'heroes', the brothers Castalio and Polydore. Both men are entirely obsessed by Monimia – as one puts it, 'To touch thee's Heav'n, but to enjoy thee, oh! / Thou Nature's whole perfection in one piece!'[25] Although she loves and becomes the wife of Castalio, it is Polydore who enjoys Monimia by a trick; he manages to substitute himself for her husband in bed on their marriage night. When the trick is discovered, Monimia, a remorseful Polydore and a despairing Castalio all commit suicide. The lack of logic in both brothers' behaviour has been commented on, but the play's aim is predominantly pathos – the rationality and logic of its plot and characterisation are therefore comparatively unimportant.[26]

Barry's 'power' in the 'Art of exciting Pity', as Cibber calls it, was fundamental to the play's success. Unlike the brothers, Monimia is purely a victim, so that this role is the one most vital to the drama's tearjerking effect. Barry's success as Monimia was achieved partly through tones of voice and partly through key gestures and actions. At times she moved her audience by her delivery; as she dies, for instance, Monimia addresses Castalio with,

> When I'm laid low in the grave, and quite forgotten,
> Mayst thou be happy in a fairer bride;
> But none can ever love thee like Monimia.
> When I am dead, as presently I shall be
> (For the grim tyrant grasps my heart already),
> Speak well of me...   (V.475–80)

These sentimental lines must have been declaimed with the emotional power of a diva at the end of Verdi's *La Traviata*. At other moments, pathos was achieved purely by Barry's actions as she wept, knelt and threw herself across the stage. At the climactic instant, for example, at which Polydore reveals her unconscious adultery to her, Monimia speaks only two words before swooning.

> POLYDORE: Within thy arms
> I triumphed. Rest had been my foe.
> MONIMIA: 'Tis done – (*she faints*)   (IV.396–7)

The playwright George Granville usefully explains the dramatic impact of such a swoon: 'in some Cases where the Passion must be presum'd so Violent or so Tender, that Words can but faintly represent it, it is then a Beauty to express it in this Manner, and by far more Pathetick, than any Speech, tho' never so Rhetorical'.[27] The most famous and moving moment of the play was apparently Monimia's simple exit line, 'Ah poor Castalio' (V.304), the line that Barry said she could never speak without weeping.[28]

Barry's remarkable success as Monimia is forcefully documented by Downes. He tells us that all the parts in *The Orphan* were 'Admirably done', but 'especially the Part of Monimia'. It was one of the three roles that gained Barry 'the Name of Famous Mrs. Barry, both at Court and City' and when she played it she 'forc'd Tears from the Eyes of her Auditory, especially those who have any Sense of Pity for the Distress't'.[29] *The Orphan* itself was not immediately a hit only because the political crisis of the Popish Plot was interfering with the success of all theatrical productions early in 1680. It later proved to be one of the most popular tragedies of the age – a major turning point for both Barry's career and the course of Restoration tragedy.

ELIZABETH BARRY AND 'SHE-TRAGEDY'

Among the very first to capitalise on Barry's success as Monimia was Nahum Tate, whose notorious adaptation of Shakespeare's *King Lear* opened a few months after *The Orphan*. Tate rewrote Shakespeare's tragedy so as to focus on Cordelia, played of course by Barry, and, as he explained in his dedication, he changed the original plot so as to heighten the 'Distress of the Story'.[30] The play became the love story of Cordelia and Edgar. Soon after it opens the heroine's wretched and pitiable situation is established – she loves Edgar, but her father has ordered her to marry Burgundy:

> Alas! What wou'd the wretched Edgar with
> The more unfortunate Cordelia?
> Who in Obedience to a Father's will
> Flies from her Edgar's Arms to Burgundy's?[31]

The overriding concern of Tate's Edgar is to prove the sincerity of his passion for Cordelia. Thus, when Edmund tells him to flee because his father has threatened his death he seems fairly unconcerned. He is far more preoccupied with the question of whether or not Lear's daughter really cares for him: 'Friend I obey you. – O Cordelia'

(p. 189). His disguise as Poor Tom becomes a means of pursuing and protecting the vulnerable Cordelia.

Instead of sending Cordelia to France as Shakespeare does, so that she is absent for much of the play, Tate has his heroine seek her father alone after he is abandoned. This allowed Barry an affecting scene in which Cordelia pleads for help for her father from Gloucester, and even Edmund is moved:

> O charming Sorrow! How her Tears adorn her,
> Like Dew on Flow'rs, but she is Virtuous,
> And I must quench this hopeless Fire i'th'kindling.   (p. 209)

As in her role as Lavinia in *Caius Marius*, Barry was here called upon to express her feelings with heightened rhetorical passion, as her Shakespearian counterpart would never have done:

> And I have only one poor Boon to beg,
> That you'd convey me to his breathless Trunk,
> With my torn Robes to wrap his hoary Head,
> With my torn Hair to bind his Hands and Feet,
> Then with a Show'r of Tears
> To wash his Clay-smear'd Cheeks and Die beside him. (p. 210)

Cordelia goes to the heath to aid her father, but is there seized by Edmund's ruffians for the rape he intends, before being rescued by Edgar. Her lover then reveals himself and explains that he took the disguise merely in the hope of supporting 'wretched Cordelia' (p. 233). At this evidence of genuine affection, Cordelia is moved to disclose her own love.

The last act of Tate's drama changes Shakespeare's tragedy utterly by having the King and Cordelia rescued from death by Edgar and Albany – that is, Cordelia is rescued by Edgar for the second time. The end of the play is a celebration of their faithful love in which Edgar and Cordelia are treated as god and goddess. 'W'are past the fire', says Edgar, 'and now must shine to Ages' (p. 233). The 'Celestial Pair' are now to rule the kingdom while Lear retires into obscurity with Kent. The play concludes appropriately with a paean of praise from Edgar to Cordelia:

> Divine Cordelia, all the Gods can witness
> How much thy Love to Empire I prefer!
> Thy bright Example shall convince the World
> (Whatever Storms or Fortune are decreed)
> That Truth and Vertue shall at least succeed.   (p. 252)

'Woman' and 'Love' triumph decisively over 'Empire', as they were to triumph in tragedies to come.

After playing Cordelia, Barry created the central role of Belvidera in Otway's last and greatest tragedy, *Venice Preserved* (1682). As we have seen, Belvidera and her relationship with her husband create the main focus of interest here. In fact, as Aline Mackenzie Taylor points out, Otway's play is a vehicle for a great actress rather than a great actor because Belvidera dominates Jaffeir morally:

> Belvidera dominates the crucial action as Pierre cannot – her role is the longest and most arduous in the old repertory of stock plays – whereas Jaffeir, who is so much under the influence of each, can very easily topple from his precarious perch as hero of the action.[32]

At the end of the play it is Belvidera who holds our attention. Jaffeir and Pierre perish, leaving Barry to perform a ranting *tour de force* of madness:

> > Hoa, Jaffeir, Jaffeir!
> Peep up and give me but a look, I have him!
> I've got him, father! Oh now how I'll smuggle him!
> My love! my dear! my blessing! Help me, help me!
> They have hold on me, and drag me to the bottom.
> Nay – now the pull so hard – farewell – (*she dies*)　　(V.iv.24–9)

Barry's next leading role was as the eponymous heroine of John Banks' *Vertue Betray'd: or, Anna Bullen* (1682), the second of his turgid pathetic tragedies loosely based on periods of Tudor history. The first, *The Unhappy Favourite* (1681), had been written for the King's Company rather than its rival (to which Barry belonged) and the major source of pathos in this play was a male character, Essex. Significantly, despite this play's success, for his next pathetic tragedy Banks changed companies and centred his play on a distressed heroine for Barry. *Anna Bullen* also represents an important development for 'she-tragedy' in being concerned solely, as *The Orphan* was not, with the suffering of its virtuous female protagonist.

Tricked into believing that her love, Piercy, has married Lady Diana Talbot, Anna Bullen is persuaded to marry King Henry VIII before she realises her mistake. She is then assailed on one side by a jealous King Henry, who recognises that she does not love him, and on the other by a reproachful Piercy, who believes her to be inconstant; at the same time she is also the victim of a plot by the evil Cardinal Wolsey and the ambitious Lady Elizabeth Blunt. Anna's function is simply to respond with appropriate anguish to each new twist in this basic situation — as she puts it:

> Was ever Virtue stormed like mine?
> Within, without, I'm haunted all alike:
> Without, tormented with a jealous King;
> Within, my Fears suggest a thousand Plagues,
> Bid me remember injur'd Piercy's wrongs.[33]

Whereas Monimia's death was only the first of three at *The Orphan*'s bloody end — Otway's play concludes with Castalio's despairing account of world chaos — the climax of Banks' action is the execution of the heroine. In a scene clearly designed as a vehicle for Barry, Anna first bids an emotional goodbye to her brother, and then, more tearfully, to her child. Each farewell is punctuated by a message that another 'traitor' has been despatched; each death brings Anna's nearer and increases the tension. Banks intensified the pathos by playing upon the emotion inherent in the idea of a woman's beheading — Anna pleads:

> My Lord, I've but a little Neck:
> Therefore I hope he'll not repeat his Blow;
> But do it, like an Artist, at one Stroke.   (p. 74)

Finally, the centre of a superb spectacle, Anna is led to her execution '*all in White*' (p. 70), followed by '*Women in Mourning*' and majestically proclaiming her virtue: 'for Innocence is still its own Reward' (p. 75). Female suffering has become the whole subject of tragedy.

Barry continued to create more roles in the Anna Bullen mould into the next century, as well as repeating her successes as Monimia and Anna again and again. Roles in this vein were added to essentially male-dominated plays for her. Dryden, for instance, added the passionate Marmoutier to his dramatisation of the French wars of religion, *The Duke of Guise* (1682), although her part is quite unnecessary to the plot and probably did not exist in the first version of this drama.[34] Crowne also created a sub-plot for his *Darius, King of Persia* (1688) which would enable Barry to delight audiences as the suffering Barzana, 'to the obvious benefit of the drama', as Crowne himself put it. There was a considerable stir at the first performance of this play, incidentally, when Barry suddenly fell ill on stage and, as one spectator later reported, 'she was forced to be carried off and instead of dying in jest was in danger of doing it in earnest'.[35]

After 1688, the vogue for 'she-tragedy' was further boosted by the emergence of Anne Bracegirdle as a leading actress for the United Company alongside Barry. When they performed together in tragedy, Bracegirdle, as the younger of the two, usually played the gentle, vulnerable heroine, while Barry played a stronger, more mature type such as a monarch or matron (such pairings are discussed in detail in chapter 7). At the same time, however, Barry never lost the position she had gained in the 1680s as the queen of pathetic tragedy and this was reinforced by her creation of the starring role of Isabella in Southerne's hugely successful *The Fatal Marriage* in 1694. In the dedication to its published edition, Southerne makes it clear that Barry was the inspiration behind the play: 'I made the Play for her part, and her part has made the Play for me.' Isabella, like Anna Bullen, does nothing but suffer as one misfortune follows another. After believing for seven years that her husband is dead she remarries to escape poverty, only to have her first husband immediately reappear. She then goes mad before finally expiring in a protracted and sentimental death scene. Again Barry produced performances of extraordinary power. In a letter of 22 March 1694 a spectator wrote, 'I never saw Mrs. Barry act with so much passion as she does in it: I could not forebear being moved even to tears to see her act.'[36]

A striking feature of both Anna and Isabella is passionate maternal feeling; a potent source of pathos lies in both suffering separation from their children. Anna, for example, is pregnant throughout, while in the most sentimental scene of Banks' play her daughter Elizabeth pleads with Henry VIII for her mother's life: 'Pray save my Mother, Dear King-Father do' (p. 68). Isabella's sufferings are magnified because her small son must share them and she is given further pain when her father-in-law offers to care for the child so long as she never sees him again. 'I live', she protests, 'but in my Child' (I.iii.265). Her death scene is rendered more affecting by her tearful farewell to her boy. Such use of children was nothing new (see, for instance, Lady Macduff's son in *Macbeth* or the little prince Mamillius in *The Winter's Tale*), but as Barry grew older and was frequently paired with the younger Anne Bracegirdle, her stage dominance resulted in a striking increase in the number of mothers as central characters in tragedy. Whereas the state of motherhood was relatively infrequently presented in Renaissance drama as against fatherhood,[37] this was reversed in the 1690s and early 1700s, and we find Barry playing a mother in at least seven plays.[38] This fashion for maternal pathos also spread to the rival theatre. When Cibber adapted Shakespeare's *Richard III* for Drury Lane in 1699, for example, he added a scene in which Queen Elizabeth weeps over the little princes as they are torn from her to be imprisoned in the Tower of London. Such weeping is typical, as, significantly, the heroine's maternity is usually not a source of strength and power but a symptom of her frailty – the bearing and rearing of children renders a woman more pitiable and easily victimised. Thus, as was shown in chapter 2, although women became central characters in tragedy, they were used in ways which reinforced a female image of weakness and femininity.

ELIZABETH BARRY AND ROWE'S *THE FAIR PENITENT*

The Fair Penitent by Nicholas Rowe, dramatist, poet and Shake-spearian editor, may be said to mark the final stage of 'she-tragedy'. As Laura Brown points out, by the beginning of the eighteenth century the genre had begun to link pathetic suffering more overtly with virtue. Rowe's play ends with a clear moral, 'If you would have the nuptial union last, / Let virtue be the bond that ties it fast.'[39] The heroine's suffering is not so much misfortune as punishment for being the victim of her seducer. However, the primary intention of this drama is the same as that of its predecessors and a comparison with its source, *The Fatal Dowry* (pub. 1632) by Philip Massinger with John Ford, highlights the way in which this play stands as the apotheosis of the Barry affective mode.

The *Fatal Dowry* is the story of Charalois, an honourable young man who is driven to kill his faithless wife, Beaumelle, and her worthless lover, is acquitted of murder, but is finally stabbed as he leaves the court by the dead lover's loyal friend. However, the true thematic centre of the play is not this individual and his misfortune, but society as a whole and the overriding importance of a formal organised system of justice. The court acquits Charalois of murder, but as he dies he acknowledges the justice of his end. This thematic emphasis is reflected in the sheer number of characters in *The Fatal Dowry*. In addition to the half a dozen memorable main characters there is a host of advocates, creditors and tradesmen, each with his own concerns and loyalties. The play also gives weight to both sides of the central conflict – it illustrates the feelings not only of those who care for Charalois, but also of those who support his rival. At the end, one is no better than the other. *The Fatal Dowry* suggests that since society is composed of many individuals, each with his own point of view, justice must be represented by an objective arbiter above them all. By contrast, like *The Fatal Marriage* or *Anna Bullen*, *The Fair Penitent* focuses on a single female character and seeks to submerge the minds of the audience in her emotions. Events are presented only in relation to Calista, the penitent. The first part of *The Fatal Dowry* (up to the marriage of Charalois and Beaumelle) is merely retold as past history in the opening scene and the killing of Lothario is shown not as an unlawful act, but as fuel for Calista's suffering. The character of the lover's father is omitted because his concern for his son would be a distraction, and similarly Rossano, Lothario's friend, is reduced to being simply the audience to whom the lover can tell the story of the heroine's seduction. The conversation of the other main characters is predominantly concerned with Calista, so that the early scenes become a build-up to her first appearance.

Rowe changed the personalities of Massinger's main characters as well as their place in the drama for the same reason. Beaumelle is in many ways the least developed of Massinger's main characters – not even mentioned until Act II and dead by the end of Act IV. She is cold, hard-headed and determined on adultery until Charalois discovers her perfidy. Faced with his sorrowful accusations she apparently repents. This penitent speech was presumably the source of Rowe's Calista:

> Though I was bold enough to be a strumpet.
> I dare not yet liue one: let those fam'd matrones
> That are canoniz'd worthy of our sex,
> Transcend me in their sanctity of life,
> I yet will equall them in dying nobly,
> Ambitious of no honour after life,
> But that when I am dead, you will forgive me.[40]

Charalois's response is, significantly, 'How pity steals upon me!' In this brief scene Rowe must have recognised Beaumelle's potential as a pathetic heroine. However, Beaumelle is always seen in action – after her marriage she loses no time in having an affair and she has little time to indulge in repentance before she is killed. Calista, by contrast, although she dominates the play, is a passive victim. Her seduction (which occurs *before* her marriage, so she is never an adultress) occurred almost against her will. Her attraction to her seducer is a complicating factor, but one which should not obscure the central fact, which is, like Anna Bullen, Isabella and others, she is essentially a noble figure on whom wrong-doing, the worst possible calamity, has fallen.

With dramatic emphasis shifted to the heroine, the Charalois equivalent in Rowe's tragedy becomes a weaker character. By having the events concerning the burial of Altamount's father narrated instead of performed, Rowe rejected the opportunity of establishing the hero's strength and nobility, as the eighteenth-century playwright and critic, Richard Cumberland, points out:

for who that compares Charalois, at the end of the second act of Massinger, with Rowe's Altamount at the opening scene of *The Fair Penitent*, can doubt which character has most interest with the spectators. We have seen the former in all the most amiable offices which filial piety could perform; enduring insults from his inveterate oppressors, and voluntarily surrendering himself to a prison to ransom the dead body of his father from unrelenting creditors. Altamount presents himself before us in his wedding suit, in the splendour of fortune and at the summit of happiness...the happy and exulting bridegroom may be an object of our congratulation, but the virtuous and suffering Charalois engages our pity, love and admiration.[41]

Cumberland's last comment is particularly important. In Rowe's play, Calista performs precisely the function he describes for Charalois. She is presented as 'virtuous and suffering' and she 'engages our pity, love and admiration'. Altamount is to be viewed only in terms of his relationship with Calista. His killing of Lothario is presented not in terms of its effect on him, but of its impact on her. He does not die at the end of the play, but merely faints, thereby helping to convey the depth of sorrow and pity to be felt for Calista's death. Altamount's feebleness also renders the character of his rival more attractive than in the Massinger original. Because Lothario is loved by the most important person in the drama, he gains in importance. Rowe's libertine has a certain charm and fascination, whereas Massinger's adulterer remains merely a vain fop with animal appetites. Lothario actually admits that he would have married

Calista had not his suit been rejected by her father, thereby adding to the sympathy the audience should feel for Calista.

The character of the heroine's father is in each case strongly affected by the dramatist's overall intention. Rochfort, in his position as the retiring premier of the court, exemplifies the honour and rectitude of official justice, and Massinger also used him to present the conflict between personal feeling and public law. Rowe employed this inner conflict to very different effect. Sciolto's stern sense of Calista's guilt contributes to her suffering and drives her on to suicide, while his pity for her emphasises the pathos of her anguish:

> I have held the balance with an iron hand,
> And put off ev'ry tender, human thought,
> To doom my child to death; but spare my eyes
> The most unnatural sight, lest their strings crack,
> And my old brain split and grow mad with horror.
>
> (V.108–12)

It is significant that Rowe did not acknowledge his Massinger source. In fact, he used *The Fatal Dowry* only for its dramatic situation; he could have chosen any earlier drama for his source so long as it had somewhere a female victim who could arouse pity. One can understand the opinion of the *London Magazine* critic in the early nineteenth century who, in his review of a revival of *The Fatal Dowry* at Drury Lane on 8 January 1825, noted that while 'Massinger's tragedy is full of poetry, downright vigorous dramatic dialogue, and full of character and stern passion', *The Fair Penitent* is simply 'a better acting piece'.[42] Rowe's true source, like that of his predecessors, Otway, Lee, Banks and Southerne, was Barry's talents.

The 'she-tragedies' of Otway, Banks, Southerne and Rowe continued to be revived throughout the eighteenth century, but very few new examples of the genre were written during this period – Rowe's *The Tragedy of Jane Shore* (1714) is among the very last. By the 1720s and 1730s the pathetic heroine had been superseded as the main protagonist of tragedy by male bourgeois heroes, such as George Barnwell in Lillo's *The London Merchant* (1713). Laura Brown's explanation for the disappearance of the defenceless woman in drama is a formal one: as literature became progressively more moralistic, so the epistolary novel proved to be a far more effective means than drama of presenting a passive, idealised, victimised female figure.[43] The virtuous heroine left tragedy to reappear in novels like Richardson's *Pamela* (1740) and *Clarissa* (1747–8). While this may be true in the long term, a more immediate cause of 'she-tragedy's' decline may simply have been the retirement from the stage of Bracegirdle in 1707 and Barry in 1710. Elizabeth Barry was largely responsible for the creation of 'she-tragedy', and when she died in 1713, it died with her.

CHAPTER 6

The actress as dramatic prostitute

This chapter traces the impact of Elizabeth Barry on comic drama between 1680 and the end of the century. Here she inspired and played a new female type which remained uniquely hers. As we have seen, the hallmark of Barry's roles in tragedy was their sexual passion, whether, as lustful villainess, she expressed freely her character's desires and sensuality; or as heroine she struggled to restrain her sexual feelings, torn, like Monimia, Belvidera and Calista, between love and duty. After 1680, Barry's powerful combination of pathos and eroticism in performance had its effect on comedy as well as tragedy. Amid a variety of roles in comedy in the last two decades of the century, Barry created a striking series of wholly original heroines, prostitutes and mistresses who are passionate, seduced and consequently doomed to unhappiness, their wild emotionalism and intense suffering contrasting with the more typically humorous activity of the other characters in their plays (and with the kind of tough professional mistresses played by Currer and Butler).

Barry's creation of a new and sympathetic image for the prostitute and the mistress in drama is significant for two reasons. First, it highlights still further her outstanding influence on Restoration drama after 1680, when comedies as well as tragedies were turned into vehicles for her talent. Secondly, her success in this sphere gave the 'whore' and society's double standard a dramatic prominence that neither had received previously on the English stage. Before 1660, the woman who permitted herself a sexual relationship outside marriage was generally a minor figure and was rarely given sympathy.[1] During the 1660s and 1670s, since the actresses themselves were perceived as prostitutes and mistresses, the situation changed and several major actresses specialised in playing whores – notably Currer. However, the fallen woman in society was still usually portrayed as unfeeling and mercenary, and even the suffering

Angellica Bianca in Aphra Behn's *The Rover* (1676) is swiftly eclipsed
by the lively Hellena, who successfully tames the rake-hero after the
courtesan has been rejected. It was only when Barry's mesmeric
talents were employed in the portrayal of prostitutes and mistresses
that their problematic situation was given detailed consideration and
their sufferings vividly realised. Although sympathy for such women
was still carefully limited and social attitudes dictated that the Barry
character could not be allowed to marry the hero, the actress's talent
and popularity did cause an interesting shift in the centre of interest
in some comedies away from the traditional heroine onto the suffering
mistress, who became the most important character in the play.
Thanks to Barry, the prostitute and the mistress became a source of
conflict and debate in the theatre and so contributed to the fresh
upsurge of interest in women and women's problems at the end of the
century.[2]

THE REVENGE AND ELIZABETH BARRY

As we have seen, during the 1670s Barry was the Duke's Company's
leading comedienne, playing first ingenues and then wives. Her most
successful role to date came in 1680 when she played Monimia in *The
Orphan*. Her success did not only have far-reaching consequences for
tragedy: six months later it led to her playing her first suffering
prostitute in a comic drama called *The Revenge*, probably by Aphra
Behn.[3] In only six months this dramatist adapted John Marston's
tragedy *The Dutch Courtesan* (1605) and its demonic central figure into
a vehicle for Barry's resoundingly proved talent for passion and
pathos, a vehicle that would also express Behn's own forceful opinions
about the plight of the prostitute in society.

   The Dutch Courtesan is the grim story of Franceschina, the fiendish
courtesan of the title who, when discarded by her lover Malheureux,
seeks bloody revenge on him, his virtuous fiancée Beatrice and his
loyal and noble friend Freevill. At the end Freevill defeats her evil
plots and she is led off to suffer a harsh whipping and gaol. Behn
turned this play into a comedy in which all the characters are finally
paired off in marriage; even the prostitute is found a husband, thanks
to a new and resourceful character called Diana. Behn's main change
to the Marston play was to transform the heartless Franceschina into
a frail victim of libertine desire for Barry to play in the same style as
she had played Monimia. Corina is, in fact, not a professional
prostitute at all but the loving mistress of Wellman (Marston's

Malheureux), who seduced her when she was a virgin and has now discarded her in favour of the heiress Marinda (Beatrice), whom he plans to marry. Corina is in a brothel not to earn money but to shelter, because no respectable house will take her in. Although the play is essentially a comedy, Corina stands out as a tragic intrusion, suffering both from Wellman's betrayal and her own sense of sin.

In the very first scene we find Corina anxiously pondering Wellman's growing coldness towards her and bewailing the loss of her virtue. She tells Wellman's companion Friendly, 'I have been false to Virtue, false to Honour, false to my Name and Friends; but was to Wellman ... a mercie, all complying sweetness.' In contrast to the condemnatory Freevill of Marston's play, Friendly is struck by Corina's goodness in comparison to Marinda and replies, 'I cou'd not slightly part with such a Jewel, or, Indian-like, barter this real Gold for shining gingling Bawbles. Marinda! Heaven, thou'rt an Angel to her!'[4] In Act II, not surprisingly, Behn extended the 'whore's' attack on her bawd, making the other woman more responsible for Corina's seduction. We hear how the corrupt Mrs Dunwell emphasised Corina's charm to Wellman and showed him the best way to persuade her to submit.

In the next scene Behn gave Barry a particularly fruitful opportunity to display her tragic talents within the comedy. In desperation Corina draws a dagger on Mrs Dunwell and then fires a pistol at Wellman. Having missed him she collapses, '*offers to stab herself; Friendly runs to her, prevents her, and she seems fainted a little while in his arms*' (p. 19). Frenzied violence and swooning in quick succession allowed Barry to combine the wild emotionalism of Lavinia in *Caius Marius* with the pathetic vulnerability of Monimia, an exciting sequence of 'passions'. Act IV was rewritten along similarly tragic lines, with Corina nearly raped by a would-be client named Trickwell. She is rescued by a disguised Wellman just in time, appearing '*disordered*' (p. 40) and in an appropriate state of anguish. A scene later she is told of the suspected death of Wellman (a ploy to free himself from her) and collapses once again, weeping bitterly.

To highlight the sufferings of Barry's character, Behn also made Marinda a much weaker and less attractive character than Marston's Beatrice. She cut a long speech by Freevill extolling Beatrice's virtue (as we have seen, Friendly praises Corina's goodness instead), as well as Beatrice's own long opening speech which shows her simplicity, good nature and grace. Significantly Behn also cut the lengthy and climactic diatribe against prostitution by Freevill in Act V of *The Dutch Courtesan*:

> What man, but worthy name of man, would leave
> The modest pleasures of a lawful bed,
> The holy union of two equal hearts,
> Mutually holding either dear as health,
> The undoubted issues, joys of chaste sheets,
> The unfeigned imbrace of sober ignorance:
> To twine th'unhealthfull loines of common loves
> The prostituted impudence of things
> Senseless like those of cataracts of Nile,
> Their use so vile takes away sense! How vile
> To love a creature, made of blood and hell,
> Whose use makes weak, whose company doth shame,
> Whose bed doth beggar, issue doth defame![5]

In any case, it would surely have been a brave actor who, before members of the Stuart court, was able to denounce a mistress as one 'whose use makes weak, whose company doth shame'.

In Act V Corina, like Franceschina, is arrested, but she accepts her unjust imprisonment nobly, 'with Joy, since Wellman lives, and lives to be perjur'd, no matter what becomes of poor lost me' (p. 52). She is rescued by the witty and cunning Diana (played by minor actress Mrs Price) who arranges for Wellman to pretend to her own foolish suitor Sir John Empty that Corina is his sister, so that Sir John will consent to marry her. Thus a grim fate for Corina is averted in favour of a traditional comic conclusion – a husband by deception. Wellman even offers his victim a sort of apology: 'it was not want of Love, my Fortune did depend upon my Marriage, but when I saw the Woman destin'd for me, I must confess, I felt new flames possess me, without extinguishing the old' (p. 61). However, Corina still stands apart from the other characters for whom the comedy ends happily. Unlike, say, the Mrs Currer type of mistress, who is happy so long as she gets a rich husband, Corina hardly cares what happens to her if she cannot have Wellman and simply marries Sir John because her lover wants her to – 'since I must lose you, and am by your Commands obliged to Life, no matter how forlorn and wretched 'tis' (p. 62). Although Corina does not die like Monimia and Calista, her future life is to be a wretched one.[6]

The tragic status of Corina marks a new departure in the treatment of the prostitute or mistress in English drama. There is only one play dated earlier than 1660 in which the main character is a prostitute who is reformed by falling in love and who then suffers through being rejected by her lover: Thomas Dekker's *The Honest Whore Parts 1 and 2* (1604). However, the heroine of this play, Bellafront, is substantially different from Corina and Barry's other subsequent roles in this mould. Although Bellafront suffers in her rejection by her seducer Hippolito, and in her marriage to the worthless Matheo, she is emphatically not an object of pathos. Dekker mitigated Bellafront's crime by the fact that she was led to the profession of prostitute through an initial seduction by Matheo, but his aim was to point out the evil of the whore and her way of life; the heroine's reform represents the moral message of the play. By contrast, the aim of Aphra Behn was to create sympathy for an essentially noble female who becomes the prey of a libertine. Corina is not a working prostitute but the innocent victim of Wellman. She does not need to reform and if anyone is at fault it is her seducer. Like the majority of tragic heroines created by Barry, Corina exists primarily to engender pity, even tears, from spectators, combining soft, erotic femininity with wild, passionate anguish. We have no record of how *The Revenge* was received, and it is not a particularly good play, but the performance of its leading character must have been successful, since both Aphra Behn and other comic dramatists went on to create more variations on the suffering mistress for Barry to play. In this way a new sequence of comedies was born.

ELIZABETH BARRY AND APHRA BEHN 1681–2

Soon after *The Revenge*, Behn produced another similar vehicle for Barry's talent in a second part to her highly successful comedy of 1676, *The Rover* (for which Barry had created the role of the witty heroine, Hellena). In *The Rover Part II* (1681), Barry played the beautiful and passionate courtesan La Nuche, who finally abandons her profitable career in favour of a permanent alliance with her love, Willmore. (Willmore, of course, married Hellena in the first part, but she is now dead.) The alliance is an unusual and romantic alternative to the typical fate of the prostitute. La Nuche could not be allowed to marry the hero but in this instance the lovers apparently live happily and faithfully together ever after. Willmore is even willing to subsist in poverty so long as it is shared with La Nuche.

Although La Nuche is a more robust heroine than either Corina or

Monimia, she shares many of the essential features of Barry's tragic roles. Initially wary of the penniless Willmore, who is famed as a womaniser, she is passionately divided between torments of jealousy and an inability to resist his amorous advances. Finally she takes Willmore as lover and turns, ranting, against her bawd Petronella (who, significantly, was played by the same obscure actress, one Mrs Novice, who played Mrs Dunwell, Corina's bawd). 'From Childhood thou hast trained me up in cunning, read Lectures to me of the use of Man, but kept me from the knowledge of the right... but oh how soon plain Nature taught me Love!'[7] This 'Love' leads La Nuche to grant Willmore a free partnership 'without the formal foppery of Marriage' (p. 81) and together she and Willmore represent a romantic ideal – a truly loving relationship beyond the mercenary and constraining limits of conventional marriage.

However, although the end of *The Rover Part II* was 'romantically satisfying',[8] it did not provide a realistic solution to the problems of a woman who gives herself to a faithless libertine and, more importantly, it did not give Barry a purely tragic role in which she could, at the end, stir audiences by a thrilling portrayal of suffering. A year later Aphra Behn remedied these deficiencies by providing the star with the outstanding 'tragic mistress' role of Lady Galliard in her cynical social comedy, *The City Heiress* (1682). The plot of this comedy bears an interesting resemblance to Etherege's famous *The Man of Mode* (1676). In both plays a libertine is in the process of casting off one mistress, seducing a second and marrying an heiress. In Etherege's play the female centre of interest is the heiress Harriet, witty and charming, who finally seems to love and be loved by Dorimant. Mrs Loveit, Dorimant's old mistress, and Bellinda, his new, are comparatively minor characters, especially Bellinda. In Behn's comedy, however, the female focus is shifted away from the heiress onto the newly seduced mistress. Charlot, the heiress, is a minor character and Lady Galliard, Barry's role, is the character who holds our attention.

Lady Galliard is a widow, young, beautiful and wealthy, with a number of admirers. She falls in love with the rake Wilding, but recognising his inability to remain faithful refuses first his proposal of marriage and then his request that she become his mistress. While Wilding is a typical comic rake, Galliard is a serious figure, and her efforts to repress her unconquerable desire for him allowed Barry to project another high-flown conflict between love and duty. When Wilding visits her at night and embraces her she struggles and breaks away, only to call him back when he cunningly '*offers to go*'. She cannot resist him and expresses the anguish of her dilemma in extravagant verse:

> A whore? A Whore! Oh, let me think of that!
> A man's Convenience, his leisure hours, his Bed of Ease,
> To loll and tumble on at idle times:
> The Slave, the Hackney of his lawless Lust!
> A loath'd Extinguisher of filthy flames,
> Made use of, and thrown by. – Oh infamous![9]

Ludicrously inflated as these lines may seem (the image of the mistress as some kind of fire extinguisher is particularly unfortunate), they express the vital, central message of Aphra Behn's play. The loving mistress is merely a rake's toy to be enjoyed until lust is satisfied and then discarded. Behn wrote in verse rather than prose and gave the lines to Barry, the queen of tragedy, in order to bring home as forcefully as possible the difficulty of the woman's position. Wilding finally manages to seduce Lady Galliard by accusing her of only pretending to care for him – something that Galliard's passionate nature cannot allow:

> What heart can bear distrust from what it loves?
> Or who can always her own Wish deny?
> My Reason's weary of the unequal strife;
> And Love and Nature will at last o'ercome.

Barry had a magnificent moment of submission – murmuring 'you must undo me if you will', she '*sinks into his Arms by degrees*' and is led to the bedchamber. Wilding, '*with his arms about her*' cries triumphantly, 'In Loves Kind Fever let me ever ly, / Drunk with Desire, and raving mad with Joy' (pp. 41–2).[10] Once the sexual act has taken place, Galliard is, of course, racked with remorse. She desperately tries to convince Wilding that she will not remain his mistress, although the scene makes plain that the affair will never end until he discards her. By merely threatening to kill himself if she rejects him Wilding is able to have his mistress in his arms again. Galliard's sigh of passion as she '*leans on him*', 'Ah, Wilding' (p. 45), seems a deliberate echo of Barry's most famous line as Monimia in *The Orphan*, the 'Ah Castalio' which she could never apparently speak without weeping and which made such a memorable impression on spectators. Thus Barry used one of her most effective tragic techniques at this crucial moment to load Galliard's renewed submission with still more emotion.

The wretchedness of Lady Galliard is immediately increased by the fact that after these love-scenes her other normally retiring suitor, Sir Charles Merriwill, emboldened by drink, attempts to rape her. She is only able to hold him off by promising to marry him the next day. The crude and drunken lovemaking of Galliard's husband-to-be contrasts painfully with her preceding seduction by Wilding. Sexual ecstasy for both man and woman is juxtaposed with the grim reality of what is for the woman a safe but loveless marriage, and this is what Galliard finally chooses for herself because she cannot contemplate life as Wilding's mistress. As Sir Charles puts it, then 'You wou'd be left to the wide World and Love, / To Infamy, to Scandal and to Wilding' (p. 58). Wilding meanwhile rids himself of his old mistress, Diana, and wins his 'city heiress' and her money. In Behn's grim comedy the only characters to benefit are the men.

THE BARRY CAST-MISTRESS 1690–1700

There followed a lapse in similar roles for Barry for eight years – between 1682 and 1689 there were on average only four new plays of any kind produced in any one year.[11] However, with the revival of the theatre at the end of the decade, Barry's influence as a tragedienne in comedy revived as well, and the 1690s saw an interesting series of variations on the Behn prototype. If he includes this period, Jocelyn Powell is quite wrong in stating that 'the cast-mistress of Restoration comedy is generally a figure of fun'.[12] The first of Barry's roles in this line was Dorinda, 'a private mistress kept by my Lord Worthy'[13] in William Mountfort's *Greenwich Park* (1691). Although Dorinda clearly resembles Corina, La Nuche and Lady Galliard, Mountfort's treatment of her character shows that it was Barry's talent and popularity that inspired the role, not an interest in the problems of seduced women in society. Unlike Aphra Behn, Mountfort had no such interest.

Dorinda's part demanded the enaction of a typical range of picturesque emotions by Barry. First came remorse and anger as the mistress accuses her aunt of arranging her seduction by Worthy when she was very young and poor:

> 'Tis true, he is the Man who first seduc'd me,
> And thou art she who first betray'd me to him:
> I then was Poor, was ignorant of Sin;
> So Innocent, that had I lov'd as now,

> I could not for the Soul of me have told
> What 'twas I long'd for more than talk and kisses. (p. 15)

Then Dorinda falls in love with a lively rake, aptly named Young
Reveller, so that in spite of pangs of conscience over the betrayal of
Worthy she cannot resist the prospect of sexual ecstasy with her new
lover.

> What harmony will be in both our Souls!
> Whilst trembling sighs bedew the willing Lips,
> And every squeeze still closer than the former.
> O Extasie!
> But hold, keep down my Joy, it were a Crime
> That I should lose my self before my time. (p. 18)

Young Reveller, in turn, is fired with passion for her – 'her every
touch distracts me' (p. 26) – and Act IV ends with their withdrawal
to the bedroom together.

However, whereas Behn portrayed such passion sympathetically in
the character of Lady Galliard, Mountfort condemns it. In following
her own sexual desires (as a man like Young Reveller does), Dorinda
has 'betrayed' her keeper Lord Worthy and is duly punished when
he discovers her affair. Absolving Young Reveller entirely, Worthy
places all the blame on Dorinda,

I did love her (to my shame I own it) above the World...and she has well
repaid me: the Ignorance, and my Breach of Friendship in not trusting thee,
makes thee unblamable; but she's sure double damn'd, to wrong me with
the only Man she knew my Friend. (p. 57)

His revenge on Dorinda is to publicly discard her, announcing to the
assembled company his future plans to live a 'sober, discreet Life' in
marriage to the heiress Violante. Unable to compete with 'a Fortune
and a Face' (p. 58), the mistress is left in isolation, railing powerlessly.
In her sorrow and her 'villainy', she is set apart from the play's comic
conclusion, which focuses on two contented couples, Lord Worthy
and Violante, and Young Reveller and his true love, Florella.

The lively Florella is in fact as important, if not perhaps as
interesting, a character as Dorinda right through the play – unlike
Marinda in *The Revenge* and Charlot in *The City Heiress*. In the first act
she offers some sharp criticism of Dorinda's past behaviour, 'I cannot
help thinking that she who will be Debauch'd to mend her condition,
will afterwards lye with any man that can better it' (p. 13), and her
combination of wit, determination and chastity constitute a positive
female image to contrast with Dorinda. Florella was played by

Susannah Mountfort, the wife of the dramatist as well as a very popular comedienne. These facts, combined with Mountfort's evident lack of concern for the plight of the discarded mistress, explain why at the end of *Greenwich Park*, Barry's character was balanced, although not overshadowed, by a conventional comic heroine.

Two years later, however, the Barry-prostitute was back in the limelight. Lady Malepert, the heroine of Southerne's bitterly cynical comedy *The Maid's Last Prayer* (1693), is both the most psychologically subtle and the most satirically acute portrayal of a reformed prostitute in Restoration comedy. Whereas Mountfort used Barry's tragic talents purely to boost his comedy's entertainment value, Southerne employed them as the mainstay of his exceptionally aggressive attack on libertinism and his society's debased attitude towards sexual behaviour.

While *The Maid's Last Prayer* is peopled with familiar comic types – cunning rakes, adulterous wives, a foolish cuckold, a silly old coquette – the play stands out in presenting every one of these as heartless and corrupt, greedily pursuing wealth and sexual conquests. Not one character, except, ironically, the prostitute Lady Malepert, and possibly the foolish old maid of the title, Lady Susan, is at all sympathetic. Lady Malepert herself is not immediately attractive, being a spoilt immature 18-year-old (Barry was actually 35 when she played the role, but this would not have worried audiences[14]), who has been married off to an ugly, stupid husband. When the play opens she is, unknown to him, a professional prostitute who sells her sexual favours to the highest bidder, under the management of her bawd Wishwell. Unlike her predecessors, she is not sentimentalised and her relationship with her bawd is not the simple affair of victim and exploiter presented by Behn. Wishwell uses Lady Malepert because she is too old to enjoy the attentions of the opposite sex herself, 'while I am Mistress of Malepert's Beauty, I am not very sensible of the loss of my own'[15] and because she wants her revenge on men. Lady Malepert allows herself to be manipulated because she enjoys the power and admiration she gains from her exploits. She is not interested in, and indeed has no need of, the money she earns, so Wishwell keeps her working by a mixture of flattery – 'Thou Charming Creature! Be for ever thus, thus dear, thus Young, thus ever killing Fair!' (II.i.126–7) – and appeals to her baser nature, 'Love your self, and then you'l Love nothing but your Interest'

(II.i.230–1). In spite of this, Lady Malepert has never been wholly converted: 'But why shou'd I do any thing against my Inclinations? I don't want the Money' (II.i.240–1). While the similarity to Barry's earlier roles is clear, the realism and lack of melodrama in Southerne's portrayal of the prostitute–bawd relationship is wholly original.

Like her predecessors, however, Lady Malepert falls in love with an attractive rake and renounces her trade. The object of her affections is a particularly heartless libertine named Gayman who is attracted to her but has no intention of paying for the privilege of sleeping with her: 'That a Woman, at Eighteen, an Age, when Love, and Pleasure us'd to rule, shou'd in the midst of plenty, value herself upon the Reputation of a Publican, and always sit at the Receit of Custom' (I.i.52–5). Gayman determines to cure Lady Malepert of her disgraceful pastime – when he has finished with her she will sleep with men because they charm her into it, not for their money. To this end he takes the place of Sir Ruff Rancounter, her next client, convinced that after a night of *his* lovemaking she will never be able to stomach the attentions of her aged customers again. The act of intercourse duly takes place and Lady Malepert does experience a joy she has never known before. However, she unfortunately remains ignorant of the exchange. Although in the dark she has tried to imagine that her partner was Gayman, she believes she has slept with Sir Ruff.

The scene once the night is over required all Barry's capacity for powerful emotion. In contrast to the language in the rest of the play, Lady Malepert expresses her discovery of love lyrically and rhetorically:

> I have slept away my life,
> My better part of it, my life of Love
>
>   ...
>
> How cou'd Sir Ruff do this? O Love!
> What canst thou not do in a Woman's Heart!
> That brutal thing [i.e. Sir Ruff], whom, as I thought, I loath'd,
> Thy gentle Fires have softened by degrees,
> And melted into Gayman.   (V.i.25–6,33–7)

Transformed by her new discovery, Lady Malepert renounces her career as a prostitute and tells 'Sir Ruff',

> Let Wishwell bear the mercinary blame –
> Her baseness wrought me to her sordid ends:
> But I'll return your Bills –   (V.i.47–9)

Significantly, she also gives her bedfellow a ring with which to 'make a better Marriage' (V.i.54) than the one she is in. As Aphra Behn does in *The Rover Part II*, Southerne hints here that an unlawful yet truly loving union is better than an arranged marriage, which is socially respectable but loveless.

Unlike *The Rover Part II*, however, Southerne's comedy represents not an ideal, but his most bitter and cynical view of libertine society. Lady Malepert's new happiness is swiftly shattered as she discovers that she really has slept with Gayman – 'then I am ruin'd' (V.i.65). Ironically, she can only enjoy the man she loves when she imagines him in someone else (or thinks she does). To give herself to such a rake in reality means the loss of her reputation and position. With appropriate symbolism, at this moment the cosy darkness which had enveloped the lovers is dispelled by the light of a candle carried by Wishwell.

Furious at Gayman's trick, the bawd locks the couple in their bedroom to be discovered by the lady's husband. But by this time Gayman has changed his mind. Embittered by the fact that his partner could not tell the difference between his lovemaking and Sir Ruff's, he no longer cares to 'reform' her. 'The Lady receiv'd me for Sir Ruff; but when I think of the pleasures that came after, that she shou'd still mistake me, for that bargaining Booby of her Bawds providing; I don't forgive her' (V.i.17–20). Far from wishing to change her mode of behaviour by exposing her adultery to her husband, he tells Lady Malepert that, coarsened by her affairs, she is fit only to be a prostitute – since 'twas impossible to have you to my self; it goes a great way in my Cure, to know that any Fool may engage you for the time' (V.i.210–13). As a result, instead of exposing his wife's affairs to Lord Malepert when that gentleman arrives, Gayman chooses to explain away his presence innocently to the gullible cuckold. He then continues his vengeance against Lady Malepert by proposing to his other 'love', Maria, in front of her – as in *The Man of Mode*, Dorimant proposes marriage to Harriet in front of Mrs Loveit. But whereas Dorimant's proposal is only partly intended to annoy his old mistress and truly signifies how far Harriet has conquered his affections, Southerne presents the traditional union of 'hero' and 'heroine' in a much more unpleasant light. Crueller than Dorimant, Gayman apparently chooses marriage neither for love, nor for parental approval, nor for a fortune, but as a calculated punishment for his mistress. He even goes so far as to ask her publicly for her opinion so that she is forced to give an assent to it – expressing her true feelings at the same time in anguished asides. The audience's attention was clearly focused in this scene not on the reforming bride-to-be but on her broken-hearted rival, Barry crying desperately to herself at one point, 'How the Tyrant Triumphs!' (V.i.355).

Unlike Harriet or Florella, Maria, Gayman's chosen wife, does not represent a charming, positive alternative to the 'whore'. She is almost the most minor female character in the play and there is little evidence of her charm, wit or good sense. Her main characteristic is a fatal love of gambling which blinds her to the fact that her so-called friends at the card-table, Lady Trickitt and Garnish, are cheating her. She makes no lively brilliant speeches and has no bouts of repartee with Gayman. She accepts him cautiously, 'Well, Sir, you may repent this rashness' (V.i.352), and reserves her enthusiasm for her beloved gaming. Southerne would seem to have deliberately deprived Maria of the usual attractions of the witty heroine in order to highlight Gayman's cruelty and to focus more sympathy on Lady Malepert. Significantly, a minor actress in the United Company at the time, Jane Rogers, took the part of Maria.

The play's conclusion typically presents the Barry tragic prostitute isolated from the rest of the cast. In this case however she is isolated, not by her guilt, but by the new moral understanding she has gained. Having discovered the value of genuine love she turns on Wishwell, 'O, I must hate you, you have undone me with the only man I ever Lov'd, or shall' (V.i.309–11). No one else has changed though. The other characters will continue as before, the cunning deluding the stupid, the stupid happy in their delusions. Lady Malepert's tragedy is that the corruption around her will inevitably reverse her reformation and propel her back into her old profession. Wishwell is unperturbed by the girl's apparent change of heart. Now that Gayman's love is no longer a threat, she is confident that she can win back her business asset, 'I am sure to keep her in my Power' (V.i.312). In view of Lady Malepert's youth and impressionable nature, the bawd is probably correct in her assumption.

The Maid's Last Prayer is the most grim and comfortless comedy in the Restoration period. 'Love', says Wishwell, summing up the attitude of most of the characters, is no more than 'Nature's Appetite Diseas'd: / Where we have no Concern, we're always pleas'd' (II.i.251–2). With all her faults, Lady Malepert is the only character in the comedy (except perhaps her husband's foolish old aunt, Lady Susan Malepert) who experiences love as more than 'Nature's Appetite Diseas'd'. For the rest of the characters, in a society founded upon the pursuit of sexual pleasure and material gain, love and affection have become pointless weaknesses. It is bitterly ironic that the prostitute in the play should show up the inadequacies of the others. Such cynicism must have been too much for audiences accustomed to comedies like *Greenwich Park*, for the play was a dismal failure. In its dedication Southerne wrote angrily, 'I have had my ends of this Play, and shou'd have been glad if it had answer'd every Bodies: I think it has its Beauties, tho' they did not appear upon the Stage' (dedication, 30–3). So far as Barry's performance was concerned, one reason for the play's failing to work well 'upon the Stage' may have been its restrained style of language. While the part of Lady Malepert clearly needed all the actress's talent for affective acting, its emotion is, for her, unusually understated, with no ranting *tours de force*, no inflated rhetoric and no melodrama. The only rhetorically heightened lines in the play are those in which Lady Malepert expresses her recognition of the power of love ('I have slept away my life'), her suffering in the final scene, for example, is exceptionally muted: 'Wou'd I might never see his Face again' (V.i.341). Similarly, when resisting Gayman's blandishments in the second act, her most emotional words are merely, 'Why will you press me thus to what will ruine me?' (II.i.160). While to the modern ear this moderate, more realistic language can seem an asset, it possibly disappointed both Barry and her listeners and made it harder for the leading lady to perform with her usual thrilling fervour. At any rate, Barry's presence at the head of the cast as a sympathetic mistress was not enough to save the play from disaster.

Interestingly, a month after *The Maid's Last Prayer*, the United Company staged Henry Higden's *The Wary Widow* which contains a crude example of the Barry type of role of the kept mistress. Panting, ranting, swooning Leonora is the opposite of Lady Malepert: she rails at her bawd, ''twas thy Flattery that first seduc'd and Debauch'd me...and foolishly barter'd away my Virgin Treasure, for Glass, Bells and Baubles'.[16] At times Leonora's speeches and actions are so ridiculously exaggerated as to suggest an unintentional parody of earlier Barry roles in this style. She is first seen, for instance, in hot pursuit of her lover, Frank, '*disguis'd in the habit of a Gentleman, running and out of Breath, looks at him, falls in a Swoond crying – He's gone, he's gone!*' (p. 15). When Frank tries to end their affair she attempts suicide by falling on her sword, before finally flinging herself on her couch. Eventually, however, she finds a more prosaic solution to her difficulties in marriage to the fool, Sir Noisy Parrat, who is convinced that she is an innocent virgin.

We have no cast list for *The Wary Widow*, but an actress named Mrs Lassells delivered its epilogue and the first lines of this address imply that she played Leonora:

> What diffring designes we Women lay
> She to avoid, and I to snap the Prey:
> Virtue, and Fortune, makes her Luster great:
> Raising that Value, I but counterfeit.

Leonora here contrasts herself with the virtuous heiress Clarinda, who spends most of the play trying to avoid the amorous advances of Sir Noisy. Lassells had only a brief career on the stage and from the variety of types she played was probably used by the company to fill in roles in plays of secondary importance when the best actresses were occupied elsewhere. Higden must have written the role of Leonora for Barry, but the United Company presumably preferred not to use their star performer in such a weak play, or perhaps the actress herself refused to play in it. Lassells played the modest and virtuous Violante in *Greenwich Park* and then the flirtatious Berenice in *The Marriage-Hater Match'd* nine months later – both supporting roles. Leonora constituted her first and only attempt at the lead and the mistress part in a play.[17] She certainly seems to have failed decisively and Higden's comedy was hissed and laughed off the stage. 'The Theatre was by Faction transformed into a Bear-Garden, hissing, mimicking, ridiculing and Catcalling.'[18] But one wonders if the play would have been mocked so heartily if Barry had played Leonora. She was to play several equally exaggerated characters in the coming years (such as Homais in *The Royal Mischief*, and Bellinda in Pix's *The Innocent Mistress*). She had the capacity to make the worst plays work on stage – as an eighteenth-century critic notes, 'she often so greatly exerted her art in an indifferent character, that her acting had given success to plays that would disgust the most patient reader'.[19] Characters like Leonora could work if played by Barry.

Perhaps the failure of *The Maid's Last Prayer* frightened most dramatists from attempting to use the 'tragic' prostitute or mistress to embody a serious satiric attack on male behaviour and the double standard. Only at the end of the decade did Congreve, in *The Way of the World*, attempt another serious and sympathetic portrayal of the discarded mistress in Mrs Fainall (played incidentally by Mrs Bowman, so that Barry was free to play Fainall's fiery mistress, Mrs Marwood). On the other hand, Barry was as popular as ever, and over the last seven years of the century she inspired three more suffering, ranting mistresses varying in virtue from the nobly suffering Bellinda in Pix's *The Innocent Mistress*, 1697, to the demonic Lady Touchwood (in Congreve's second comedy *The Double-Dealer*, 1693). A glance at these roles suggests the ingenious variations dramatists extracted from the basic theme, in order to create more vehicles for Barry's talent.[20]

Lady Touchwood is a straightforward lustful villainess. Tired of adultery with the equally villainous Maskwell she pursues the play's hero Mellefont who remains, however, the faithful suitor of the heroine Cynthia. Although Lady Touchwood is in the mould of previous Barry 'tragic' mistresses – she speaks in heightened rhetoric and burns with sexual passion – she is wholly unsympathetic, which contrasts with Barry's next mistress role a few months later as the unwilling adulteress Mrs Lovely in Crowne's interesting late comedy *The Married Beau* (1694). Mrs Lovely is an essentially loyal wife who succumbs on one fatal occasion to the temptation of sleeping with her husband's friend Polidor. (Could his name be an ironic reminder of the adulterous Polidor of Otway's *The Orphan?*) Her behaviour when being seduced is highly reminiscent of that of Lady Galliard when seduced by Wilding. She cries, 'What shall I do with him? I'm yielding! yielding...' as he *'pulls her off the Stage, and bolts the Door'*.[21] However, while Mrs Lovely typically expresses her shame and remorse in a tragic style of verse:

> Oh, Madam! I confess I've been surpriz'd
> By wicked Polidor; he forc'd himself
> Into my Chamber, and he wou'd not leave me
> Till he had ruin'd me. Oh spare me! spare me   (p. 36)

Crowne's play is predominantly comic in tone. Mr Lovely deserved to be made a cuckold. He boastfully begged Polidor to try and seduce his wife in order to hear how thoroughly his friend was rebuffed and he himself adored. And Mrs Lovely is not excluded from the play's happy ending; she manages to keep her act of adultery a secret from her husband and is thankful to have the opportunity to remain faithful thereafter. The rake Polidor marries the strong-minded and pious Camilla who is to reform him thoroughly. Crowne's happy ending contradicted prevailing convention by suggesting sensibly that a woman need not be 'ruined' for ever by once giving in to temptation.

After three years during which she played a variety of roles,[22] Barry created a completely fresh version of her usual tragic mistress role as Bellinda in Pix's unusual comedy *The Innocent Mistress* (1697). As the title of the play suggests, Bellinda and her married lover, although mutually adoring, have a purely platonic relationship. This time the rhetorical lines that Barry was called upon to deliver were all profoundly, even ludicrously, virtuous. For instance, at one point Bellinda pledges that she will retire from society and in suitably elevated tones instructs that her faithful lover be told the news:

Tell him, lest he should take it ill of you, that I have ... resolv'd to fly from him and all the World, and in my Father's house remain as in a Cloister ... I have the Goal in view, bright Honour leads me on, the part is glorious, but, oh! 'tis painful too.[23]

In spite of Bellinda's virtue, the couple's efforts to resist their overwhelming desire for each other provide an opportunity for a sexual scene comparable to those of previous Barry plays. Bellinda's efforts to part from her lover provoke moments of frantic sexual passion: in Act V Sir Charles cannot restrain himself from embracing Bellinda, 'What! uncontroul'd clasp thee thus! Oh, Extasie! with wild Fury run o'er each trembling beauteous Limb, and grasp thee, as drowning Men the dear Bark from whence they are thrown.' Bellinda at this stage breaks away with the modest cry, 'Away, away! What are we doing? Divide him, Heaven, from my fond guilty Eyes' (p. 41). Virtue is finally rewarded. At the end Sir Charles discloses that he never consummated the marriage to his present wife, and a little later it is revealed that the lady actually possesses another husband who predates Sir Charles. The lovers embrace passionately at the news and in an ecstasy of wildly exaggerated emotion, Bellinda swoons. Sir Charles exclaims, 'Ha! the transporting Joy has caught her Rosie Breath, and those bright Eyes are in their snowy Lids retir'd ... Wake my Bellinda, 'tis thy Beauclair calls.' Recovering, Bellinda delicately withdraws, 'I fear I have offended my Virgin Modesty by me still practis'd and ador'd; now we must stand on forms, till time and decency shall crown our Wishes' (p. 51). This time, uniquely, audiences had the pleasure of seeing the Barry 'mistress' marry her lover.

Aphra Behn's *The Revenge* and Mary Pix's *The Innocent Mistress* have very different heroines and use the idea of love outside marriage in very different ways. What links these heroines, and all the related mistress roles that came in between, is not the issue of the fallen woman in society (only a very few dramatists were concerned with that) but the leading actress whose personality and extraordinary abilities were the reason such parts existed. We understand such plays best if we compare Barry to a Hollywood idol like Bette Davis, who similarly inspired a stream of female roles of a particular kind, good and bad, because she and her distinctive style of performance were what the public wanted to see:

She has survived because of the rare quality that keeps the viewer mesmerized by her performances and fascinated to learn what she will do next and how she'll do it, even when her material is less than superb. Through sheer force of personality she can make you think she's beautiful, make you weep for her, make you loathe her. As an actress she has courageously run the gamut of roles and genres.[24]

So her biographer describes Bette Davis, but his account bears a remarkable similarity to Elizabeth Barry.

CHAPTER 7

The angel and the she-devil

Drama's tendency to depict woman as angel or devil, patient Griselda or temptress Eve, has been much commented on in recent years.[1] As Flamineo notes succinctly in *The White Devil* (1612), 'woman to man / Is either a god or a wolf'.[2] However, while both types recur steadily throughout the seventeenth century, they are most prominent in Restoration tragedy because of the combined influence of two successive pairs of actresses: first Rebecca Marshall and Elizabeth Boutell, then Elizabeth Barry and Anne Bracegirdle. During the 1670s Marshall and Boutell popularised a type of tragedy with two female leads, usually in competition for the same man, yet wholly dissimilar in attitude and behaviour. One would be chaste and gentle, the other wild and passionate: Boutell played the former, Marshall the latter. While this type of pairing largely disappeared when Marshall left the stage in the late 1670s, it was powerfully revived at the end of the 1680s with Barry and Bracegirdle. So great was the effect of these two actresses playing together that two-thirds of the new tragedies produced by their company between 1695 and 1706 contain a pair of contrasting leading roles for them. The history of this pairing from 1660 to the beginning of the eighteenth century reveals the outstanding impact of the actress on Restoration drama.[3]

ANGELS AND DEVILS 1660–5

There is no one production during the 1660s in which the success of two particular actresses as contrasting characters may be said to have initiated a whole series of imitations in the next decade: several factors led to the later potent combination of Marshall and Boutell as unbridled passion and gentle purity, respectively. In 1662 the King's Company revived Beaumont and Fletcher's *The Maid's Tragedy* and this fine play remained a firm and influential favourite throughout the next forty years.[4] The play has two leading and contrasting female characters, the bold and sexually experienced Evadne, mistress of the king, who marries the noble Amintor and finally stabs her former royal lover, and her rival for the love of Amintor, the passive, chaste and suffering Aspatia. Evadne in particular offered an actress several marvellous scenes, such as her sharing her bed with Amintor but refusing to let him touch her on their wedding night, and her murder of the king, whom she ties up and regales with his sins before stabbing him three times. Rebecca Marshall was very effective in this role as early as 1666, when Pepys wrote appreciatively of a production that year, 'a good play, and well acted, especially by the younger Marshall'.[5] The play must have inspired later incarnations of the two female types.

The angel and the she-devil existed both separately and together in new plays as well as revivals of the 1660s. By 1670 the gentle vulnerable virgin and what Eric Rothstein calls the 'lustful villainess' type had emerged as the two most popular kinds of female character in new plays.[6] The 'lustful villainess' was not in fact necessarily lustful, nor wholly villainess, but, like Evadne, she was invariably flawed, passionate and sexually experienced. Her most immediate sources lie in Renaissance drama – Shakespeare's Tamora, Cleopatra and Lady Macbeth, Marston's Insatiate Countess, Webster's Vittoria and Middleton's Beatrice-Joanna all reappeared on the stage after 1660 and presumably influenced dramatists. The innocent virgin was, of course, a standard figure, used again and again in all styles of Restoration tragedy.

The first appearance of the 'lustful villainess' in a new Restoration play was Davenant's influential introduction of Roxolana into the second version of *The Siege of Rhodes* in 1661. With actresses now at his disposal, Davenant transformed the original, clandestinely produced version of 1656 by adding a foil for the virtuous Ianthe (Mary Betterton) in the empress Roxolana (Hester Davenport), whose insane jealousy of her husband Solyman's love for Ianthe provokes the liveliest scenes in the play. Having added a scene to the first part in which Roxolana wildly attacks Solyman for inconstancy and is dismissed, Davenant had her plan Ianthe's murder in the second part. Grimly she approaches the sleeping Ianthe, '*a Turkish Embroidered Handkerchief in her left hand, And a naked Ponyard in her right*'.[7] However, when she is on the point of gagging her rival with the handkerchief and stabbing her with the dagger, Ianthe wakes and, in a highly dramatic reversal, persuades her enemy to spare her. The dagger is thrown aside and the two kiss in friendship. The play concludes happily; Roxolana is reconciled with Solyman and Ianthe returned to her true love, Alphonso. The dagger motif was to be used again and again in future colourful battles between female rivals.

This version of *The Siege of Rhodes* was enormously successful. Pepys, of course, began to refer to Mary Betterton as 'Ianthe' in his diary and to Hester Davenport as 'Roxolana'. The next appearance of such a pair of women came in Dryden's *The Indian Queen* (1664) where, surely in imitation of Davenant (and ever with an eye to show business), Dryden gave his timorous heroine, Orazia, a fearsome rival named Zempoalla. Zempoalla (probably played by Anne Marshall, elder sister of Rebecca[8]) has a central role as the usurping Indian queen of the title, not only intriguing for political power, but also suffering unrequited love for the hero, Montezuma, who rejects her and loves the meek and retiring Orazia. She is a more prominent character than Orazia and she expresses her complex and passionate emotions at length. She struggles at first to resist love because it is for an unworthy object (Montezuma is her prisoner) and therefore dishonourable:

> 'Tis love, 'tis love, that thus dishonours me!
> How pride and love tear my divided soul!
> For each too narrow, yet both claim it whole.

Nevertheless, Zempoalla eventually seeks a charm to make Montezuma love her. When this fails, like Roxolana she seizes a dagger and prepares to plunge it into the breast of her rival.[9] This time the victim of the dagger survives because another of Orazia's admirers saves her just in time.

It is interesting to find Dryden criticising *The Siege of Rhodes*, among other things, for a want of 'variety of Characters'.[10] His modifications to the Roxolana type make her less simplistic and reveal new possibilities in the character of the 'darker woman' (because Zempoalla and later equivalents are not always wholly evil, this seems a fairer description than 'lustful villainess'). Dryden's queen is not merely a jealous rival for the love of the hero – her passion is complicated by a desire for power and a pride which conflict with her love. This struggle is symbolised by the moment in which Zempoalla raises her dagger again, this time to stab Montezuma, but then cuts the cords that bind him instead. Finally, in a potentially moving scene, thwarted in love and in ambition, she stabs herself with the dagger announcing, 'All that cou'd render Life desir'd is gone / Orazia has my Love, and you my Throne.'[11] Dryden's play suggested that the unsuccessful rival could be made as sympathetic as the conventional heroine, and later this became an important feature of the tragic pairing.

Characteristically, Dryden cashed in on the success of *The Indian Queen* by producing a sequel called *The Indian Emperour* the following year. In this play he provided Zempoalla's equivalent in Almeria, her daughter, who contrasts with another meek heroine, Cydaria. In this play an aged Montezuma now ironically loves Almeria (Orazia being dead) but she and Cydaria both love the hero of this play, Cortez. Almeria reminds audiences of the earlier drama when, like Zempoalla, she falls in love against her reason with an enemy: 'My Mother's Pride must find my Mother's Fate.'[12] Cortez, of course, loves Cydaria.

Dryden developed both rivals in new directions suggesting less admirable qualities in the frail heroine and more sympathetic traits in her passionate opposite. Cydaria, for instance, is a coward. When Almeria draws a dagger on her (implying that the dagger device had become very popular by this time) Cydaria, unlike the brave Ianthe, shows great fear and is glad to obey Cortez's command that she hide behind him so that he is stabbed. Similarly, when both women express a wish to stay with Cortez as he goes into battle, it is Cydaria who for a cowardly reason begs against separation: 'Leave me not here alone, and full of fright, / Amidst the Terrors of a Dreadful night' (VI.iv.133–4). Almeria, on the other hand, is full of selfless courage:

> Then stay and take me with you; though to be
> A Slave to waite upon your Victory.
> My Heart unmov'd, can Noyse, and Horrour bear,
> Parting from you is all the Death I fear.   (IV.iv.141–4)

Exploiting the dagger motif still further, Dryden also reintroduced it into the final act when Almeria again threatens Cydaria with the weapon and the victim shows a most unheroic terror: 'I yet am Tender, Young and full of Fear / And dare not Dye, but fain would tarry here' (V.ii.277–8). This time Almeria stabs first Cydaria and then herself. When actually believing that she is about to die Cydaria does show some courage, but this proves unnecessary since Almeria only intended her own wound to be fatal. The 'darker woman' dies forgiven by Cortez and her rival whose hands she joins just before she expires. She also repeats her willingness to die for Cortez who cries remorsefully, 'You for my sake, Life to Cydaria give: / And I could dye for you, if you might Live' (V.ii.329–30).

Almeria reveals a positive side to the 'darker woman's' aggression. In this case the unsuccessful rival seems perhaps more attractive than the pure heroine. This shift is reflected in the casting. The cowardly Cydaria was played by Nell Gwyn the comedienne, whom Pepys found quite wrong for the part: 'I find Nell come again, which I am glad of, but was most infinitely displeased with her being put to act the Emperours daughter; which is a great and serious part, which she doth more basely.'[13] According to Downes, Anne Quin (née Marshall) played Almeria, having already played Zempoalla and Evadne in a very early revival of *The Maid's Tragedy*. Anne Quin was by no means restricted to villainous roles. She played Celia in Jonson's *Volpone* (1661), and the noble heroines Edith in Fletcher's *Rollo, Duke of Normandy* (1661) and Alizia in Boyle's *The Black Prince* (1667). Audiences would, in fact, have been more accustomed to seeing her in virtuous roles. Already the tragic pairing was no simple conflict between good and evil. Once the 'darker woman' began to be played by actresses as popular and talented as Rebecca Marshall and Elizabeth Barry, dramatists would develop the sympathetic potential of this character still further.

Around the same time as *The Indian Queen* and *The Indian Emperour* were produced, Davenant adapted *Macbeth* (*c*.1664), partly in order to produce another typical pair of contrasting female roles. The part of Lady Macduff was substantially increased so as to become a foil to Lady Macbeth and in a series of new scenes their differing attitudes to power and honour are opposed. For instance, the heartless ambition of Lady Macbeth is emphasised by contrast to Lady Macduff's rejection of such aims:

> The world mistakes the glories gain'd in war,
> Thinking their Lustre true: alas, they are
> But Comets, Vapours! by some men exhal'd
> From others blood.

Whereas Lady Macbeth incites her husband to regicide, Lady Macduff persuades her husband to ignore the witches' prophesy of his success,

> He that believes ill news from such as those
> Deserves to find it true: their words are like
> Their shape, nothing but fiction.[14]

Overall, the adaptation is not an effective one. Lady Macduff is merely a wooden idealisation of feminine virtues, perfunctorily added to capitalise on a fashionable trend.

THE IMPACT OF REBECCA MARSHALL AND ELIZABETH BOUTELL

Over the next five years, from 1665 to 1670, there were no more pairs of heroines and villainesses, only a series of contrasting pairs of virtuous female characters (usually supporting roles), such as the strong-minded rulers Queen Timandra and Princess Elizabeth and their shy shrinking pages Calanthe and Charlot in Howard's *The Usurper* (1664) and Caryll's *The English Princess* (1667).[15] The next important development came in 1670 when Rebecca Marshall and Elizabeth Boutell first appeared together in Joyner's *The Roman Empress* (1670). From this first appearance it is plain that they were a remarkable acting combination, for they earned special praise from the author:

The ancient Phaedra is here set off in a real Fulvia... This Character has been ever much extoll'd: if my art had fail'd in the writing of it, it was highly recompenc'd in the scenical presentation; for it was incomparably acted. I have for the greater variety of the Stage divided this Character, conferring some share of it on Aurelia, which though a great, various and difficult part, was excellently performed.[16]

Joyner gave the traditional female pair a new twist by having Boutell undergo a radical change of type halfway through. Initially Aurelia seems meekly virtuous, weeping and pleading with her father:

> Sir let these tears
> Soften that breast, which the age, war and custom
> Seem to have armed so against compassion.

However, at the news that her lover has killed her brother, she is transformed into a bloodthirsty plotter for revenge, working in union with the passionate and sadistic Fulvia (played by Marshall):

> hereafter
> These fountains of my eyes be ever dry:
> My hand, and tongue audacious to commit
> Mischiefs to terrifie mankind.[17]

The change was purely for entertainment value, to offer a pleasing shock of novelty for spectators: as Joyner explained, he did it 'for the greater variety of the stage'.

The 'incomparable' acting of Marshall and Boutell triggered a series of roles for them as women in conflict. In the same year (1670) as *The Roman Empress*, Dryden cast them in leading, opposed roles in *The Conquest of Granada*. Marshall played the lively and wicked Lyndaraxa, Boutell was the loving and virtuous Benzayda. Lyndaraxa gave Pepys' favourite tragic actress an especially good role, as she shamelessly exploits the fatal attraction she has for her two wooers, Abdalla and Abdelmech, in order to obtain her ambition to be queen. One of them exclaims:

> A glancing smile allur'd me to command;
> And her soft fingers gently prest my hand,
> I felt the pleasure glide through every part.[18]

Dryden developed the character of Lyndaraxa far beyond anything suggested by sources of the play, such as La Calprenède's *Cassandra* and *Cleopatra*. In his study of La Calprenède and Dryden, Herbert Wynford Hill has noted that 'Lyndaraxa was probably intended to be the stock unscrupulous rival of the heroine, but this capable and fascinating woman develops so rapidly under the hand of the entranced author that she quite outstrips her type and challenges in interest the heroine herself.'[19] This is what one would expect, considering Dryden's treatment of Lyndaraxa's predecessors in *The Indian Queen* and *The Indian Emperour* and the fact that he had Marshall to play his villainess.

Marshall and Boutell next appeared together as the corrupt Poppea and the pure Cyara in Nathaniel Lee's *The Tragedy of Nero* (1674), the passionate Berenice and pious Clarona in Crowne's *The Destruction of Jerusalem* (1677) and, most successfully, as Roxana and Statira in Lee's *Alexander the Great* (1677).[20] The latter became one of the most popular, oft-repeated tragedies of the whole period, and the roles of Roxana and Statira were later played by Barry and Bracegirdle. Apart from Alexander's death, the scenes of conflict between the two queens – Roxana battling for her rights as Alexander's first wife, and Statira defending herself as his second, most beloved – are the most dramatic and memorable in the play. This plot recalls that of *The Siege of Rhodes*: Lee even revived the dagger device, which was taken to its limits. The scene in which Roxana attacks Statira with her dagger is elaborately prepared. In the

preceding act Roxana graphically describes the torments of jealousy
she suffers and makes plans to kill her rival. The fatal encounter
between the queens opens with Statira's vision prophesying her
coming death: '*Statira is discover'd sleeping in the Bower of Semiramis. The
Spirits of Queen Statira her Mother, and Darius, appear standing on each side
of her, with Daggers threatning her.*'[21] Finally, the women face each other
and Roxana manages to stab Statira just before help arrives. The
latter nevertheless survives long enough to take farewell of Alexander
and to forgive her rival. Once Statira is dead, Roxana has a dramatic
and taxing scene in which, clinging to his robe, she begs for
Alexander's love and pleads on behalf of the child she carries within
her. Here the villainess took the centre of the stage and made
audiences pity her, in spite of her horrific activities only moments
before.

With Marshall and Boutell together scoring successes for the
King's Company, the other house quickly began to offer similar
pairings in their tragedies, mainly using their two best tragediennes,
Mary Betterton and Mary Lee. Their response to *The Roman Empress*
and *The Conquest of Granada* was Samuel Pordage's *Herod and Mariamne*
(1671), with Betterton as the virtuous Mariamne and Lee as the
heartless Salome, and Crowne's *The History of Charles the Eighth* (also
1671) which set the gentle goodness of Julia (Mrs Dixon) against the
vengeful ranting of Isabella (Mrs Betterton). A perhaps surprising
change of casting is to be noted in Crowne's drama as Betterton,
whose line was normally that of a virtuous heroine, here created the
role of Isabella. However, clearly she had no difficulty with evil roles.
Cibber says that she was a better Lady Macbeth, for instance, than
Barry.

Even Mrs. Barry, who acted the Lady Macbeth after her, could not in that
Part, with all her superior Strength, and Melody of Voice, throw out those
quick and careless Strokes of Terror, from the Disorder of a guilty Mind,
which the other gave us, with a Facility in her Manner, that render'd them
at once tremendous, and delightful.[22]

Betterton was also cast as the devilish Empress of Morocco in
Settle's play of that name two years later, in which she was called
upon to perish, like Isabella, bloody and ranting. In Settle's play
Mary Lee, who had created the wicked Salome in Pordage's *Herod
and Mariamne*, also changed line to play the honourable Mariamne.
Three years later, in Settle's *Ibrahim the Illustrious Bassa* (1676),

Betterton reverted to her usual type, playing the Christian captive princess Isabella, opposite Lee's proud and jealous queen Roxolana, in yet another version of the plot of Davenant's *The Siege of Rhodes*. In this case, Roxolana has tamed her husband Solyman, but loses her power over him when Isabella appears on the scene. Settle rang the changes by having Roxolana draw a dagger on Solyman before finally taking a dish of poison herself, in the ignominy of rejection. Solyman is reformed by her act; too late he consigns Isabella to her true love and swears to spend his life mourning Roxolana.

A year later, like further episodes to a popular modern soap opera, the Duke's Company answered Nathaniel Lee's *The Rival Queens* with Samuel Pordage's feeble melodrama *The Siege of Babylon* (1677). In this play Betterton played Statira and Lee played Roxana, both now widows of Alexander and rivals for the love of Orontes, who, of course, loves Statira. Like Dryden's Almeria, Roxana wrestles with her passion but cannot bring herself to stab the man she loves. Pordage revived the dagger device once again by having Statira bravely 'shew her Breast' to Roxana's knife in the third act. Defeated in the final act, Roxana flourishes the fateful dagger for the last time, to hold the enemy at bay and to stab herself. Statira points the moral of her end, 'Thus Gods their Judgement show', and Roxana is '*carried off the Stage Raveing*'.[23] Pordage's rival queens seem in every way inferior to Nathaniel Lee's. The conflict between them is less exciting and the sympathy Lee managed to create for Roxana is lacking in Pordage's much more simplistic character portrayal. The play, which failed, seems just a poor effort to cash in on the success of Marshall and Boutell at the other theatre.

In the meantime, the King's Company began to suffer the dire financial problems from which it never recovered. One of the first of its players to defect was Marshall; by 21 May 1677 she was playing Maria in Durfey's *A Fond Husband* for the Duke's Company. She cannot have been happy there, however, as for some reason she left the stage soon after. Losing Marshall cannot have helped the fading fortunes of the King's Company and it was in no state to initiate a fresh tragic partnership between Boutell and another actress. There was, in any case, no tragedienne in the company of Marshall's stature and abilities with whom to pair Boutell.

In Nathaniel Lee's plays, in particular, the disappearance of a pair of balanced, contrasting female characters is very marked after Marshall's departure. In *Mithridates* (1678), Boutell's virtuous character, Semandra, was simply paired opposite another equally virtuous female, Monima, created by Mrs Corbett, another specialist in pure roles, with no talent for playing villainesses. Lee then began to write for the Duke's Company and in *Oedipus* (1678) Betterton had a central senior role as the doomed Jocasta and Mary Lee a supporting, rather than opposing, role as the proud and constant Eurydice, a generation younger than Jocasta. *Caesar Borgia* (1679) has only one leading female part – that of Bellamira, who was played by Lee. Then came Barry's success in Otway's *The Orphan* (1680) so that Mary Lee's next few plays, *Theodosius* (1680), *Lucius Junius Brutus* (1680), *The Princess of Cleve* (1680?) and *Constantine the Great* (1683) each have only one starring part, for her. There were then only a tiny number of new plays produced at all for the remainder of the decade.

THE BARRY–BRACEGIRDLE PARTNERSHIP 1689–1700

Anne Bracegirdle's first known role was a leading one, as Antelina in Mountfort's *The Injur'd Lovers* (1688). The part equals that of Oryala, her rival, who was played by Elizabeth Barry. Antelina is gentle, suffering and chaste, Oryala, bold and passionate. Thus, with the revival of London theatre at the end of the 1680s, the United Company seem to have deliberately chosen Bracegirdle to emulate with Barry the Marshall–Boutell successes of the early 1670s. Personal friendship may have been one reason why such a balanced partnership existed between Barry and Bracegirdle from the very start of the latter's career. They were apparently always good friends; Barry did not feel threatened by her younger colleague, Bracegirdle had no wish to oust Barry from her position of tragic supremacy. Cibber records that when the patentees of The United Company, in an attempt to cut actors' wages, offered several of Barry's and Thomas Betterton's chief parts to the younger players George Powell and Bracegirdle

farther their first Project did not succeed; for tho' the giddy Head of Powell, accepted the Parts of Betterton; Mrs. Bracegirdle had a different way of thinking, and desir'd to be excus'd, from those of Mrs. Barry; her good Sense was not to be misled by the insidious Favour of the Patentees; she knew the Stage was wide enough for her Success, without entring into any such rash, and invidious Competition, with Mrs. Barry, and therefore wholly refus'd acting any Part that properly belong'd to her.[24]

The very fact that Barry and Bracegirdle were close friends and worked well together must have encouraged Mountfort and others to write plays in which they could both star.

The pattern of Barry–Bracegirdle typecasting set up in *The Injur'd Lovers* never varied. The two actresses did not swap types like Mary Betterton and Mary Lee. Although Barry played a wide spectrum of roles from evil to good, Bracegirdle always played the innocent virgin, whether she was cast as Barry's rival, friend or daughter. (The nearest they came to an exchange was, of course, Granville's *Heroic Love*, in which Barry played the dignified and virtuous Chruseis and Bracegirdle her lighthearted and coquettish rival.) As was shown in chapter 4, this division was partly the result of public perception of their personalities in real life. Barry was known to have been the mistress of at least one man, but Bracegirdle never lost her famed reputation for chastity. The casting also corresponds to their looks. Barry was no conventional beauty whereas Bracegirdle, as well as being younger, seems to have been extremely attractive. Aston describes her as being 'of a lovely Height, with dark-brown Hair and Eye-brows, black and sparkling Eyes, and a fresh blushy Complexion…a chearful Aspect, and a fine set of even white Teeth'. In spite of her right shoulder being 'a little protended', she was 'finely shap'd, and had very handsome Legs and Feet'.[25] Her portrait as the goddess Flora with Barry as Ceres by Kneller at Hampton Court certainly shows an attractive woman (see plate 12). Naturally perhaps, no one wished to see this 'Cara, the Darling of the Theatre'[26] play anything but heroines.

The division of roles may also be attributed to a difference in acting skills. As we have seen, Barry was very versatile and effective in tragedy and even when playing a villainess could still make spectators weep for her. Curll reports of her performances in Roxana's climactic scene in a revival of Lee's *Alexander the Great* some time after 1690:

I cannot conclude without taking notice that tho' before our Eyes we had just seen Roxana with such Malice murder an innocent Person, because better beloved than herself; yet, after Statira is dead, and Roxana is following Alexander on her knees, Mrs. Barry made this Complaint in so Pathetic a Manner, as drew Tears from the greatest Part of the Audience.

> O! Speak not such harsh words, my Royal Master:
> But take, dear Sir, O! take me into Grace;
> By the dear Babe, the Burden of my Womb,
> That weighs me down when I would follow faster.
> O! do not frown, but clear that angry brow;

12 *William III on Horseback*, by Godfrey Kneller, with Elizabeth Barry as Ceres and Anne Bracegirdle as Flora.

> Your Eyes will blast me, and your Words are Bolts
> That strike me dead; the little Wretch I bear,
> Leaps frightened at your Wrath, and dies within me.

In Congreve's *The Mourning Bride* the passionate Zara played by Barry even eclipsed the heroine Almeria, played by Bracegirdle, when Congreve had deliberately created Almeria to give the younger actress (his favourite) the star role – as Anthony Aston explains: 'Mrs. Barry out-shin'd Mrs. Bracegirdle in the Character of Zara in *The Mourning Bride*, altho' Mr. Congreve design'd Almeria for that Favour.'[27] Barry was the obvious choice for the often more interesting and unexpected 'darker woman'. Bracegirdle was an excellent comedienne but her tragic range seems to have been limited. It seems significant that the one surviving record of her tragic style of performance is a parody. In 1696 Christopher Rich's company produced an anonymous satiric parody of tragedy, *The Female Wits*, at Thomas Betterton's rival theatre. The play shows rehearsals for a ridiculous melodrama which soon emerges as a thinly disguised *Royal Mischief*. Here the actress who represents Bracegirdle (played by Jane Rogers) is told:

Give me leave to instruct you in a moving Cry. Oh! there's a great deal of Art in crying; Hold your Handkerchief, thus; let it meet your Eyes, thus; your Head declin'd, thus; now in a perfect whine, crying out these words, 'By these Tears, which never cease to Flow.'[28]

The exaggerated gestures and the whining – so clearly creating the opposite of a truly moving cry – suggest that Bracegirdle's may have been a somewhat clichéd, uninspired style of tragic acting. In his general account of the actress, Cibber discusses only her playing of Millamant and the lack of accounts of her tragic performances suggests that none was particularly outstanding. Possibly Barry's presence in the same company inhibited her from developing skills as a tragedienne.

For nearly twenty years, Barry and Bracegirdle dominated the form of female characterisation in tragedy, as dramatists wrote plays around them and their stereotypes. Between 1688 and 1706, when they created complementary roles for the last time as the sisters Almyna and Zoradia in Delariviere Manley's melodrama *Almyna* (soon after which, Bracegirdle retired from the stage), they were cast together in at least thirty new tragedies.[29] A brief survey of some of these shows how variously and entertainingly their partnership set its stamp on the tragedy of nearly two decades.

It is a tribute to both the inventiveness of many Restoration dramatists and the acting skills of the two women that, in spite of the limitations of typecasting, they performed a remarkable range of different roles over the years. Mountfort's *The Injur'd Lovers* (1688) is the story of King Rhusanes who loves the chaste and beautiful Antelina, but who is tricked into marrying her rival, the ruthless and vengeful Oryala. That the play is clearly indebted to *The Indian Emperour* model is shown by the character of Oryala who, in contrast to the virtuous yet passive Antelina, is flawed but not unsympathetic – a woman who is divided between her warring passions of love and

pride and whose solution to her problems is ultimately to stab herself.
Oryala could be said to represent a halfway point in the spectrum of
female characters played by Barry as a foil to Bracegirdle's purity.
Towards one end of the spectrum, so to speak, Barry's roles could be
a good deal more evil – as the plotting queen-mother Isabella, for
instance, in John Bancroft's historical tragedy *King Edward III*
(1690), or as Homais in Manley's *The Royal Mischief*. Towards the
other end of the spectrum, Barry played a range of wholly
sympathetic, wholly virtuous characters, although her roles still
contrasted with Bracegirdle's. The contrast was here generally
achieved by making the Barry roles markedly more strongminded,
more passionate and more dominant, as when she played the fighting
queen of Britain and Bracegirdle was cast as her pathetically raped
daughter in Charles Hopkins' *Boadicea* (1697) or when Barry played
Penelope in Rowe's *Ulysses* (1705) and Bracegirdle played her son's
beloved.

In *Cyrus the Great* (1695) John Banks had the innovative idea of
making Barry's character the beloved of the two rivals and
Bracegirdle's the sufferer of unrequited love. Barry as Panthea is
pursued by Cyrus, while Bracegirdle as Lausaria hopelessly pursues
him and is driven distracted in a picturesque manner. Banks would
seem to have derived the idea for this development from Thomas
Durfey's casting of Bracegirdle as the frustrated Marcella in *The
Second Part of the Comical History of Don Quixote* earlier in the year. As
Marcella, Bracegirdle sang a song about her frustrated love to
tumultuous applause (she was also an extremely talented soprano) –
'a song so incomparably well sung and acted by Mrs. Bracegirdle,
that the most Envious do allow, as well as the most Ingenious affirm,
that 'tis the best of that kind ever done before'.[30] Banks exploited
Bracegirdle's voice to similar effect. In *Cyrus* she sang two such songs,
'*distracted*' and '*drest like Cupid*' – a novel twist. Although *Cyrus the
Great* was apparently written years earlier,[31] Banks must have revised
Lausaria's role for its 1695 production so as to capitalise on
Bracegirdle's success in Durfey's play. The similarity between
Lausaria and Marcella is too close to be accidental.

Occasionally Barry was paired with Bowman instead of Bracegirdle, presumably because the latter, also the company's leading
comedienne, was too busy with other roles. In Pix's *The Czar of
Muscovy* (1701), for example, Barry played the passionate Zarriana
who bravely defies the Czar's attempt to rape her and survives to rule

Russia, while Bowman played the gentle Marina, possibly because
Bracegirdle had been occupied playing Portia in Granville's *The Jew
of Malta* the month before. Barry and Bowman played other similar
parts in a handful of indifferent tragedies, Jane Wiseman's *Antiochus
the Great* (1701), Charles Boyle's *Altemira* (1701) and John Oldmixon's
The Governour of Cyprus (1703). All these dramatists, except perhaps
Pix, would have been considered minor so, although they may have
written their plays with Bracegirdle in mind, they had to accept a less
popular actress (though Bowman was good and experienced) in her
stead. After Bracegirdle's retirement Barry played opposite a variety
of actresses, including Anne Oldfield (in Rowe's *The Royal Convert*,
1707) and Jane Rogers (in *Irene* by Charles Goring, 1708). It is
interesting to find that although the Marshall–Boutell partnership
could not survive the departure of Marshall, this time the tradition of
female pairing continued. This suggests that the strength in both
partnerships lay with the passionate, versatile 'darker woman' and
that she was much harder to replace.

The Barry–Bracegirdle successes generated more female pairings
on similar lines at the rival theatre in Drury Lane. Frances Mary
Knight was the actress that Rich's company used for their Barry-type
roles, with Jane Rogers playing parts similar to Bracegirdle's.
(Rogers, as we have seen, played the Bracegirdle role in *The Female
Wits*, and Knight played 'Mrs Barry' opposite her.) In 1695 there
appeared an anonymous version of the Boadicea story, *Bonduca the
British Heroine*, with Knight as Bonduca and Rogers as her daughter
Claudia (Thomas Betterton's company of course countered this with
Hopkins' *Boadicea* two years later), Robert Gould's *The Rival Sisters*,
in which Knight and Rogers played the sisters of the title, and
Catherine Trotter's *Agnes de Castro*, in which Rogers played the
heroine, Agnes, and Knight the murderous Elvira. In the following
year there were more third-rate plays on a similar theme in which
Rogers and Knight played rivals, such as Richard Norton's classical
drama *Pausanias, the Betrayer of his Country* (1696) in which Knight
played the mother of Pausanias and Rogers his mistress. (Knight,
like Barry, was significantly older than her colleague.) In 1699 competition between the two theatres raged so fiercely that both put on
tragedies about Iphigenia at about the same time – Bracegirdle took
the role in Dennis's *Iphigenia* at Lincoln's Inn Fields and Rogers
played the same part in Abel Boyer's translation of Racine's *Iphigenia
en Aulide* at Drury Lane. No tributes to the tragic acting of either

Knight or Rogers survive, though the number of roles they performed
together suggests that both were competent actresses. They were
clearly only pale shadows of Barry and Bracegirdle, the endurance of
their partnership in tragedy only a measure of their rivals' success.

The pairing of contrasting female types was not restricted to tragedy.
Although the feature is far less marked here, some dramatists also
provided two different styles of comic heroine, the contrast most
usually being between the bold and witty character and another who
is gentler and more restrained. The idea was not new; Shakespeare's
Much Ado About Nothing, for example, has such characters in Beatrice
and Hero, and this comedy was revived after 1660. As actresses in
both companies tended to play one sort of heroine or the other it was
natural that new comedies began to be written to this pattern and
they occur throughout the period. In 1667, for example, *Flora's
Vagaries* appeared, by Richard Rhodes, with Nell Gwyn as the lively
Flora and Mrs Knepp as her more timorous cousin, Otrante. In
Thomas Shadwell's *The Sullen Lovers* the following year, two heroines
are characterised in a manner reminiscent of Jonsonian humours
characters – Emilia (Mrs Shadwell) a retiring manhater, Carolina
(actress unknown) cheerful and witty. Each has a lover suitable to
her disposition. Similar pairings occurred in comedies up to the 1690s
but no particular pair of actresses such as Marshall and Boutell
emerged to make such pairings their speciality and these pairings
occurred relatively infrequently.[32] There is no obvious reason for this.
The idea of two exaggeratedly polarised kinds of womanhood, one
angelic, the other demonic, would seem to belong in tragedy, rather
than in the more prosaic, commonsense world of comedy, but
presumably if two gifted and popular actresses had specialised
successfully as contrasting comic rivals, they might have established
a strong trend. What did occur, however, were occasional attempts to
introduce the Marshall–Boutell and Barry–Bracegirdle tragic partnerships, with varying degrees of success, into comedy.

Wycherley experimented with the idea first in *The Plain Dealer*
(1676), in which Rebecca Marshall was cast as the villainous Olivia,
unfaithful mistress of the hero Manly, while Elizabeth Boutell played
Manly's constant lover Fidelia. The latter proves her devotion by
serving him disguised as a page and finally wins him. Olivia is both
heartless and lustful; she tries to seduce the disguised Fidelia and is

fiercely vengeful when finally defeated. The chaste Fidelia is still more obviously an outcast from serious drama – her disguise as a page belongs to the tragicomic world of Beaumont and Fletcher rather than to Restoration London. She even speaks in verse, the only character to do so:

> But did there never any love like me,
> That, untried tortures, you must find me out?
> Others, at worst, you force to kill themselves,
> But I must be self-murderess of my love,
> Yet will not grant me power to end my life,
> My cruel life, for, when a lover's hopes
> Are dead and gone, life is unmerciful.
> (*Sits down and weeps*)

Wycherley's use of Marshall and Boutell in their traditional tragic roles contributes to the dark, at times disturbing, nature of the main plot of the 'comedy', just as the behaviour of the male characters Manly and Vernish (Olivia's husband) often seems too vicious and savage to belong comfortably in a comic work. Vernish, for instance, attempts to rape Fidelia:

FIDELIA: Oh, oh! Rather than you shall drag me to a death so horrid and so shameful I'll die here a thousand deaths; but you do not look like a ravisher, Sir.
VERNISH: Nor you like one would put me to't but if you will...[33]

Even the happy ending, in which Manly and Fidelia retreat from society entirely, seems out of place in a comedy. Wycherley clearly intended the play's tragic elements to have a thought-provoking effect, and so contribute to his scathing condemnation of greed, lust and corruption. Unfortunately both women, especially Fidelia, fit so awkwardly into the comic context that they serve to render the play a puzzling hotchpotch rather than a powerfully integrated attack on social evils. The play failed and there were no more attempts to shift the Marshall–Boutell pairing into another genre (Rebecca Marshall, in fact, seldom performed in comedy). While all kinds of tragic behaviour might be parodied in comedy – Mrs Loveit, Harriet's rival in *The Man of Mode*, for instance, rants in tragic style and is an object of ridicule – Wycherley's remained the only comedy before 1690 in which a tragic female partnership was transferred, wholesale, from one genre to another. In general, the contrasting heroines, even rivals, of comedy seem unrelated to those of tragedy.

However, during the 1690s, Barry and Bracegirdle were cast together in a number of comedies both before and after the break away from the United Company. These actresses, of course, were not known solely as contrasting rivals and they played other types of comic role together. In Shadwell's *The Scowrers* (1690), for example, their two parts bear little or no relation to the way in which they were cast together in tragedy – the parts are just two, equally attractive, star roles. Although in *The Wives' Excuse*, a year later, Southerne clearly designed the two main female roles with some of Barry's and Bracegirdle's tragic associations in mind, their traditional opposition – purity versus passion – was not one of them. Barry created the part of the virtuous heroine, Mrs Friendall, who nobly suffers in resisting the efforts of rakish Lovemore to seduce her, in spite of the fact that she is attracted to him and dislikes her husband. Bracegirdle played her unmarried friend Mrs Sightly, who is pursued by Friendall (Barry's husband in the play) in the hope that society will believe that he is having an affair with her, even if he is not. Like Bracegirdle's usual tragic parts, Mrs Sightly is chaste and virtuous, the innocent victim of a rapacious male, but the similarities between her role and Barry's are more marked than the contrasts. Together, Mrs Friendall and Mrs Sightly strengthen Southerne's satiric message about the plight of women in a male-dominated libertine society. Barry and Bracegirdle also took similar, as opposed to contrasting, parts in Vanbrugh's best play *The Provok'd Wife* in 1697, Barry playing the patient, good-humoured Lady Brute, chained to a boorish husband, and Bracegirdle her equally sensible, lively friend Bellinda. It is, however, interesting to see that as the wife in both the Southerne and the Vanbrugh plays, Barry still tended to play the senior character and the non-virgin.

One of Durfey's finest comedies, *The Marriage-Hater Match'd* (1692) is the first of a series of plays in which the traditional Barry–Bracegirdle partnership of tragedy was deliberately recalled to make a point. In this play Bracegirdle played the virtuous Phaebe who has been debauched by and is determined to marry the 'marriage-hater', Sir Philip. Barry played Lady Subtle, a haughty widow who has jilted Sir Philip and from whom he attempts to recover a fortune. Lady Subtle is proud and passionate and she rants vengefully, 'Oh, I could tear my Flesh, burn, Stab, or poyson.'[34] Thus, as in many tragedies, Barry's character and Bracegirdle's are involved with the same man, the Barry character is wild and passionate and the Bracegirdle heroine a (comparatively) innocent victim. Surprisingly, however, in this comic context Phaebe and Lady Subtle unite in their opposition to Sir Philip and enjoy triumphing over him. Phaebe, unlike the Bracegirdle heroines of tragedy, is a plotter. She even tricks Lady Subtle out of her fortune, although she compensates her for this by getting her a rich husband, the fool Van Grin. At the end Sir Philip is reconciled to the idea of marriage to Phaebe and returns to Lady Subtle the money that properly belongs to her. These deviations from tradition highlight important features of the play: that the 'hero', won by the Bracegirdle heroine, is no hero at all, but basically a corrupt libertine (although Durfey did allow him a romantic change of heart at the very end): that the heroine in libertine society must exercise independence and great cunning in order to survive and cannot afford to behave in a traditionally feminine, passive way. Like Fidelia, Phaebe is a victim of male lust, but she extricates herself from her predicament on her own. Durfey's satire, like Wycherley's, is strengthened by an arresting use of a tragic formula in a comic context.

Durfey also cast Barry and Bracegirdle as contrasting rivals in *The Richmond Heiress* a year later, but again altered the usual formula by uniting, instead of opposing them. Bracegirdle played the sensible, virtuous Fulvia, Barry the highminded, passionate Sophronia. Sophronia loves the hero Frederick but loses him to Fulvia (because the latter has a fortune). 'He's gone,' she rants, 'and tears my Heartstring as he goes.'[35] However, when Sophronia then goes on to prove Frederick's inconstancy to Fulvia, the two women combine to scorn the hero who exits in a fury – 'Hell take all Heiresses, and all the Sex besides' (p. 62). Fulvia finally decides never to marry, a decision warmly commended by her friend:

thou art a dear Example for all thy Sex to copy out thy Virtue, for that a kind and tender heart like thine, moulded for Love and softened with Endearments, should generously on the account of honour, resist a Traytor, that with strong Enchantments of Vows and Oaths, had long time made Impression, is a performance heightened to a wonder, and will be reverenc'd in succeeding ages. (pp. 63–4)

In tragedy, audiences were accustomed to seeing Barry and Bracegirdle fighting over the same man. Durfey drove home his satiric message – that in a libertine society where men are out for what they can get from women, financially and sexually, women must band together to protect themselves – by having them forget their rivalry and unite to defeat the man. The play's epilogue, spoken by a woman, emphasised the point, addressing the men:

> This Theam occasions our new Scenes to Night,
> To Shew a Woman once was in the right:
> The Satyr's gentle, and I think 'tis new,
> And only meant to teach ye to be true.[36]

CONGREVE'S USE OF BARRY AND BRACEGIRDLE

It was Congreve, however, who most effectively inserted the tragic partnership of Barry and Bracegirdle into comedy. Whereas Wycherley and Durfey seem to have introduced this element into their comedy to strengthen its satiric message, Congreve aimed, I believe, to go further and to give two of his comedies, *The Double-Dealer* (1693) and *The Way of the World* (1700), an additional tragic dimension through 'tragic' roles.

In *The Double-Dealer* Congreve made an obvious attempt to move beyond the conventional limits of comedy, towards a more serious conflict between good and evil. The play's motto, from Horace's *Ars Poetica*, is '*interdum tamen, a vocem Comoedia tollit*' – 'now and then however, even Comedy raises its voice'.[37] The drama has a contemporary setting and is peopled with familiar comic types – the cuckold Sir Paul Plyant and his promiscuous wife, the foolish Froths, the coxcomb Brisk, a sensible, loving hero and heroine. However, the plot seems reminiscent of tragedy; it is centred on an Iagoesque villain, Maskwell, and his associate and mistress, Lady Touchwood, and their wicked intrigues are finally discovered and punished. The tragic parallel was strongly emphasised by the fact that Barry and Bracegirdle were cast as contrasting rivals. Bracegirdle played the heroine Cynthia who loves and is loved by the hero Mellefont. As we have seen, Barry played the wildly emotional Lady Touchwood, also in love with Mellefont whom she has unsuccessfully tried to seduce. When he rejected her, 'she flew to my Sword, and with much ado I prevented her doing me or herself a Mischief: Having disarm'd her, in a Gust of Passion she left me' (pp. 126–7). Like Cassandra in Dryden's *Cleomenes* the year before, Lady Touchwood desperately seeks revenge when her act of seduction fails, 'Oh Mellefont! I burn; married to Morrow! Despair strikes me. Yet my Soul knows I hate him too: Let him but once be mine, and next immediate Ruin seize him' (p. 135). Barry's character thus speaks and behaves as she would in a tragic role, ranting rhetorically and even finally drawing a dagger on her husband when he discovers her perfidy. Lord Touchwood himself is no foolish cuckold, that stock figure of comedy. He is a noble character who, once he learns of his wife's betrayal, casts her off with dignity and authority, 'Go, and thy own Infamy pursue thee' (p. 210). Here too the casting reinforced the parallel with tragedy, for Lord Touchwood was played by Kynaston, an actor associated far more with tragedy than with comedy.

Beside the more decidedly comic characters the Touchwoods and Maskwell stand out as intruders from another world. Even Maskwell's plan to win Cynthia for himself recalls the plotting of villains, such as the king in *The Injur'd Lovers* and Genselaric in Brady's *The Rape* (1692), to seduce the Bracegirdle heroine: 'Cynthia, let thy Beauty gild my Crimes; and whatsoever I commit of Treachery or Deceit, shall be imputed to me as a Merit' (p. 149). But the comic framework contains these savage emotions. Cynthia seems never to be in serious danger and all is happily resolved at the end. Nevertheless, by carrying over conventions such as the Barry–Bracegirdle typecasting from one genre to another, Congreve offered a new perspective on the precepts of comedy. Adultery – of Maskwell and Lady Touchwood – is shown as an evil, and harshly condemned, whereas this is an act taken lightly in most other comedies.

Congreve's 'Epistle Dedicatory' to the printed play highlights both his serious intention and its lack of success with audiences. He stresses first his moral purpose – 'I design'd the Moral first, and to that Moral I invented the Fable' – and his effort 'to preserve the three Unities of the Drama' (p. 114). Then he defends Maskwell's Iagoesque soliloquies, which had apparently come under attack, as a perfectly acceptable dramatic contrivance. This may be so, but Maskwell's style of speech belongs more commonly to tragedy than to comedy and so perhaps seemed unnatural to some spectators. Similarly the fact that Mellefont, the hero, was deceived and 'made a fool' (p. 115) was apparently resented. In Restoration comedy the hero or 'truewit' traditionally tricks others; he is never gulled himself. In tragedy, on the other hand, the hero is often deceived by the plausible villain (see, for example, Lee's *Theodosius*, Otway's *Venice Preserved*, Mountfort's *The Injur'd Lovers* and innumerable other contemporary tragedies). Congreve's epistle implies that *The Double-Dealer* was an experiment in combining comedy and tragedy, which unfortunately proved unsuccessful with the public. As regards the casting of Barry and Bracegirdle, however, it remains an interesting exploration of how genre could be carried over by these actresses so as to give comedy a new dimension.

In one sense *The Way of the World* may be seen as an improvement on the 'tragicomedy' that Congreve had attempted more crudely in *The Double-Dealer*.[38] The plot and characters can be seen as having a tragic dimension, but this is assimilated into the whole rather than standing out as an intrusion. For example, Barry and Bracegirdle were again cast in contrasting roles: Bracegirdle created the part of the charming heroine Millamant and Barry that of the passionate villainess Mrs Marwood. The two are rivals for the love of Mirabell, who of course loves Millamant, so that Marwood seeks revenge for her rejection. However, Marwood does not appear as an outcast from tragedy as she talks and behaves like the other comic characters. She does not soliloquise like Maskwell nor rave like Lady Touchwood or a Mary Pix tragedy queen. She possesses all the jealous pride and vicious thirst for revenge of a traditional villainess, but these emotions are contained and hidden, and even when they burst forth – as in her exchanges with her lover Fainall in Act III – they are not expressed in inflated, melodramatic rhetoric and are the more powerful for that. When Fainall, for instance, mocks her for her hypocritical friendship with his wife, she loses control and threatens to reveal their affair in this way: 'It shall all be discover'd. You too shall be discover'd; be sure you shall. I can't but be expos'd – if I do it my self I shall prevent your Baseness' (p. 365).

As rivals, Millamant and Marwood attack each other as fiercely as Statira and Roxana, but they use the weapons appropriate to their society – barbed words beneath a semblance of elaborate good manners. In their vicious confrontation in Act III Marwood first tries to embarrass her opponent by revealing that she knows Mirabell and Millamant are in love: 'The Secret is grown too big for the Pretence: 'Tis like Mrs. Primly's great Belly; she may lace it down before, but it burnishes on her Hips' (p. 387). However, Millamant knows the depth of Marwood's own feelings for Mirabell and retaliates more than effectively:

MAR: Mr. Mirabell and you both may think it a Thing impossible, when I shall tell him by telling you ...
MIL: O dear, what? for it is the same thing, if I hear it – Ha, ha, ha.
MAR: That I detest him, hate him Madam.
MIL: O Madam, why so do I – And yet the Creature loves me, ha, ha, ha. How can one forbear laughing to think of it – I am a Sybil if I am not

amaz'd to think what he can see in me. I'll take my Death, I think you
are handsomer – and within a Year or two as young. – If you cou'd but
stay for me, I shou'd overtake you – But that cannot be – Well, that
Thought makes me melancholick – Now I'll be sad.

MAR: Your merry Note may be chang'd sooner then you think.

MIL: D'ye say so? Then I'm resolv'd I'll have a Song to keep up my Spirits.
(pp. 388–9)

Marwood cannot maintain Millamant's tone of good humour. She
exposes her feelings with her intense 'detest him, hate him' and with
her dark threat – 'Your merry Note may be chang'd.' Millamant's
long speech is a brilliant series of jibes – about the differences in their
ages and about Mirabell's preference for herself. Finally Marwood is
forced to hear a song that rams home the triumph of her rival:

> Then I alone the Conquest prize,
> When I insult a Rival's Eyes:
> If there's Delight in Love, 'tis when I see
> That Heart which others bleed for, bleed for me.   (p. 390)

In tragedy Bracegirdle's character tended to be the passive victim of
the villainess Barry's spite and cunning: in sophisticated London
society the tables are turned.

This change to the usual Barry–Bracegirdle battles has, I suggest,
two important effects. First, it highlights the point made throughout
the play that success in libertine society requires wit, cunning and the
concealment of one's real feelings. (Even Millamant's acceptance of
Mirabell's proposal of marriage is couched in terms of a jesting series
of provisos which keep the expression of their total commitment at
bay.) The weapons that work well for a Barry villainess in tragedy,
such as a bloodthirsty willingness to commit murder with one's
dagger, are ineffectual here; at the end of the play Fainall draws his
sword on his wife, but Sir Wilfull holds him off and Mirabell's
cunning wins the day. Secondly, the tragic parallel gives *The Way of
the World* a gravity which sets it apart from most other comedies.
Beneath the wit and repartee burn passionate love and hatred.
Familiar comic figures – the cuckold, the coquette heroine, the
mistress – are portrayed with a new depth of feeling.

This potent absorption of tragic elements within a comic framework was perhaps one reason for the play's modest success. Congreve
was surprised that it achieved even this. 'That it succeeded on the
Stage, was almost beyond my Expectation; for but little of it was
prepar'd for that general Taste which seems now to be predominant

in the Pallats of our Audience' (p. 336). In fact, however much comic tastes might have changed by the end of the century, the popularity of the Barry–Bracegirdle pairing never waned. *The Way of the World* offered audiences a brilliantly entertaining version of a familiar partnership within an effective blend of comedy and tragedy and this perhaps helped rescue the play from total failure.

Conclusion: the achievement of the first English actresses

Did not the Boys Act Women's Parts Last Age?
Till we in pitty to the Barren Stage
Came to Reform your Eyes that went astray,
And taught you Passion the true English Way
Have not the Women of the Stage done this?
Nay took all shapes, and used most means to Please.

(Epilogue to Settle's *The Conquest of China by the Tartars*
(1676), spoken by leading lady Mary Lee)

What did the first English actresses achieve? What were the consequences of their introduction for English drama and English theatre? Did the arrival of actresses encourage a fuller and more vigorous dramatic exploration of 'feminist' issues than heretofore and provoke, on the stage at least, more equality between the sexes? Some answers to these questions are already apparent. Commercially the actresses proved highly successful for the theatre and a number of them possessed a rapport with spectators that no male actor could emulate – they became, in the modern sense, stars. Even after the novelty of their presence on the stage had worn off, the women remained, arguably, the most popular single element of London theatre: 'the additional Objects...of real, beautiful Women, could not but draw a proportion of new Admirers to the Theatre'.[1] The demand for these 'real, beautiful Women' had its negative side as well, of course. The Restoration actress was exploited sexually on and off the stage, promoting gratuitous titilation in the drama and prostitution behind the scenes.

The status of the actresses within the companies was low. They were paid significantly less than their male counterparts and not one of them became a theatre manager. Even the exceptional Barry almost always wielded power in private, without official recognition. As members of the acting profession, the women did eventually achieve some rights, as they received liveries plus immunity from debt and a few of them were granted company shares and benefits. However, this limited success can hardly have affected contemporary attitudes to working women in general, even if the presence of actresses in the theatre possibly encouraged women such as Aphra Behn, Mary Pix and Catherine Trotter to expose themselves as professional playwrights.

Jacqueline Pearson has rightly pointed out that one of the most striking differences between male and female performers is that the former often became playwrights, the latter did not. While many successful actors such as Betterton, Lacy, Powell, Mountfort and Cibber also succeeded as dramatists, successful actresses like Barry, Bracegirdle and Mrs Mountfort wrote nothing.

It seems that male players were felt to have an authority denied to their female colleagues. They could be men of letters, controlling language on their own account as well as using the language of others. Actresses were simply the mouthpieces of words they had hardly ever written.[2]

However, Pearson surely overestimates the importance of this fact. Although the dramatists were the artists whose work lived after them and who are perceived to 'have an authority' in literary and academic terms, at the time, in the eyes of the public, it was the player, not the playwright, who held sway. As theatre historians Judith Milhous and Robert Hume explain, 'plays were not... thought of as particularly individual creations'. In a letter of 4 March 1699, Dryden mentions that the playbill of Congreve's *The Double-Dealer*, printed that day, was the first in England to have the author's name included.

The difference between late seventeenth-century and twentieth-century views of the play could hardly be made clearer. In Dryden's theatre plays were thought of not as art but as a necessary commodity – and the skilful contriver of useable scripts was regarded as an artificer worthy of his far from extravagant hire.[3]

In the Restoration theatre, as in film and television today, it was the star performer whom people remembered and wanted to see, not the writers, and as such the actresses were certainly more than mere 'mouthpieces'.

'FEMINIST' COMEDY

What of the drama itself? Do plays post-1660 present greater equality between the sexes and, if so, how far can this be attributed to the introduction of actresses? We need to answer the first part of the question before we can respond to the second. In the past, a kind of critical myth of sexual equality has been attached to Restoration comedy, under whose influence C. V. Wedgewood, for instance, contrasts the position of women in Shakespearian and Restoration comedy:

The old system of chivalry, in which women were chattels – precious chattels, but chattels nonetheless – to be protected and possessed, had in an attenuated form governed the moral outlook of the upper classes well into the seventeenth century. A new morality had not yet been worked out to fit a society which now finally came unmoored from feudalism and chivalry. With all their cynicism, the morals of the fast set in the later seventeenth century represent a move towards greater justice between men and women. The capacity to meet a man on equal terms, which had been the prerogative of an occasional Brunhild or Britomart, was now open to any woman of quick wits. It can hardly be sustained that the morality depicted by Wycherley, Etherege, Congreve and Vanbrugh is an advance on that depicted by Spenser, Shakespeare, Massinger, or even Ford. But at least theirs is a society in which neither Hero or Imogen could be so scandalously mistreated by their lovers with the full approval of society.[4]

Although this passage highlights the greater *appearance* of sexual equality than the cynicism of the anti-platonic gay couple often gives, Wedgewood's view of Restoration society and its drama is fundamentally mistaken. Very many recent studies – for instance, Laurence Stone's *The Family, Sex and Marriage in England*, David Roberts' *The Ladies* and Angeline Goreau's *Reconstructing Aphra* – have presented a very different picture of female submission in a male-dominated society. Whatever the social changes that resulted as England under a restored monarchy just emerged from the chaos of civil war, no substantial shift towards true sexual equality in society occurred and no such shift appears in the drama. Women like Mrs Sightly in Southerne's *The Wives' Excuse* and Lady Brute in Vanbrugh's *The Provok'd Wife* could be just as much victims of slander, in their own way, as Shakespeare's Imogen. In Restoration comedy, as in Restoration society, however wittily a girl might defeat her lover in conversation, her real freedom was severely limited. She had to remain a virgin until she became a wife, and, once married, as *The Wives' Excuse* illustrates, she was technically chained to the man for life. Even after separation from one's husband, to love another man openly spelt ruin. Under the double standard, the Restoration male had all the sexual freedom women lacked, his reputation sometimes even enhanced by the number of affairs he was known to have had. This is the situation in the majority of comedies and by and large the actresses were called upon to reinforce traditional images of woman-hood – the girl guarding her reputation, in search of a happy and secure marriage, and the mistress also in need of marriage as the only means of redeeming her honour.

More comedies than ever before continued the convention of a resourceful girl disguised as a man who organises the action, but the Restoration breeches heroine generally achieves no more freedom than her Renaissance predecessors. As before, most Restoration heroines assume male disguise to pursue the men they love with marriage in view. Those married already return to their husbands and former subordinate positions after their adventures are over. So far as the gay couple is concerned, its apparent sexual equality is sustained by the woman's ability to hold her own in bouts of wit and to maintain her man's affection: his is the only true freedom. The 'gay' female may not scorn or dread marriage at all and her anti-matrimonialism is often no more than an expedient pose to capture an elusive libertine.

But if the Restoration saw no feminist revolution, either in life or on the stage, a significant quantity of its comedy does deal, directly or indirectly, with a perception of sexual inequalities in society. The Restoration heroine may not possess any *new* rights, but she is more vociferous than her Renaissance counterpart in asserting the few rights she may already possess. Catherine Belsey has attributed this fact (along with other feminist developments of the period) to the late seventeenth-century establishment of the family as a 'private realm of retreat' from the masculine world of public affairs.[5] As the centre of this private sphere of the family, women finally gained a recognised place in society from which they were able to protest forcefully and to make demands – hence we find female characters in comedy attacking sexual injustices, for instance. Belsey's argument makes good sense, but I would also argue that the introduction of actresses itself brought about the stronger expression of an exclusively female viewpoint in comedy. The establishment of the gay couple, for instance, stemming directly from Nell Gwyn's successes with Charles Hart, gave the comic heroine an opportunity to forcibly express her own needs in battles with her lover, even if she did not possess his freedom. The Hart–Gwyn formula may have begun, in *Secret Love*, as a series of bantering, romantic exchanges between lovers, but in plays like *She Would If She Could* and *The Rover* it became an important satiric means of conveying the female viewpoint in a relationship. Similarly, the emergence of popular and talented comediennes like Bracegirdle and Mountfort fostered plays that were focused on women and gave dramatists like Southerne and Behn the necessary materials for presenting the 'feminist' debate in comic form.

A stronger female voice is most often heard in Restoration comedy's portrayal of marital conflict, as the genre 'increasingly exhibits an awareness of the drawbacks and possible pitfalls of matrimony'.[6] Whether the plot concerns a gay couple, or a husband and wife at odds with one another, the focus of Restoration comedy is on conflict between the sexes rather than on harmonious union. The development of the proviso-scene, for example, shows couples' increased awareness of the difficulties and disadvantages of the marriage bond. Elsewhere, as at the close of Southerne's *The Wives' Excuse* and Durfey's *The Richmond Heiress*, heroines reject marriage entirely. In many of the comedies lively young girls accept marriage while bitterly regretting the loss of their freedom and in those comedies concerned with adultery, a final reconciliation between husband and wife is portrayed as distinctly temporary, if it occurs at all – whether the play presents marital discord lightheartedly, as in George Farquhar's boisterous *The Beaux' Stratagem* (1707), or with bleaker realism, as in *The Wives' Excuse* and *The Provok'd Wife*. While the major cause of this questioning of marriage lies in the general challenge to patriarchal institutions which occurred as a result of the Civil War and Interregnum,[7] such questioning in the drama is partly attributable to the actresses, whose vocal presence on the stage encouraged lively portrayals of marital conflict.

'SEXIST' TRAGEDY

As in Renaissance drama, sexual equality is much less evident in Restoration tragedy than it is in comedy. Although, as we have seen, actresses like Marshall and Barry encouraged dramatists to make the traditional villainess of tragedy more sympathetic, still in this genre she is forceful and assertive, while the heroine is distinguished by her frailty, passivity and helplessness. In general, the arrival of actresses seems to have achieved very little modification of conventional stereotypes, and in many ways their exploitation intensified them. The presence of women's bodies on the stage encouraged lurid, eroticised presentations of female suffering, and was designed to tantalise, rather than to attack violent masculine behaviour. While 'she-tragedy', inspired by Elizabeth Barry, did make women rather than men the main focus, at the same time this genre strengthened the popular female image of virtuous suffering passivity. The majority of heroines in she-tragedy, for example Monimia, Anna Bullen and Isabella, are all physically weak, victimised characters, and compare unfavourably with a character like John Webster's Duchess of Malfi (in *The Duchess of Malfi*, written 1612/13, published 1623), who projects a much more active, positive image of female heroism. In death, for instance, Anna Bullen's victimisation is what is emphasised, whereas the Duchess's end, in similar circumstances, is courageous and assertive: 'pull and pull strongly, for your able strength / Must pull down heaven upon me'.[8] The tendency of Restoration tragedy to characterise women as frail and incapable is perhaps a result of the increasingly popular image of women as a soft, domestic opposite to the ruling male sex. It might also be seen as a reaction against the radical, potentially alarming development of actually allowing women on to the stage. If consistently portrayed as weaker than men in the public spheres which are the dominion of tragedy, the female player posed no threat to male-dominated society.

CONCLUSION

The legacy of the first English actresses to drama, to theatre and to their own sex is a mixed one. Actresses provided both new literary opportunities to explore female needs and desires on stage, and new opportunities for female exploitation. They influenced some of the worst melodrama of the period and a number of its finest plays. As the mouthpieces of other people's words, their effect for good or bad was ultimately as strong, or weak, as the dramatists who wrote for them. Inevitably, they themselves adapted to the status quo in order to survive. As working professionals, like the first English women playwrights, they faced prejudice, antagonism and a variety of patriarchal laws and traditions, all of which made sexual equality in the theatre (as elsewhere) an impossibility. Given these disadvantages, the power and influence that Barry and Bracegirdle achieved within their companies by the end of the century is impressive.

Drama, perhaps because it is the most public and social of literary forms, has always constituted the field of literary endeavour that women have found hardest to penetrate. While certain women have achieved notable success as poets and particularly as novelists, in theatre the number of male playwrights, roles, directors and producers still enormously outweighs the female. The move towards greater theatrical and dramatic equality of the sexes has proved almost as slow and difficult after 1700 as it was during the last forty years of the seventeenth century. Seen in this light, the achievement of the Restoration actresses is not without substance: if nothing else, they made women an unstoppable presence on stage, creating a foundation on which succeeding generations built, and are still building.

Major actresses and their roles in new plays

(S) Supporting role
(B) Breeches role
(R) suffers rape or attempted rape
(P) probably (actress's casting in this role is not absolutely certain)
  * 'young girl' signifies a virginal and virtuous young heroine

ELIZABETH BARRY

Year	Play	Dramatist	Role	Type
1675	*Alcibiades*	Thomas Otway	Draxilla	maid(S)
1676	*Abdelazer*	Aphra Behn	Leonora	young girl*
	The Wrangling Lovers	Edward Ravenscroft	Elvira	young girl
	Tom Essence	Thomas Rawlins	Theodocia	young girl
	Madam Fickle	Thomas Durfey	Constantia	young girl
	Titus and Berenice	Thomas Otway	Phaenice	young girl(S)
	The Cheats of Scapin	Thomas Otway	Lucia	young girl
1677	*The Rover*	Aphra Behn	Hellena(B)	young girl
	A Fond Husband	Thomas Durfey	Emilia	wife
	The French Conjuror	Thomas Porter	Clovinia	young girl
	The Constant Nymph	Anon.	Phillisides(B)	young girl
1678	*Friendship in Fashion*	Thomas Otway	Mrs Goodvile	wife
	The Counterfeits	John Leanerd	Clara(B)	maid
	Squire Oldsapp	Thomas Durfey	Sophia	young girl
	The Destruction of Troy	John Banks	Polyxena	young girl
1679	*The Feign'd Curtezans*	Aphra Behn	Cornelia	young girl
	The Woman Captain	Thomas Shadwell	Mrs Gripe(B)	wife
	The Virtuous Wife	Thomas Durfey	Olivia(B)	wife
	Caius Marius	Thomas Otway	Lavinia	young girl
1680	*The Loving Enemies*	Lewis Maidwell	Camilla(B)	young girl
	The Orphan	Thomas Otway	Monimia	young girl
	The Souldiers Fortune	Thomas Otway	Lady Dunce	wife
	The Revenge	Aphra Behn	Corina	passionate mistress
	The Princess of Cleve	Nathaniel Lee	Princess	wife
	Theodosius	Nathaniel Lee	Athenais	young girl
	The Spanish Friar	John Dryden	Leonora	young girl
	Lucius Junius Brutus	Nathaniel Lee	Teraminta	young girl
1681	*The Second Part of the Rover*	Aphra Behn	La Nuche	passionate mistress
	King Lear	Nahum Tate	Cordelia	young girl
	The Lancashire Witches	Thomas Shadwell	Isabella	young girl
	The London Cuckolds	Edward Ravenscroft	Arabella	wife
1682	*Venice Preserved*	Thomas Otway	Belvidera	wife
	Vertue Betray'd	John Banks	Anna Bullen	wife

Year	Play	Dramatist	Role	Type
	The City Heiress	Aphra Behn	Lady Galliard	passionate mistress
	The Duke of Guise	John Dryden	Marmoutier	young girl
1683	*The Atheist*	Thomas Otway	Porcia	young girl
	Constantine the Great	Nathaniel Lee	Fausta	young girl
1684	*Valentinian*	Earl of Rochester	Lucina	wife
1685	*Sir Courtly Nice*	John Crowne	Leonora	young girl
1686	*The Banditti*	Thomas Durfey	Laura	young girl
	The Lucky Chance	Aphra Behn	Lady Fulbank	wife
1688	*The Injur'd Lovers*	William Mountfort	Oryala	'darker woman'
	Darius	John Crowne	Barzana	wife
1689	*The Massacre of Paris*	Nathaniel Lee	Marguerite	passionate mistress
	Don Sebastian	John Dryden	Almeyda	young girl
1690	*Amphitryon*	John Dryden	Alcmena	wife
	Distress'd Innocence	Elkanah Settle	Orundana	villainess
	King Edward III	John Bancroft	Isabella	villainess
	The Scowrers	Thomas Shadwell	Eugenia	young girl
1691	*Win Her & Take Her*	John Smyth	Florella	young girl
	Greenwich Park	William Mountfort	Dorinda	passionate mistress
	The Wives' Excuse	Thomas Southerne	Mrs Friendall	wife
1692	*The Marriage-Hater Match'd*	Thomas Durfey	Lady Subtle	widow
	Cleomenes	John Dryden	Cassandra	villainess
	Henry II	John Bancroft	Queen Eleanor	wife
1693	*The Maid's Last Prayer*	Thomas Southerne	Lady Malepert	passionate mistress
	The Old Bachelor	William Congreve	Laetitia	wife
	The Richmond Heiress	Thomas Durfey	Sophronia	young girl
	The Double-Dealer	William Congreve	Lady Touchwood	villainess
1694	*Love Triumphant*	John Dryden	Victoria	young girl
	The Fatal Marriage	Thomas Southerne	Isabella	wife
	The Ambitious Slave	Elkanah Settle	Celestina	villainess
	The Married Beau	John Crowne	Mrs Lovely	wife
1695	*Love for Love*	William Congreve	Mrs Frail	'woman of the town'
	She Ventures & He Wins	'A Young Lady'	Urania	wife
	Cyrus the Great	John Banks	Panthea	wife
	The She-Gallants	George Granville	Lady Dorimen	older spinster
1696	*The Country-Wake*	Thomas Doggett	Lady Testie	wife
	The Royal Mischief	Delariviere Manley	Homais	villainess
	Love's a Jest	Peter Motteux	Lady Single	old spinster
	The City Lady	Thomas Dilke	Lady Grumble	wife
1697	*The Mourning Bride*	William Congreve	Zara	'darker woman'
	The Provok'd Wife	John Vanbrugh	Lady Brute	wife
	The Intrigues at Versailles	Thomas Durfey	Madame de Vendosme	whore
	The Novelty, Act IV, 'The Unfortunate Couple'	Peter Motteux	Elvira	wife
	The Innocent Mistress	Mary Pix	Bellinda	young girl
	Boadicea	Charles Hopkins	Boadicea	ruler
	The Deceiver Deceiv'd	Mary Pix	Olivia	wife
1698	*Heroick Love*	George Granville	Chruseis	young girl
	Beauty in Distress	Peter Motteux	Laura	young widow
	Fatal Friendship	Catherine Trotter	Lamira	'darker woman'
	Queen Catharine	Mary Pix	Queen Catharine	ruler
	Rinaldo & Armida	John Dennis	Armida	wife
1699	*Xerxes*	Colley Cibber	Tamira	wife
	The Princess of Parma	Henry Smith	Julia	villainess
	The False Friend	Mary Pix	Adellaida	wife
	Friendship Improv'd	Charles Hopkins	Semanthe	wife
	Iphigenia	John Dennis	Queen of Scythians	'darker woman'
1700	*The Way of the World*	William Congreve	Mrs Marwood	villainess

Year	Play	Dramatist	Role	Type
	The Beau Defeated	Mary Pix	Mrs Rich	widow
	The Fate of Capua	Thomas Southerne	Favonia	wife
	The Ambitious Stepmother	Nicholas Rowe	Artemisa	villainess
1701	The Ladies Visiting Day	William Burnaby	Lady Lovetoy	young girl
	The Double Distress	Mary Pix	Leamira	young girl
	The Czar of Muscovy	Mary Pix	Zarriana(R)	young girl
	Love's Victim	Charles Gildon	Queen of Bayonne	villainess
	Antiochus the Great	Jane Wiseman	Leodice	'darker woman'
	Tamerlane	Nicholas Rowe	Arpasia	wife
	Altemira	Roger & Charles Boyle	Altemira	young girl
1702	The Stolen Heiress	Susannah Centlivre	Lucasia	young girl
1703	The Governor of Cyprus	John Oldmixon	Issamanea	wife
	The Fickle Shepherdess	author unknown	Clarinda	fickle shepherdess
	As You Find It	Charles Boyle	Eugenia	young girl
	The Fair Penitent	Nicholas Rowe	Calista	'darker woman'
1704	Liberty Asserted	John Dennis	Sakia	mother
	Zelmane	author unknown	Zelmane	'darker woman'
	The Biter	Nicholas Rowe	Mrs Clever	bawd
1705	The Gamester	Susannah Centlivre	Lady Wealthy	widow
	The Confederacy	John Vanbrugh	Clarissa	wife
	Ulysses	Nicholas Rowe	Penelope	wife
1706	The Revolution of Sweden	Catherine Trotter	Constantia	wife
	The British Enchanters	George Granville	Arcabon	enchantress
	Adventures in Madrid	Mary Pix	Clarinda	wife
	Almyna	Delariviere Manley	Almyna	young girl
1707	Phaedra & Hippolitus	Edmund Smith	Phaedra	young girl
	The Royal Convert	Nicholas Rowe	Rodogune	'darker woman'
	The Lady's Last Stake	Colley Cibber	Lady Wronglove	wife
1708	Irene	Charles Goring	Sultana Valide	mother

MARY BETTERTON

Year	Play	Dramatist	Role	Type
1661	The Siege of Rhodes	William Davenant	Ianthe	young girl
	The Cutter of Coleman Street	Abraham Cowley	Aurelia	young girl
1662	The Villain	Thomas Porter	Bellmont(R)	young girl
	The Adventures of Five Hours	Samuel Tuke	Porcia	young girl
1663	The Slighted Maid	Robert Stapylton	Pyramena	wife
	The Stepmother	Robert Stapylton	Caesarina	young girl
1664	The Comical Revenge	George Etherege	Graciana	young girl
1665	Mustapha	Roger Boyle	Roxalana	wife
1668	Henry the Fifth	Roger Boyle	Princess Katharine(P)	young girl
1669	The Roman Virgin	Thomas Betterton?	Virginia	young girl
	Mr. Anthony	Roger Boyle	Mrs Isabella	young girl
1670	Sir Salomon	John Caryll	Julia	young girl
	The Forc'd Marriage	Aphra Behn	Erminia	wife
	The Womens Conquest	Edward Howard	Parisatis	ruler
	The Amorous Widow	Thomas Betterton	Lady Laycock	widow
1671	Cambyses	Elkanah Settle	Mandana	young girl
	The Six Days Adventure	Edward Howard	Serina	ruler
	Juliana	John Crowne	Juliana(B)	young girl
	Charles the Eighth	John Crowne	Isabella	villainess
1672	The Citizen Turn'd Gentleman	Edward Ravenscroft	Lucia	young girl
	The Fatal Jealousy	Henry Nevil Payne	Eugenia(R)	seduced girl
	Epsom Wells	Thomas Shadwell	Mrs Jilt	whore
1673	Macbeth	adapt. Wm. Davenant	Lady Macbeth	villainess

Year	Play	Dramatist	Role	Type
	The Reformation	Joseph Arrowsmith	Juliana	wife
	The Empress of Morocco	Elkanah Settle	Laula	villainess
1674	*Love and Revenge*	Elkanah Settle	Aphelia	young girl
1675	*The Conquest of China*	Elkanah Settle	Orunda	young girl
	Alcibiades	Thomas Otway	Timandra	young girl
1676	*The Countrey Wit*	John Crowne	Lady Faddle	aunt
	Ibrahim	Elkanah Settle	Isabella	young girl
	The Man of Mode	George Etherege	Bellinda	seduced girl
	The Virtuoso	Thomas Shadwell	Miranda	young girl
	Abdelazer	Aphra Behn	Florella	wife
	Pastor Fido	Elkanah Settle	Amaryllis	young girl
1677	*Antony and Cleopatra*	Charles Sedley	Octavia	wife
	The Rover	Aphra Behn	Florinda	young girl
	Circe	Charles Davenant	Iphigenia	young girl
	The Constant Nymph	author unknown	Alveria	young girl
	The Siege of Babylon	Samuel Pordage	Statira	young widow
1678	*Timon of Athens*	Thomas Shadwell	Evandra	young girl
	Sir Patient Fancy	Aphra Behn	Isabella	young girl
	Oedipus	Dryden & Lee	Jocasta	mother
	The Destruction of Troy	John Banks	Andromache	wife
1679	*Troilus and Cressida*	John Dryden	Andromache	wife
1680	*The Misery of Civil-War*	John Crowne	Lady Grey	widow
	Theodosius	Nathaniel Lee	Pulcheria	young girl
	The Spanish Friar	John Dryden	Elvira	wife
	The Princess of Cleve	Nathaniel Lee	Elianor	wife
	Lucius Junius Brutus	Nathaniel Lee	Lucretia	wife
1682	*The Royalist*	Thomas Durfey	Camilla	wife
	Henry the Sixth	John Crowne	Elianor	wife
1689	*The Massacre of Paris*	Nathaniel Lee	Queen Mother	villainess
1692	*The Rape*	Nicholas Brady	Amalazontha	mother
	Cleomenes	John Dryden	Cratisclea	mother
1693	*The Maid's Last Prayer*	Thomas Southerne	Wishwell	bawd
1694	*Love Triumphant*	John Dryden	Ximena	mother

ELIZABETH BOUTELL

Year	Play	Dramatist	Role	Type
1670	*The Roman Empress*	William Joyner	Aurelia(B)	young girl
	The Conquest of Granada Part 2	John Dryden	Benzayda(B)	young girl
1671	*Love in a Wood*	William Wycherley	Christina	young girl
	The Generous Enemies	John Corye	Lysander(B)	young girl
1672	*Marriage à la Mode*	John Dryden	Melantha(B)	affected girl
	The Assignation	John Dryden	Laura	young girl
1673	*The Spanish Rogue*	Thomas Duffett	Alcinda	young girl
1674	*The Amorous Old Woman*	Thomas Duffett	Clara(B)	young girl
	Nero	Nathaniel Lee	Cyara(B)	young girl
1675	*The Country Wife*	William Wycherley	Margery(B)	wife
	Sophonisba	Nathaniel Lee	Rosalinda(B)	young girl
	Love in The Dark	Francis Fane	Bellinganna	wife
1676	*The Plain Dealer*	William Wycherley	Fidelia	young girl
1677	*Destruction of Jerusalem*	John Crowne	Clarona	young girl
	Alexander the Great	Nathaniel Lee	Statira	wife
	Wits Led by the Nose	William Chamberlayne	Glorianda	young girl
	King Edgar & Alfreda	Edward Ravenscroft	Matilda	young girl
	All for Love	John Dryden	Cleopatra	mistress
1678	*Mithridates*	Nathaniel Lee	Semandra	young girl
	Trick for Trick	Thomas Durfey	Cellida	young girl
1688	*A Fool's Preferment*	Thomas Durfey	Aurelia	wife
	The Squire of Alsatia	Thomas Shadwell	Mrs Termagant	mistress

Year	Play	Dramatist	Role	Type
1689	Bury Fair	Thomas Shadwell	Mrs Fantast	young girl
1690	The Treacherous Brothers	George Powell	Semanthe	wife
	The English Frier	John Crowne	Lady Credulous	'bigoted papist'
1695	She Ventures & He Wins	author unknown	Dowdy	wife
	Cyrus the Great	John Banks	Thomyris	mother
	The She-Gallants	George Granville	Constantia(B)	young girl
1696	The City Bride	Joseph Harris	Clara	mistress
	Love's a Jest	Peter Motteux	Francilia	young girl

ANNE BRACEGIRDLE

Year	Play	Dramatist	Role	Type
1688	The Injured Lovers	William Mountfort	Antelina(R)	young girl
	The Squire of Alsatia	Thomas Shadwell	Lucia	seduced girl(S)
1689	The Widow Ranter	Aphra Behn	Semernia(B)	young girl
1690	The Successful Straingers	William Mountfort	Biancha	young girl
	The Treacherous Brothers	George Powell	Marcelia	young girl
	The English Frier	John Crowne	Julia	young girl
	The Amorous Bigotte	Thomas Shadwell	Rosania	young girl
	Sir Anthony Love	Thomas Southerne	Charlote	young girl
	Distress'd Innocence	Elkanah Settle	Cleomira(R)	young girl
	King Edward III	John Bancroft	Maria	young girl
	Alphonso, King of Naples	George Powell	Urania(R)	young girl
	The Scowrers	Thomas Shadwell	Clara	young girl
	The Mistakes	Joseph Harris	Miranda	young girl
1691	Love for Money	Thomas Durfey	Mirtilla	young girl
	Bussy D'Ambois	Thomas Durfey	Tamira	wife
	King Arthur	John Dryden	Emmeline(R)	young girl
	The Wives' Excuse	Thomas Southerne	Mrs Sightly	young girl
1692	The Marriage-Hater Match'd	Thomas Durfey	Phaebe	young girl
	The Rape	Nicholas Brady	Eurione(R)	young girl
	The Traytor	Anthony Rivers	Amidea	young girl
	Cleomenes	John Dryden	Cleora	wife
	Regulus	John Crowne	Elisa	young girl
	Henry II	John Bancroft	Rosamond	seduced girl
	The Volunteers	Thomas Shadwell	Clara	young girl
1693	The Maid's Last Prayer	Thomas Southerne	Lady Trickett	wife
	The Old Bachelor	William Congreve	Araminta	young girl
	The Richmond Heiress	Thomas Durfey	Fulvia	young girl
	The Female Vertuoso's	Thomas Wright	Mariana	young girl
	The Double-Dealer	William Congreve	Cynthia	young girl
1694	Love Triumphant	John Dryden	Celidea	young girl
	The Fatal Marriage	Thomas Southerne	Victoria	young girl
	The Ambitious Slave	Elkanah Settle	Clarismunda	young girl
	The Married Beau	John Crowne	Camilla	young girl
	Don Quixote – Part 1	Thomas Durfey	Marcella	coquette
	Don Quixote – Part 2	Thomas Durfey	Marcella	young girl
1695	Love for Love	William Congreve	Angelica	young girl
	She Ventures & He Wins	author unknown	Charlot(B)	young girl
	The Lover's Luck	Thomas Dilke	Mrs Purflew	young girl
	Cyrus the Great	John Banks	Lausaria	young girl
	The She-Gallants	George Granville	Angelica(B)	young girl
1696	The Country-Wake	Thomas Doggett	Flora	young girl
	The Royal Mischief	Delariviere Manley	Bassima	young girl
	Love's a Jest	Peter Motteux	Christina	young girl
	The Loves of Mars & Venus	Peter Motteux	Venus	young girl
1697	The Mourning Bride	William Congreve	Almeria	young girl
	The Provok'd Wife	John Vanbrugh	Bellinda	young girl
	The Intrigues of Versailles	Thomas Durfey	Countess de Sanserre	wife

Year	Play	Dramatist	Role	Type
	The Innocent Mistress	Mary Pix	Mrs Beauclair(B)	widow
	Boadicea	Charles Hopkins	Camilla(R)	young girl
	The Deceiver Deceiv'd	Mary Pix	Ariana	young girl
1698	*Heroick Love*	George Granville	Briseis	young girl
	Beauty in Distress	Peter Motteux	Placentia(R)	young girl
	Fatal Friendship	Catherine Trotter	Felicia	wife
	Queen Catharine	Mary Pix	Isabella(R)	young girl
1699	*Princess of Parma*	Henry Smith	Almira	young girl
	The False Friend	Mary Pix	Lovisa	young girl
	Friendship Improved	Charles Hopkins	Locris(B)	young girl
	Iphigenia	John Dennis	Iphigenia	young girl
1700	*Measure for Measure*	adapt. Charles Gildon	Isabella	young girl
	The Way of the World	William Congreve	Millamant	young girl
	The Beau Defeated	Mary Pix	Lady Landsworth	widow
	The Ambitious Stepmother	Nicholas Rowe	Amestris	young girl
1701	*The Ladies Visiting Day*	William Burnaby	Fulvia	young girl
	The Jew of Venice	George Granville	Portia	young girl
	The Double Distress	Mary Pix	Cytheria	young girl
	The Judgement of Paris	William Congreve	Venus	young girl
	Love's Victim	Charles Gildon	Guinoenda	wife
	Tamerlane	Nicholas Rowe	Selina	young girl
1703	*Love Betrayed*	Charles Burnaby	Villaretta(B)	young girl
	The Fickle Shepherdess	author unknown	Amintas(B)	young man
	As You Find It	Charles Boyle	Orinda	young girl
	The Fair Penitent	Nicholas Rowe	Lavinia	wife
1704	*Abra Mulé*	Joseph Trapp	Abra Mulé	young girl
	Liberty Asserted	John Dennis	Irene	young girl
	Squire Trelooby	Congreve, Vanbrugh & Walsh	Julia	young girl
	Zelmane	author uncertain	Antimora	young girl
	The Biter	Nicholas Rowe	Mariana	wife
1705	*The Gamester*	Susannah Centlivre	Angelica(B)	young girl
	The Confederacy	John Vanbrugh	Flippanta	maid
	Ulysses	Nicholas Rowe	Semanthe	young girl
1706	*The British Enchanters*	George Granville	Oriana	young girl
	The Temple of Love	Peter Motteux	Phillis	young girl
	Adventures in Madrid	Mary Pix	Laura(B)	young girl
	The Platonick Lady	Susannah Centlivre	Lucinda	young girl
	Almyna	Delariviere Manley	Zoradia	young girl
1707	*Marriage à la Mode*	Colley Cibber	Melantha(B)	young girl

CHARLOTTE BUTLER

Year	Play	Dramatist	Role	Type
1675	*Calisto* (at court)	John Crowne	Plenty	nymph(S)
1680	*The Orphan*	Thomas Otway	Serina	young girl(S)
	The Revenge	Aphra Behn	Marinda	young girl(S)
1682	*The City Heiress*	Aphra Behn	Charlot	young girl
	Romulus and Hersilia	author unknown	Felicana(P)	young girl
1683	*Dame Dobson*	Edward Ravenscroft	Mrs Cleremont	wife
	The Atheist	Thomas Otway	Lucretia(B)	young girl
1689	*The Fortune-Hunters*	James Carlile	Sophia	young girl
	Bury Fair	Thomas Shadwell	Philadelphia(B)	young girl
1690	*The Treacherous Brothers*	George Powell	Statilia(B)	young girl
	The English Frier	John Crowne	Airy	mistress
	The Amorous Bigotte	Thomas Shadwell	Levia	whore
	Sir Anthony Love	Thomas Southerne	Floriante(B)	young girl
	Amphitryon	John Dryden	Night	goddess
	The Mistakes	Joseph Harris	Astella(B)	young girl
1691	*Love for Money*	Thomas Durfey	Betty Jiltall	whore
	King Arthur	John Dryden	Philidel	'Airy Spirit'

Year	Play	Dramatist	Role	Type
1692	The Marriage-Hater Match'd	Thomas Durfey	La Pupsey	affected girl
	The Rape	Nicholas Brady	Agilmond(B)	young girl

ELIZABETH CURRER

Year	Play	Dramatist	Role	Type
1675	The Conquest of China	Elkanah Settle	Alcinda	young girl(S)
1676	The Countrey Wit	John Crowne	Betty Frisque	mistress
	Ibrahim	Elkanah Settle	Asteria	young girl
	The Virtuoso	Thomas Shadwell	Clarinda	young girl
1677	The Counterfeit Bridegroom	Aphra Behn	Mrs Hadland(B)	wife
1678	Sir Patient Fancy	Aphra Behn	Lady Fancy	wife
	Squire Oldsapp	Thomas Durfey	Madame Tricklove	wife
1679	The Feign'd Curtezans	Aphra Behn	Marcella	young girl
	The Virtuous Wife	Thomas Durfey	Jenny Wheedle	whore
	The Loyal General	Nahum Tate	Queen	villainess
1680	The Misery of Civil-War	John Crowne	Lady Elianor Butler(B)	mistress
1681	The Rover Part 2	Aphra Behn	Ariadne(B)	young girl
	The False Count	Aphra Behn	Isabella	foolish girl
	The London Cuckolds	Edward Ravenscroft	Eugenia	wife
1682	Mr. Turbulent	author unknown	Lady Medler	matchmaker
	Venice Preserved	Thomas Otway	Aquilina	courtesan
	The City Heiress	Aphra Behn	Diana	mistress
1683	Dame Dobson	Edward Ravenscroft	Mrs Featly	wife
	The Atheist	Thomas Otway	Sylvia	wife
1684	A Duke and No Duke	Nahum Tate	Isabella	wife
1689	The Widow Ranter	Aphra Behn	Widow Ranter(B)	widow

MARY ('MOLL') DAVIS

Year	Play	Dramatist	Role	Type
1662	The Law Against Lovers	William Davenant	Viola	young girl
1663	The Stepmother	Robert Stapylton	Violinda	young girl
1664	The Comical Revenge	George Etherege	Aurelia	young girl
	Henry the Fifth	Roger Boyle	Princess Anne	young girl
1665	Mustapha	Roger Boyle	Queen of Hungary	widow
1667	Feign'd Innocence	John Dryden	Millisent	young girl
	The Tempest	Dryden & Davenant	Ariel	spirit
1668	She Would If She Could	George Etherege	Gatty	young girl

NELL GWYN

Year	Play	Dramatist	Role	Type
1665	The Indian Emperour	John Dryden	Cydaria	young girl
1667	The Chances	Duke of Buckingham	Second Constantia(P)	young girl
	Secret Love	John Dryden	Florimel(B)	young girl
	All Mistaken	James Howard	Mirida	young girl
1668	The Great Favourite	Robert Howard	Maria	young girl
	The Mulberry Garden	Charles Sedley	Olivia(P)	young girl
	An Evening's Love	John Dryden	Donna Jacintha	young girl
	The Damoiselles à la Mode	Richard Flecknoe	Lysette(P)	maid
1669	Tyrannick Love	John Dryden	Valeria	young girl
1670	The Conquest of Granada Part 2	John Dryden	Almahide	young girl

FRANCES MARIA KNIGHT

Year	Play	Dramatist	Role	Type
1684	*The Disappointment*	Thomas Southerne	Angelline	young girl(S)
1685	*A Commonwealth of Women*	Thomas Durfey	Aglaura	young girl(S)
1688	*The Squire of Alsatia*	Thomas Shadwell	Teresia	young girl
1689	*The Fortune-Hunters*	James Carlile	Mrs Spruce	wife(S)
	The Massacre of Paris	Nathaniel Lee	Queen of Navarre	ruler(S)
	The Widow Ranter	Aphra Behn	Madam Surelove	wife(S)
1690	*The Successful Straingers*	William Mountfort	Dorothea	young girl(S)
	Sir Anthony Love	Thomas Southerne	Volante	young girl(S)
1691	*Love for Money*	Thomas Durfey	Miss Jenny	'overgrown romp'(S)
	Greenwich Park	William Mountfort	Mrs Raison(B)	wife(S)
1692	*The Volunteers*	Thomas Shadwell	Teresia	affected girl
1693	*The Richmond Heiress*	Thomas Durfey	Madam Squeamish	affected girl
	A Very Good Wife	George Powell	Widow Lacy	widow(S)
	The Female Vertuoso's	Thomas Wright	Lovewitt	affected girl
1694	*The Fatal Marriage*	Thomas Southerne	Julia	wife(S)
	The Ambitious Slave	Elkanah Settle	Herminia	wife(S)
	Don Quixote Part 1	Thomas Durfey	Dorothea	young girl
	Don Quixote Part 2	Thomas Durfey	Duchess	wife
	The Canterbury Guests	Edward Ravenscroft	Arabella(B)	young girl
1695	*The Mock-Marriage*	Thomas Scott	Lady Barter	mistress
	Bonduca	author unknown	Bonduca	ruler
	The Rival Sisters	Robert Gould	Catalina	villainess
	Oroonoko	Thomas Southerne	Widow Lackit	widow
	Agnes de Castro	Catherine Trotter	Elvira	villainess
	Philaster	Elkanah Settle	Arethusa	young girl
1696	*The Young Brother*	Aphra Behn	Mirtilla	jilt
	Neglected Virtue	Charles Hopkins	Thermusa	villainess
	The Lost Lover	Delariviere Manley	Belira	mistress
	Pausanias	Richard Norton	Pandora	mistress
	Ibrahim	Mary Pix	Sheker Para	villainess
	The Female Wits	author unknown	Lady Loveall	villainess
1697	*Woman's Wit*	Colley Cibber	Leonora	coquette
	The Sham Lawyer	James Drake	Olympia	young widow
1698	*The Fatal Discovery*	author unknown	Berengaria	mother
	Caligula	John Crowne	Cesonia	wife
	Phaeton	Charles Gildon	Althea	wife
	The Campaigners	Thomas Durfey	Angelica	seduced girl
1699	*King Richard III*	Colley Cibber	Queen Elizabeth	mother
1700	*The Reform'd Wife*	William Burnaby	Astra	wife
	Love at a Loss	Catherine Trotter	Lesbia	seduced girl
	Love Makes a Man	Colley Cibber	Elvira	young girl
1701	*The Bath*	Thomas Durfey	Lydia	wife
1702	*She Wou'd & She Wou'd Not*	Colley Cibber	Vileta	maid(S)
1703	*The Old Mode and The New*	Thomas Durfey	Probleme	nurse
	The Fair Example	Richard Estcourt	Florinda	wife
	Vice Reclaim'd	Richard Wilkinson	Mrs Haughty	mistress
1704	*Love the Leveller*	author unknown	Princess Dowager	villainess
	The Albion Queens	John Banks	Queen Elizabeth	ruler
	Faithful Bride of Granada	William Taverner	Abenede	villainess
	The Careless Husband	Colley Cibber	Lady Easy	wife
1708	*The Maid's the Mistress*	William Taverner	Lady Fancy	wife
1709	*Appius & Virginia*	John Dennis	Cornelia	aunt
1710	*Elfrid*	Aaron Hill	Ordelia	young girl
	A Bickerstaff's Burying	Susannah Centlivre	Lady Mezro	wife
1711	*Injured Love*	author unknown	Lady Outside	wife

Year	Play	Dramatist	Role	Type
	The City Ramble	Elkanah Settle	Common-Councilman's Wife	wife
1712	*The Distrest Mother*	Ambrose Philips	Cephisa	confidante(S)
1713	*The Humours of the Army*	Charles Shadwell	Mrs Bloodmore	mother
	Cinna's Conspiracy	author unknown	Livia	wife(S)
1714	*The Victim*	Charles Johnson	Clytemnestra	wife
1715	*The Perplex'd Couple*	Charles Molloy	Lady Thinwit	wife
1716	*The Northern Heiress*	Mary Davys	Lady Ample	wife
1717	*The Artful Husband*	William Taverner	Lady Upstart	widow
	Mangora	Thomas Moore	Lucy de Miranda	wife
1719	*'Tis Well If It Takes*	William Taverner	Mrs Wishit	widow

MARY LEE

Year	Play	Dramatist	Role	Type
1670	*The Forc'd Marriage*	Aphra Behn	Olinda	young girl(S)
	The Womens Conquest	Edward Howard	Doranthe	young girl(S)
1671	*The Six Days Adventure*	Edward Howard	Eugenia	young girl(S)
	The Town-Shifts	Edward Revet	Leticia	young girl
	Herod and Mariamne	Samuel Pordage	Salome	villainess
1673	*The Reformation*	Joseph Arrowsmith	Aemilia	mistress
	The Empress of Morocco	Elkanah Settle	Mariamne	young girl
1674	*Love and Revenge*	Elkanah Settle	Nigrello(B)(R)	seduced girl
1675	*The Conquest of China*	Elkanah Settle	Amavanga(B)	ruler
	Alcibiades	Thomas Otway	Deidamia	villainess
1676	*The Countrey Wit*	John Crowne	Christina	young girl
	Ibrahim	Elkanah Settle	Roxalana	wife
	The Man of Mode	George Etherege	Mrs Loveit(P)	passionate mistress
	Don Carlos	Thomas Otway	Queen of Spain	wife
	Abdelazer	Aphra Behn	Isabella	villainess
	Madam Fickle	Thomas Durfey	Madam Fickle(B)	wife
	Titus and Berenice	Thomas Otway	Berenice	young girl
	Pastor Fido	Elkanah Settle	Corisca	villainess
1677	*Antony and Cleopatra*	Charles Sedley	Cleopatra	passionate queen
	Circe	Charles Davenant	Circe	villainess
	The Constant Nymph	author unknown	Astatius(B)	young girl
	The Siege of Babylon	Samuel Pordage	Roxana	'darker woman'
1678	*The Counterfeits*	John Leanerd	Elvira(B)	seduced girl
	Oedipus	Dryden & Lee	Eurydice	young girl
	The Destruction of Troy	John Banks	Cassandra	young girl(S)
1679	*The Feign'd Curtezans*	Aphra Behn	Laura Lucretia	young girl
	Troilus and Cressida	John Dryden	Cressida	young girl
	Caesar Borgia	Nathaniel Lee	Bellamira	young girl
	The Loyal General	Nahum Tate	Arviola	young girl
1680	*The Loving Enemies*	Lewis Maidwell	Julia(B)	young girl
	The Misery of Civil-War	John Crowne	Queen Margaret	wife
	The Princess of Cleve	Nathaniel Lee	Marguerite	passionate mistress
	Lucius Junius Brutus	Nathaniel Lee	Sempronia	mother
	King Lear	Nahum Tate	Regan	villainess
1682	*Mr. Turbulent*	author unknown	Lucia	young girl
	Romulus and Hersilia	author unknown	Tarpeia(B)	young girl
	The Duke of Guise	Dryden & Lee	Queen Mother	ruler
1683	*Dame Dobson*	Edward Ravenscroft	Lady Noble	wife
1685	*A Commonwealth of Women*	Thomas Durfey	Clarinda	young girl

JANE LONG

Year	Play	Dramatist	Role	Type
1661	*Cutter of Coleman Street*	Abraham Cowley	Laughing Jane	servant(S)
1663	*The Adventures of Five Hours*	Samuel Tuke	Flora	maid(S)

Year	Play	Dramatist	Role	Type
	The Slighted Maid	Robert Stapylton	Diacelia	young girl(S)
	The Stepmother	Robert Stapylton	Brianella	maid
1664	*The Comical Revenge*	George Etherege	Widow	widow
	Henry the Fifth	Roger Boyle	Queen of France	ruler(S)
	The Rivals	William Davenant	Leucippe	maid
1665	*Mustapha*	Roger Boyle	Zarma	maid
1667	*The Tempest*	Dryden & Davenant	Hypolito(B)	young man
1669	*Mr. Anthony*	Roger Boyle	Mrs Nell	young girl
1670	*The Woman made a Justice*	Thomas Betterton	The Justice	young girl?
	The Women's Conquest	Edward Howard	Mandana	ruler
	The Amorous Widow	Thomas Betterton	Mrs Brittle	wife
1671	*Cambyses*	Elkanah Settle	Osiris(B)	young man
	The Six Days Adventure	Edward Howard	Crispina	young girl
	The Town-Shifts	Edward Revet	Fickle	young girl
	Juliana	John Crowne	Paulina(B)	young girl
1672	*The Morning Ramble*	Henry Nevil Payne	Betty Rash	young girl
1673	*Macbeth*	adapt. Wm. Davenant	Lady Macduff	wife

REBECCA MARSHALL

Year	Play	Dramatist	Role	Type
1667	*The Chances*	Duke of Buckingham	First Constantia(P)	young girl
	Secret Love	John Dryden	Queen of Sicily	passionate queen
	The Black Prince	Roger Boyle	Plantaginet	young girl
1668	*The Damoiselles à la Mode*	Richard Flecknoe	Anne(P)	young girl
1669	*Tyrannick Love*	John Dryden	Berenice	young girl
1670	*The Roman Empress*	William Joyner	Fulvia	villainess
	The Conquest of Granada Part 2	John Dryden	Lyndaraxa	villainess
1671	*The Generous Enemies*	John Corye	Jaccinta	young girl
1672	*Marriage à la Mode*	John Dryden	Doralice(B)	wife
	The Assignation	John Dryden	Lucretia	young girl
1673	*Amboyna*	John Dryden	Isabinda	young girl
1674	*Nero*	Nathaniel Lee	Poppea	villainess
1675	*Aureng-Zebe*	John Dryden	Nourmahal	villainess
1676	*Gloriana*	Nathaniel Lee	Gloriana	young girl
	The Plain Dealer	William Wycherley	Olivia	villainess
1677	*Destruction of Jerusalem*	John Crowne	Berenice	passionate queen
	The Country Innocence	John Leanerd	Lady Lovely	widow
	Alexander the Great	Nathaniel Lee	Roxana	villainess
	A Fond Husband	Thomas Durfey	Maria	vengeful girl

SUSANNAH MOUNTFORT

Year	Play	Dramatist	Role	Type
1681	*Sir Barnaby Whigg*	Thomas Durfey	Winifred	'jilt'(S)
1683	*Dame Dobson*	Edward Ravenscroft	Mrs Susan	country girl(S)
	The Atheist	Thomas Otway	Phillis	maid(S)
1684	*The Disappointment*	Thomas Southerne	Juliana	seduced girl(S)
	A Duke and No Duke	Nahum Tate	Prudentia	young girl
1685	*Cuckolds-Haven*	Nahum Tate	Girtred	affected girl(S)
	A Commonwealth of Women	Thomas Durfey	Julietta	young girl
1686	*The Banditti*	Thomas Durfey	Lucia	young girl(S)
	The Devil of a Wife	Thomas Jevon	Nell	wife
	The Lucky Chance	Aphra Behn	Diana	young girl
1687	*The Emperour of the Moon*	Aphra Behn	Bellemante	young girl
	The Island Princess	Nahum Tate	Panura	maid

Year	Play	Dramatist	Role	Type
1688	*The Squire of Alsatia*	Thomas Shadwell	Isabella	young girl
1689	*The Fortune-Hunters*	James Carlile	Maria	young girl
	Bury Fair	Thomas Shadwell	Gertrude	young girl
	Don Sebastian	John Dryden	Morayma	young girl
1690	*The Successful Straingers*	William Mountfort	Feliciana	young girl
	Sir Anthony Love	Thomas Southerne	Sir Anthony(B)	mistress
	Amphitryon	John Dryden	Phaedra	maid
1691	*Greenwich Park*	William Mountfort	Florella	young girl
	The Wives' Excuse	Thomas Southerne	Mrs Wittwoud	wife
1692	*The Volunteers*	Thomas Shadwell	Eugenia	young girl
1693	*The Maid's Last Prayer*	Thomas Southerne	Lady Susan	old woman
	The Old Bachelor	William Congreve	Belinda	affected girl
	A Very Good Wife	George Powell	Annabella(B)	wife
	The Female Vertuoso's	Thomas Wright	Catchat	old woman
	The Double-Dealer	William Congreve	Lady Froth	coquette
1694	*Love Triumphant*	John Dryden	Dalinda	mistress
	The Married Beau	John Crowne	Lionell	young girl
	Don Quixote Part 1	Thomas Durfey	Mary the Buxom	country girl
	Don Quixote Part 2	Thomas Durfey	Mary the Buxom	country girl
	The Canterbury Guests	Edward Ravenscroft	Hillaria(B)	young girl
1695	*The Mock-Marriage*	Thomas Scott	Clarinda(B)	young girl
	The Rival Sisters	Robert Gould	Ansilva	evil maid(S)
	Don Quixote Part 3	Thomas Durfey	Mary the Buxom	country girl
	Oroonoko	Thomas Southerne	Charlot(B)	young girl
1696	*Love's Last Shift*	Colley Cibber	Narcissa	young girl
	The Younger Brother	Aphra Behn	Olivia(B)	young girl
	The Lost Lover	Delariviere Manley	Olivia	wife
	Pausanias	Richard Norton	Demetria	widow
	Ibrahim	Mary Pix	Achmet(B)	eunuch
	The Female Wits	author unknown	Marsilia	playwright
	The Spanish Wives	Mary Pix	Governor's wife(P)	wife
	The Relapse	John Vanbrugh	Berinthia	coquette
	Aesop	John Vanbrugh	Nurse	nurse
1697	*The World in the Moon*	Elkanah Settle	Jacintha	young girl
1698	*The Fatal Discovery*	author unknown	Margaretta	wife
	The Campaigners	Thomas Durfey	Madam la Marquise	wife
1699	*Love Without Interest*	William Penkethman?	Letitia	young girl
	The Constant Couple	George Farquhar	Lurewell	coquette
1700	*The Reform'd Wife*	William Burnaby	Lady Dainty	wife
	Love at a Loss	Catherine Trotter	Miranda	coquette
	Love Makes a Man	Colley Cibber	Louisa	'darker woman'
1701	*The Humour of the Age*	Thomas Baker	Lucia	young girl
	Sir Harry Wildair	George Farquhar	Lady Lurewell	wife
	The Bath	Thomas Durfey	Gillian	country girl
	The Funeral	Richard Steele	Lady Brumpton	widow
1702	*The Modish Husband*	William Burnaby	Lady Cringe	wife
	The Inconstant	George Farquhar	Bisarre	'whimsical lady'
	She Wou'd and She Wou'd Not	Colley Cibber	Hypolita	young girl
1703	*The Fair Example*	Richard Estcourt	Mrs Whimsey	wife
	Tunbridge Walks	Thomas Baker	Hillaria	young girl

JANE ROGERS

Year	Play	Dramatist	Role	Type
1692	*The Volunteers*	Thomas Shadwell	Winifred	affected girl(S)
1693	*The Maid's Last Prayer*	Thomas Southerne	Maria	young girl(S)
	The Female Vertuoso's	Thomas Wright	Lucy	maid(S)
1694	*The Ambitious Slave*	Elkanah Settle	Mirvan(B)	eunuch(S)
	The Canterbury Guests	Edward Ravenscroft	Jacinta	young girl

Year	Play	Dramatist	Role	Type
1695	*The Mock-Marriage*	Thomas Scott	Marina	young girl
	Bonduca	author unknown	Claudia(R)	young girl
	The Rival Sisters	Robert Gould	Berinthia	young girl
	Oroonoko	Thomas Southerne	Imoinda	young girl
	Agnes de Castro	Catherine Trotter	Agnes	young girl
	Philaster	Elkanah Settle	Bellario(B)	young girl
1696	*Love's Last Shift*	Colley Cibber	Amanda	wife
	Neglected Virtue	Charles Hopkins	Alinda	young girl
	The Lost Lover	Delariviere Manley	Marina	young girl
	Pausanias	Richard Norton	Anchilthea	mother
	Ibrahim	Mary Pix	Morena(R)	young girl
	The Unhappy Kindness	Thomas Scott	Evanthe(R)	young girl
	The Relapse	John Vanbrugh	Amanda	wife
1697	*Woman's Wit*	Colley Cibber	Emilia	young girl
	The Triumphs of Virtue	author unknown	Bellamira	young girl
	A Plot and No Plot	John Dennis	Sylvia	young girl
	The Sham Lawyer	James Drake	Florella	wife
1698	*The Island Princess*	Peter Motteux	Quisara	young girl
	Love and a Bottle	George Farquhar	Lucinda	young girl
1699	*Love Without Interest*	William Penkethman?	Honoria	young girl
	Massaniello	Thomas Durfey	Duchess(R)	wife
	The Constant Couple	George Farquhar	Angelica	young girl
	King Richard III	Colley Cibber	Ann	wife(S)
	Achilles	Abel Boyer	Iphigenia	young girl
1700	*The Grove*	John Oldmixon	Aurelia	young girl
	The Reform'd Wife	William Burnaby	Clarinda	young girl
	Courtship à la Mode	David Craufurd	Flora	young girl
1701	*The Unhappy Penitent*	Catherine Trotter	Margarita	young girl
	The Humours of the Age	Thomas Baker	Tremilia(R)	young girl
	Sir Harry Wildair	George Farquhar	Angelica(B)	young girl
	The Virgin Prophetess	Elkanah Settle	Cassandra	young girl
	The Bath	Thomas Durfey	Sophronia	wife
	The Funeral	Richard Steele	Lady Harriot	young girl
	The Generous Conqueror	Bevil Higgons	Armida	young girl
1702	*The Modish Husband*	William Burnaby	Lady Promise	wife
	The Inconstant	George Farquhar	Oriana	young girl
	The False Friend	John Vanbrugh	Leonora	young girl
	All for the Better	Francis Manning	Isabella	young girl
	The Patriot	Charles Gildon	Teraminta	young girl
	The Twin-Rivals	George Farquhar	Constance	young girl
1703	*Tunbridge Walks*	Thomas Baker	Belinda	young girl
	Love's Contrivance	Susannah Centlivre	Lucinda	young girl
	Vice Reclaim'd	Richard Wilkinson	Annabella	young girl
	The Lying Lover	Richard Steele	Penelope	young girl
1704	*Love the Leveller*	author unknown	Princess Constantia	young girl
	The Faithful Bride of Granada	William Taverner	Zelinda(R)	young girl
1705	*The Basset Table*	Susannah Centlivre	Lady Lucy	young girl
1706	*The Recruiting Officer*	George Farquhar	Melinda	young girl
1707	*The Double Gallant*	Colley Cibber	Clarinda	young girl
	The Lady's Last Stake	Colley Cibber	Lady Gentle	wife
1708	*Irene*	Charles Goring	Irene(R)	young girl
1709	*Appius and Virginia*	John Dennis	Virginia(R)	young girl
	The Busie Body	Susannah Centlivre	Isabinda	young girl
1711	*The City Ramble*	Elkanah Settle	Lucia	young girl
	The Wife's Relief	Charles Johnson	Cynthia	wife
1716	*The Perfidious Brother*	Lewis Theobald	Luciana	wife
	A Woman is a Riddle	Christopher Bullock	Lady Outside	young widow
1717	*The Artful Husband*	William Taverner	Mrs Winwife	wife

Plays in which Barry and Bracegirdle appeared together

William Mountfort	*The Injur'd Lovers: or, The Ambitious Father* (1688)
Elkanah Settle	*Distress'd Innocence: or The Princess of Persia* (1690)
John Bancroft	*King Edward the Third, with The Fall of Mortimer, Earl of March* (1690)
Thomas Shadwell	*The Scowrers* (1690)
Thomas Southerne	*The Wives' Excuse: or, Cuckolds Make Themselves* (1691)
Thomas Durfey	*The Marriage-Hater Match'd* (1692)
John Dryden	*Cleomenes, The Spartan Heroe* (1692)
John Bancroft	*Henry II, with the Death of Rosamond* (1692)
Thomas Southerne	*The Maid's Last Prayer: or, Any Rather than Fail* (1693)
William Congreve	*The Old Bachelor* (1693)
Thomas Durfey	*The Richmond Heiress: or, A Woman Once in the Right* (1693)
William Congreve	*The Double-Dealer* (1693)
John Dryden	*Love Triumphant* (1694)
Thomas Southerne	*The Fatal Marriage: or, The Innocent Adultery* (1694)
John Crowne	*The Married Beau: or, The Curious Impertinent* (1694)
Elkanah Settle	*The Ambitious Slave: or, A Generous Revenge* (1694)
William Congreve	*Love for Love* (1695)
'A Young Lady'	*She Ventures and He Wins* (1695)
John Banks	*Cyrus the Great: or, The Tragedy of Love* (1695)
George Granville	*The She-Gallants* (1695)
Thomas Doggett	*The Country-Wake* (1696)
Delariviere Manley	*The Royal Mischief* (1696)
Peter Motteux	*Love's a Jest* (1696)
Thomas Durfey	*The Intrigues at Versailles: or, A Jilt in all Humours* (1697)
Mary Pix	*The Innocent Mistress* (1697)
Mary Pix	*The Deceiver Deceiv'd* (1697)
William Congreve	*The Mourning Bride* (1697)

John Vanbrugh	*The Provok'd Wife* (1697)
Charles Hopkins	*Boadicea, Queen of Britain* (1697)
George Granville	*Heroick Love* (1698)
Peter Motteux	*Beauty in Distress* (1698)
Catherine Trotter	*The Fatal Friendship* (1698)
Mary Pix	*Queen Catharine: or, The Ruines of Love* (1698)
Henry Smith	*The Princess of Parma* (1699)
Mary Pix	*The False Friend: or, The Fate of Disobedience* (1699)
Charles Hopkins	*Friendship Improv'd: or, The Female Warriour* (1699)
John Dennis	*Iphigenia* (1699)
William Congreve	*The Way of the World* (1700)
Mary Pix	*The Beau Defeated* (1700)
Nicholas Rowe	*The Ambitious Stepmother* (1700)
William Burnaby	*The Ladies Visiting Day* (1701)
Mary Pix	*The Double Distress* (1701)
Charles Gildon	*Love's Victim: or, The Queen of Wales* (1701)
Nicholas Rowe	*Tamerlane* (1701)
Anon.	*The Fickle Shepherdess* (1703)
Charles Boyle	*As You Find It* (1703)
Nicholas Rowe	*The Fair Penitent* (1703)
John Dennis	*Liberty Asserted* (1704)
Anon	*Zelmane: or, The Corinthian Queen* (1704)
Nicholas Rowe	*The Biter* (1704)
Susannah Centlivre	*The Gamester* (1705)
John Vanbrugh	*The Confederacy* (1705)
Nicholas Rowe	*Ulysses* (1705)
George Granville	*The British Enchanters: or, No Magick Like Love* (1706)
Mary Pix	*The Adventures in Madrid* (1706)
Delariviere Manley	*Almyna: or, The Arabian Vow* (1706)

Notes

Plays cited individually in the notes and not listed separately in the bibliography will be found in the collected works of the dramatist concerned.

INTRODUCTION: THE RESTORATION THEATRE

1 See *The London Stage*, Part I, *1660–1700*, ed. William Van Lennep (Carbondale 1965), introduction, pp. xxii–iii; Robert Hume, *The Development of English Drama in the Late Seventeenth Century* (Oxford, 1976), p. 341, and John Loftis, Richard Southern, Marion Jones and A. H. Scouten, *The Revels History of Drama in English V 1660–1750* (1976), pp. 123–4.

2 See *London Stage*, Part I, p. cxxx, and Peter Holland, *The Ornament of Action* (Cambridge University Press, 1979), p. 33.

3 See *London Stage*, Part I, pp. lxxxv–lxxxvii.

4 See Jocelyn Powell, *Restoration Theatre Production* (1984), pp. 54–5.

5 See John Harold Wilson, *All the King's Ladies* (Chicago, 1958), p. 23.

6 Samuel Pepys, *The Diary of Samuel Pepys*, ed. Robert Lanier and William Matthews (1970–83), vol. VII, pp. 76–7.

7 See Holland, *The Ornament of Action*, p. 15.

8 Ibid., pp. 16–17.

9 See Emmett L. Avery, 'The Restoration Audience', *Philological Quarterly*, 45 (1966), pp. 54–61; Harold Love, 'The Myth of the Restoration Audience', *Komos*, 1 (1967), pp. 49–56, and Holland, *The Ornament of Action*, chapter 1.

10 See Loftis *et al.*, *Revels History of Drama*, pp. 13–14, and *London Stage*, Part I, pp. xxix–xxx.

11 Pepys, *Diary*, vol. VIII, pp. 71–2.

12 Colley Cibber, *An Apology for the Life of Mr. Colley Cibber*, ed. with an introduction by B. R. S. Fone (Ann Arbor, 1968), pp. 77–8.

13 See *London Stage*, Part I, pp. lvii–lix.

14 Wilson, *All the King's Ladies*, p. 9.

15 Ibid., pp. 34–5.

16 See Allardyce Nicoll, *A History of English Drama 1660–1900*, vol. I, *Restoration Drama 1660–1700* (Cambridge University Press, 1952), p. 324.

17 Judith Milhous and Robert Hume, *Producible Interpretation: Eight English Plays 1675–1707* (Carbondale and Edwardsville, 1985), p. 39.

18 Figures from *London Stage*, Part I, and Part II *1700–29*, ed. Emmett L. Avery (Carbondale, 1960).

19 See Wilson, *All the King's Ladies*, p. 37.

20 Nicoll, *Restoration Drama*, p. 365.

21 Ibid., p. 324.

22 Thomas Betterton, *The History of the English Stage from the Restauration to the Present Time. Including the Lives, Characters and Amours of the most Eminent Actors and Actresses*, a compilation by Edmund Curll and William Oldys, from the notes of Thomas Betterton (1741), p. 15. For details of nurseries, see Wilson, *All the King's Ladies*, pp. 48–9.

23 Nicoll, *Restoration Drama*, p. 324.

24 See Holland, *The Ornament of Action*, p. 65.

25 Colley Cibber, *Woman's Wit* (1697), preface.

26 Thomas Southerne, *The Dramatic Works of Thomas Southerne*, ed. Robert Jordan and Harold Love (Oxford, 1988), vol. I, *Sir Anthony Love: or, the Rambling Lady*, dedication, 18.

27 Ibid., vol. II, *The Fatal Marriage: or, the Innocent Adultery*, dedication, 35.

28 John Dryden, *The Letters*, ed. C. E. Ward (Durham, N. Carolina, 1942), pp. 23–4. Cited in Holland, *The Ornament of Action*, p. 76.

29 See *London Stage*, Part I, p. clv.

30 See Milhous and Hume, *Producible Interpretation*, pp. 59–64.

31 Charles Gildon, *Life of Mr. Thomas Betterton* (1710), pp. 15–16.

32 Holland, *The Ornament of Action*, pp. 58–9.

33 Gildon, *Life of Betterton*, p. 33. As Holland points out, there is no evidence that Betterton had anything to do with the rules of acting that Gildon ascribes to him (*The Ornament of Action*, p. 259, n. 13).

34 Gildon, *Life of Betterton*, p. 113.

35 Ibid., pp. 67, 53–4. Cibber, *Apology*, p. 59.

36 See *London Stage*, Part I, p. clx.

37 Milhous and Hume, *Producible Interpretation*, p. 42.

38 In *The Prostituted Muse: Images of Women and Women Dramatists 1642–1737* (Hemel Hempstead, 1988), p. 252, Jacqueline Pearson cites additional reasons for the arrival of women playwrights at this time.

39 Quoted in ibid., pp. 7 and 9.

40 Ibid., p. 193. For further information on these and other playwrights, see also Fidelis Morgan (ed.), *The Female Wits: Women Playwrights on the London Stage 1660–1720* (1981).

41 See Pearson, *The Prostituted Muse*, p. 254.

42 Loftis *et al.*, *Revels History of Drama*, p. 131.

1 THE ARRIVAL OF THE ACTRESS

1 See T. S. Graves, 'Women on the Pre-Restoration Stage', *Studies in Philology*, 22 (1925), pp. 184–7.

2 Thomas Jordan, 'A Prologue to introduce the first Woman that came to Act on the Stage in the Tragedy, call'd the Moor of Venice', in *A Royal Arbor of Loyal Poesie* (1664), p. 21.

3 Andrew Newport to Sir Richard Leveson, 15 December 1660, cited in Wilson, *All the King's Ladies*, p. 3. Pepys, *Diary*, vol. II, p. 5.

4 See Rosamund Gilder, *Enter the Actress: The First Women in the Theatre* (Boston, 1931), pp. 50–99.

5 Cibber, *Apology*, p. 55.

6 *Restoration and Georgian England 1660–1788*, compiled and introduced by David Thomas and Arnold Hare (Cambridge University Press, 1989), p. 138. Henry Wynsham Lanier, *The First English Actresses from 1660–1700* (New York, 1930), p. 31. Other critics who have assumed that actresses must automatically be better than boys are Gilder, *Enter the Actress*, pp. 134–5, and Wilson, *All the King's Ladies*, p. 90. A lively discussion of the topic is Stephen Orgel's article 'Nobody's Perfect: Or Why did the English Stage Take Boys for Women?' *South Atlantic Quarterly*, 88 (Winter 1989), no. 1, pp. 7–29.

7 Letter translated from the Latin, quoted by Geoffrey Tillotson, '*Othello* and *The Alchemist* at Oxford in 1610', *The Times Literary Supplement* (20 July 1933), p. 494.

8 Quoted by Gilder, *Enter the Actress*, p. 137.

9 Pepys, *Diary*, vol. II, p. 7.

10 Katharine Eisaman Maus, '"Playhouse Flesh and Blood": Sexual Ideology and the Restoration Actress', *English Literary History*, 46 (1979), p. 609.

11 See Sophie Tomlinson, 'Theatrical Women: the Emergence of Women as Actors in English Theatre and Drama before the Restoration', Ph.D. dissertation, Cambridge University, in progress.

12 See Alfred Harbage, *Cavalier Drama* (1936), p. 15.

13 James Shirley, *The Dramatic Works and Poems of James Shirley*, now first collected; with notes by the late William Gifford Esq. (New York, 1966), vol. III, p. 79. See also Shirley's *Bird in a Cage* (1633), Richard Brome's *The Court-Beggar* (1640) and William Cartwright's *The Lady-Errant* (1628–43?).

14 Martin Butler, *Theatre and Crisis 1632–42* (Cambridge University Press, 1984), p. 100.

15 See Harbage, *Cavalier Drama*, p. 20.

16 See Leslie Hotson, *The Commonwealth and Restoration Stage* (Cambridge, Mass., 1928), pp. 136–7, 171–2.

17 Petition of 13 October 1660, quoted in Thomas (ed.), *Restoration and Georgian England*, p. 13. Davenant's agreement given in Hotson, *Commonwealth and Restoration Stage*, p. 207.

18 See Wilson, *All the King's Ladies*, p. 8. Wilson suggests (pp. 6–7) that Anne Marshall or Mary Saunderson are the most likely candidates for the role of Desdemona – apparently forgetting that Saunderson was always a member of Davenant's company.

19 Ibid., p. 7.
20 Pepys, *Diary*, vol. II, p. 35.
21 Ibid., vol. I, p. 224 and vol. II, p. 7.
22 Cibber, *Apology*, p. 71.
23 Cited in Thomas (ed.), *Restoration and Georgian England*, pp. 17–18.
24 Leo Hughes, *The Drama's Patrons* (Austin, 1971), p. 140.
25 See Alice Clark, *Working Life of Women in the Seventeenth Century* (1982), especially pp. 38–40, 234–5, 286–9 and 295–308.
26 Maus, '"Playhouse Flesh and Blood"', p. 600.
27 See the lists of company members for each season in *London Stage*, Part I.
28 Quoted in Pearson, *The Prostituted Muse*, p. 32.
29 Ibid.
30 Nicoll, *Restoration Drama*, p. 383.
31 See Wilson, *All the King's Ladies*, p. 40.
32 Cibber, *Apology*, p. 218. It should be noted that Pepys mentions being invited to a collective benefit performance for the actresses of the King's Company on 28 September 1668 (*Diary*, vol. IX, p. 322).
33 See Nicoll, *Restoration Drama*, p. 375.
34 Eleanor Boswell, *The Restoration Court Stage 1660–1702* (Cambridge, Mass., 1932), p. 172.
35 Nicoll, *Restoration Drama*, p. 369.
36 Ibid., pp. 369–70 and 384. Cibber also gives an account, *Apology*, vol. I, pp. 186–94.
37 Nicoll, *Restoration Drama*, pp. 384–5.
38 Betterton, *History of the English Stage*, p. 21.
39 Thomas Brown, *The Works of Mr. Thomas Brown* (1708), vol. III, p. 43. Satire, 'To the most Virtuous and most devoted Overkind, Notorious Madm Barry', quoted in Wilson, *All the King's Ladies*, p. 116.
40 *The Letters of Sir George Etherege*, ed. Frederick Bracher (Berkeley, 1974), p. 186. According to a satire called 'The School of Venus' (1715), the Earl of Dorset is reputed to have had an affair with Barry.
41 The phrase used to describe Barry in the 'Satyr on the Players' (*c.* 1684) quoted in *A Biographical Dictionary of Actors, Actresses, Musicians... etc. in London 1660–1800*, ed. Philip H. Highfill Jr., Kalman A. Burnim and Edward A. Langhans (Carbondale and Edwardsville, 1973–), vol. I, p. 318.
42 Ibid., vol. II, pp. 275–81.
43 Jordan, 'Prologue to introduce the first Woman', *A Royal Arbor of Loyal Poesie*, pp. 21–2.
44 Pepys, *Diary*, vol. VIII, p. 463.
45 Ibid., vol. IX, p. 189.
46 See Wilson, *All the King's Ladies*, p. 28.
47 Nicoll, *Restoration Drama*, p. 324.
48 Brown, *Works*, vol. II, *Second Part of the Letters from the Dead to the Living*, p. 166.
49 See Wilson, *All the King's Ladies*, pp. 27–8.

50 Ibid., p. 26.

51 Maus, '"Playhouse Flesh and Blood"', p. 601.

52 Cibber, *Apology*, p. 98.

53 John Downes, *Roscius Anglicanus*, ed. Judith Milhous and Robert D. Hume (1987), p. 55. Anon., *A Comparison Between Two Stages*, generally considered to be by Charles Gildon (1702), p. 18.

54 See Wilson, *All the King's Ladies*, pp. 153, 172.

55 *Biographical Dictionary*, ed. Highfill *et al.*, vol. II, p. 279.

56 Brown, *Works*, vol. II, *Second Part of the Letters from the Dead to the Living*, p. 166. Anon., *Comparison Between Two Stages*, p. 17.

57 Lesley Ferris, *Acting Women: Images of Women in Theatre* (1990), p. 70. See also Harold M. Weber, *The Restoration Rake-Hero: Transformations in Sexual Understanding in Seventeenth-Century England* (Wisconsin, 1986), p. 152.

2 SEX AND VIOLENCE

1 Harold M. Weber, *The Restoration Rake-Hero*, p. 152.

2 The best account of the diverse range of Restoration tragedy is Hume's *Development of English Drama*, chapters 4 and 5.

3 John Crowne, *The History of Charles the Eighth of France: or, the Invasion of Naples by the French* (1672), p. 47.

4 Samuel Pordage, *Herod and Mariamne* (1673), pp. 10, 52, 61.

5 Thomas Southerne, *Works*, vol. II, *The Fate of Capua*, 3.v.13–18. Shakespeare, *The Complete Works*, ed. Peter Alexander (1951), *Cymbeline*, II.ii.14–17.

6 There are, of course, plenty of Elizabethan and Jacobean plays full of sensational violence. However, the element of titillation associated with the Restoration's use of women in tragedy is absent.

7 John Dryden, *The Works of John Dryden*, ed. E. Niles Hooker, H. T. Swedenburg *et al.* (Berkeley and Los Angeles, 1954–), vol. X, *Tyrannick Love*, V.i.245–53.

8 Nathaniel Lee, *The Works of Nathaniel Lee*, ed. with introduction and notes by Thomas B. Stroup and Arthur L. Cooke (New Brunswick, 1954, 1955), vol. I, *Oedipus*, V.413. Robert Gould, *The Rival Sisters: or, the Violence of Love* (1696), p. 53.

9 Eric Rothstein, *Restoration Tragedy: Form and the Process of Change* (Madison, 1967), p. 157.

10 For a full account of rape in these plays, see Suzanne Gossett, '"Best Men are Molded out of Faults": Marrying the Rapist in Jacobean Drama', *English Literary Renaissance*, 14 (1984), pp. 305–27.

11 See appendix 1 for plays containing rape.

12 Dryden criticised the female characters of Fletcher: 'Let us applaud his scenes of love; but let us confess, that he understood not either greatness or perfect honour in the parts of any of his women.' *Essays of John Dryden*, ed. W. P. Ker (Oxford, 1900), vol. I, p. 177.

13 John Dennis, *Original Letters, Familiar, Moral and Critical* (1721), vol. I, pp. 63–4.

14 John Dryden, *Amboyna: or, the Cruelties of the Dutch* (1673), p. 45.
15 Such illustrations were frequently taken from actual stage productions.
16 Mary Pix, *Ibrahim, the Thirteenth Emperour of the Turks* (1696), p. 28.
17 Nahum Tate, *The Ingratitude of a Commonwealth* (1682), p. 55.
18 Beaumont and Fletcher, *The Dramatic Works*, ed. Fredson Bowers (Cambridge, 1966–89), vol. IV, *Valentinian*, I.i.92–4. Other references to this play are given in the text.
19 John Fletcher, *Valentinian: A Tragedy As 'tis Alter'd by the late Earl of Rochester* (1685), p. 6.
20 John Dryden, *Aureng-Zebe*, ed. Frederick M. Link (1972), IV.ii.146–52.
21 Nathaniel Lee, *Works*, vol. II, *Caesar Borgia, Son of Pope Alexander the Sixth*, I.i.29–32.
22 Dryden, *Works*, vol. IX, *Secret Love: or, the Maiden Queen*, I.ii.48–9.
23 James Shirley, *The Traitor*, ed. John Steward Carter (1965), II.i.165–79.
24 Quoted from Morgan's edition of the play in *The Female Wits*, p. 229.
25 Ibid., pp. 209, 210.
26 Thomas Otway, *Venice Preserved: or, A Plot Discovered*, ed. Malcolm Kelsall (1969), III.ii.242–6.
27 *The Spectator*, ed. with introduction and notes by Donald F. Bond (Oxford, 1965), vol.I, p. 217.
28 Hume, *Development of English Drama*, p. 144.
29 Edward Ravenscroft, *The London Cuckolds* (1682), pp. 26–7.
30 The play's author is not definitely known, but is now usually assumed to be Aphra Behn. For a discussion see H. A. Hargreaves, 'The Life and Plays of Mrs Aphra Behn', unpublished Ph.D. dissertation, Duke University, 1960.
31 Richard Brome, *A Mad Couple Well Match'd* (1653), IV.iii. Aphra Behn, *The Debauchee: or, the Credulous Cockold* (1677), p. 47.
32 *The Counterfeit Bridegroom* (1677), p. 52. For a discussion of the play's authorship see Hargreaves, 'The Life and Plays of Mrs. Aphra Behn', pp. 260–71.
33 Pat Rogers, 'Breeches Roles', in *Sexuality in Eighteenth-Century Britain*, ed. Paul-Gabriel Boucé (Manchester, 1982), p. 255.
34 Thomas Rawlins, *Tom Essence: or, the Modish Wife* (1677), p. 41. Aphra Behn, *The Younger Brother: or, the Amorous Jilt* (1696), p. 48.
35 Dryden, *Works*, vol. VIII, *The Rival Ladies*, IV.iii.52.
36 *Court Satires of the Restoration*, ed. John Harold Wilson (Columbus, Ohio, 1976), p. 206, stanza 9.
37 See Wilson, *All the King's Ladies*, p. 73.
38 John Crowne, *The Misery of Civil-War* (1680), p. 63. Pepys *Diary*, vol. VIII, p. 101.
39 See *London Stage*, Part I, p. 84.
40 Both prologue and epilogue quoted in *Covent Garden Drolery; or, A Collection of all the Choice Songs, Poems, Prologues and Epilogues ... never in Print before* (1672), pp. 1, 5.
41 Linda Woodbridge, *Women and the English Renaissance: Literature and the Nature of Womankind, 1540–1620* (Brighton, 1984), p. 154. Juliet

Dusinberre, *Shakespeare and the Nature of Women* (1975), p. 233. See also Phyllis Racklin, 'Androgyny, Mimesis, and the Marriage of the Boy Heroine on the English Renaissance Stage' in *Speaking of Gender*, ed. Elaine Showalter (1989), pp. 113–33.

42 Pearson, *The Prostituted Muse*, p. 104.

43 Pearson, ibid., pp. 110–13, is able to discuss only a handful of potentially 'feminist' breeches roles.

44 Southerne, *Works*, vol. I, *Sir Anthony Love*, I.i.17–22.

45 Pearson, *The Prostituted Muse*, p. 116.

46 Cibber, *Apology*, p. 94. Satire cited in the *Biographical Dictionary*, ed. Highfill *et al.*, vol. II, p. 449.

47 Gerard Langbaine the Younger, appendix to *Account of the English Dramatick Poets* (1691). *The Gentleman's Journal*, January 1691/2, p. 33.

48 Katharine Eisaman Maus, 'Arcadia Lost: Politics and Revision in the Restoration *Tempest*', *Renaissance Drama*, 13 (1982), p. 200.

49 The women in the Duke's Company who could have played Miranda in 1667 were Winifred Gosnell (although she probably did not, since she later replaced Moll Davis as Ariel), Mrs Jennings – one of the three actresses whom Downes says were 'by force of Love … Erept the stage' (Downes, *Roscius Anglicanus*, p. 74) – and Anne Gibbs Shadwell, who was attacked for her behaviour in youth in 'A Satyr on the Players' with the phrase 'none was a greater Whore' (quoted in Wilson, *All the King's Ladies*, p. 187). The last two seem the most likely candidates for Miranda and Dorinda.

50 Dryden, *Works*, vol. X, *The Tempest*, I.ii.319–20, 332–3.

51 J. L. Styan, *Restoration Comedy in Performance* (Cambridge, 1986), p. 89.

52 Pearson, *The Prostituted Muse*, p. 50.

53 Styan, *Restoration Comedy in Performance*, p. 89.

3 THE ACTRESS, THE DRAMATIST AND COMEDY

1 See Loftis *et al.*, *The Revels History of Drama*, p. 131.

2 Holland, *The Ornament of Action*, p. 82.

3 See John Harrington Smith, *The Gay Couple in Restoration Comedy* (Cambridge, Mass., 1948), pp. 3–9.

4 James Howard, *All Mistaken: or, the Mad Couple* (1672), p. 23.

5 Pepys, *Diary*, vol. VIII, p. 594.

6 Although there is no absolute proof that Nell Gwyn played the female half of Buckingham's gay couple, the weight of evidence is overwhelmingly in favour.

7 Beaumont and Fletcher, *The Dramatic Works*, vol. IV, *The Chances*, IV.iii.136–7.

8 George Villiers, Duke of Buckingham, (1682), pp. 59, 62.

9 See Dryden, *Works*, vol. IX, *Secret Love*, I.ii.48–9.

10 Pepys, *Diary*, vol. VIII, p. 91.

11 Prologue to *Philaster*, quoted in John Harold Wilson, *Nell Gwyn, Royal Mistress* (1952), p. 67.

12 See Philip Massinger, *A City Madam* (1632?), John Fletcher's *Rule a Wife and have a Wife* (1624) and Brome's *A Mad Couple Well Match'd* (1637?–9).

13 As Holland notes (*The Ornament of Action*, p. 262, n. 109), although we have no cast list for this play, there was no one else in the company at the time suitable to perform these roles.

14 Dryden, *Works*, vol. x, *An Evening's Love*, IV.i.139–42.

15 Pepys, *Diary*, vol. vii, p. 102.

16 See David Bond, 'Nell Gwyn's Birthdate', *Theatre Notebook*, 40 (1986), pp. 3–9.

17 Pepys, *Diary*, vol. ix, p. 422.

18 Betterton, *History of the English Stage*, p. 21.

19 Dryden, *Marriage à la Mode*, ed. Mark S. Auburn (1981), p. xvi.

20 Downes, *Roscius Anglicanus*, pp. 60, 65.

21 Ibid., p. 65.

22 Thomas Betterton, *The Amorous Widow* (1706), p. 69.

23 Thomas Durfey, *Two Comedies by Thomas Durfey*, ed. Jack A. Vaughn (Cranbury, New Jersey and London, 1976), *Madam Fickle: or, the Witty False One*, IV.ii.386. See, for comparison, Elkanah Settle, *Love and Revenge* (1675), end of Act IV.

24 Durfey, *Two Comedies*, ed. Vaughn, p. 39.

25 John Crowne, *The Countrey Wit: or, Sir Mannerly Shallow* (1675), pp. 58, 86.

26 Aphra Behn, *The Town-Fopp: or, Sir Timothy Tawdrey* (1677), final speeches.

27 Dryden, *The Kind Keeper: or, Mr. Limberham* (1680), p. 65.

28 Thomas Durfey, *Squire Oldsapp: or, the Night Adventurers* (1679), final lines.

29 There were revivals of *The Man of Mode: or, Sir Fopling Flutter* with Barry as Mrs Loveit in November 1706 and April 1708. Also in April 1708, incidentally, was a revival of *The Rover* in which Barry played another discarded mistress, Angellica Bianca. Since Barry played the heroine of the latter in 1677 it would seem natural that she played also the heroine of *The Man of Mode* at that time.

30 Aphra Behn actually split Killigrew's *Thomaso* into two characters, Willmore and his serious companion Bellvile. Bellvile is paired with Florinda and they form a contrast to the 'gay couple', Willmore and Hellena.

31 Aphra Behn, *The Rover*, ed. F. M. Link (1967), V.413–16.

32 Ibid., V.453–4.

33 For a full list of Barry's roles in comedy up to 1681, see appendix 1.

34 Hume, *Development of English Drama*, p. 340.

35 Anon., *Comparison Between Two Stages*, p. 200.

36 For some reason, the two were not paired together in Mountfort's other comedy *The Successful Straingers*. Here Mountfort was paired with Mrs Knight as the serious lovers, and his wife paired with George Powell as the gay couple Feliciana and Antonio.

37 Cibber, *Apology*, p. 95.

38 Southerne, *Works*, vol. i, *Sir Anthony Love*, dedication, 14–20.

39 William Mountfort, *Greenwich Park* (1691), p. 47.

40 Cibber, *Apology*, pp. 95, 94–5.

41 Southerne, *Works*, vol. i, *The Maid's Last Prayer*, I.i.70–2.

42 Thomas Durfey, *The Three Parts of the Comical History of Don Quixote* (1729), p, 99.

43 Durfey, *The Bath* (1701), the Epistle Dedicatory. Cibber, *Apology*, p. 95.

44 All details from *Biographical Dictionary*, ed. Highfill *et al.*, vol. ii, pp. 269–71.

45 Cibber, *Apology*, p. 98.

46 I should emphasise that the typical Bracegirdle heroine here described is the one which recurs with such frequency as to make a significant impact upon comic form. Bracegirdle did on occasion play other kinds of women in comedy – for example, in Durfey's *The Intrigues at Versailles* (1697) she played a wayward wife, and she played a vigorous heroine of the Mountfort type in Pix's *The Innocent Mistress* (1697).

47 Durfey, *The Richmond Heiress* (1693), p. 64.

48 William Congreve, *Comedies*, ed. Bonamy Dobrée (Oxford, 1925), p. 331.

4 LIFE OVERWHELMING FICTION

1 Ben Jonson, *Volpone*, ed. Philip Brockbank (1968), prologue 1–2, 8, 25 and 31.

2 The prologue is tailored to what the public already knows about Hart. With the line, 'But though our Bayes's battles oft I've fought', he reminded spectators that he played heroes in several of John Dryden's tragedies (the name 'Bayes' was used to refer to Dryden in *The Rehearsal* of 1671, Villiers' (Duke of Buckingham) satiric parody of his tragedies). See Wycherley, *The Plays of William Wycherley*, ed. Peter Holland (Cambridge, 1981), *The Country Wife*, prologue, 11.

3 Ibid., 5, 6.

4 Jeremy Collier, *A Short View of the Immorality and Profaneness of the English Stage* (1698), p. 13.

5 Pepys, *Diary*, vol. ix, p. 260.

6 Wilson, *All the King's Ladies*, pp. 89–90.

7 Durfey, *Love for Money* (1691), cast list.

8 A reference to Barry's playing the title role in Thomas Dilke's *The City Lady* (1696).

9 Comic roles of this kind created by Bracegirdle included Fulvia in Durfey's *The Richmond Heiress* (1693), Angelica in Congreve's *Love for Love* (1695), Mrs Purflew in Thomas Dilke's *The Lover's Luck* (1695), Flora in Thomas Doggett's *The Country-Wake* (1696) and Millamant in *The Way of the World* (1700).

10 Congreve, *Comedies*, ed. Dobrée, p. 371.

11 Durfey, *The Three Parts of the Comical History of Don Quixote*, preface to the second part.

12 Currer's breeches roles include Mrs Hadland in *The Counterfeit Bridegroom* (1677), Ariadne in *The False Count: or, A New Way to Play an Old Game* (1681) and the title role in *The Widow Ranter: or, the History of Bacon in Virginia* (1689), all by Aphra Behn.

13 Thomas Davies, *Dramatic Miscellanies* (1784), vol. III, p. 215.

14 Crowne, *The Misery of Civil-War* (1680), pp. 33–4.

15 See Wilson, *All the King's Ladies*, p. 136.

16 Ibid., pp. 107–8.

17 John Dennis, *Critical Works*, ed. E. N. Hooker (Baltimore, 1939–45), vol. I, p. 418.

18 Cibber, *Apology*, p, 138.

19 William Chetwood, *A General History of the Stage* (1749), p. 28. Barry created the role of Cordelia in Tate's *Lear* in 1681, Bracegirdle played the role in October 1706. (See *London Stage* Parts I and II.)

20 Cibber, *Apology*, ed. Robert W. Lowe (1889), vol. I, pp. 135–6. The epilogue is quoted from Lowe's notes here.

21 Betterton, *History of the English Stage*, p. 21.

22 Wilson, *All the King's Ladies*, p. 106.

5 ELIZABETH BARRY AND THE DEVELOPMENT OF RESTORATION TRAGEDY

1 The term 'she-tragedy' was probably coined by Nicholas Rowe, its first known usage being in the epilogue to *The Tragedy of Jane Shore* (1714): 'If the reforming stage should fall to shaming / Ill-nature, pride, hypocrisy and gaming, / The poets frequently might move compassion, / And with she-tragedies o'errun the nation' (*The Tragedy of Jane Shore*, ed. Henry William Pedicord (1975), epilogue, 26–9). It can however be applied to all the pathetic tragedies of the Restoration focusing on the suffering of a female protagonist. See also Hume, *Development of English Drama*, pp. 216–17.

2 Rothstein, *Restoration Tragedy*, p. 141 and Hume, *Development of English Drama*, p. 220; Nicoll, *Restoration Drama*, p. 72; Powell, *Restoration Theatre Production*, pp, 157, 158.

3 Cibber, *Apology*, p. 92.

4 Laura Brown, *English Dramatic Form, 1660–1760: An Essay in Generic History* (New Haven and London, 1981), pp. 81–93, and Susan Staves, *Players' Scepters: Fictions of Authority in the Restoration* (Lincoln, Nebraska, 1979), especially chapter 1, pp. 87–8 and 172–86.

5 Staves, *Players' Scepters*, p. 187.

6 See ibid., p. 172.

7 Rothstein, *Restoration Tragedy*, pp. 27–46.

8 See Emmett L. Avery, 'The Restoration Audience', *Philological Quarterly*, 45 (1966), pp. 54–61.

9 See, for instance, Nathaniel Lee's portrayal of Hannibal as the devoted lover of his mistress Rosalinda, rather than as mighty conqueror, in

Sophonisba (1675), or Dryden's focus on Antony as lover in his adaptation of *Antony and Cleopatra*, aptly named *All for Love: or, the World Well Lost* (see plate 10).

10 Pepys *Diary*, vol. v, pp. 224, 240.
11 Ibid., vol. vii, p. 399, vol. viii, p. 235.
12 Ibid., vol. viii, p. 399, vol. ix, p. 37.
13 Ibid., vol. ix, p. 94.
14 Otway, *The Works of Thomas Otway*, ed, J. C. Ghosh (Oxford, 1932), vol. i, pp. 41–2.
15 Downes, *Roscius Anglicanus*, p. 76.
16 See Betterton, *History of the English Stage*, p. 14; Cibber, *Apology*, vol. i, p. 159, and Anthony Aston, *A Brief Supplement to Colley Cibber Esq; His Lives of the Late Famous Actors and Actresses* (1747?), p. 8.
17 According to Betterton, *History of the English Stage*, p. 14, and Thomas (ed.), *Restoration and Georgian England*, p. 143.
18 Betterton, *History of the English Stage*, p. 16.
19 Ibid., pp. 16–18. Curll's biographical facts, supposedly culled from Betterton's notes, may be shaky in that they seem to be based largely on hearsay and gossip. However, his accounts of Barry's performances, since they are so much in accord with other accounts of her talent, seem reliable.
20 Davies, *Dramatic Miscellanies*, vol. iii, p, 121. Aston, *Brief Supplement*, p. 7; John Dennis, *Liberty Asserted* (1704), preface, and Gildon, *Life of Betterton*, p. 40.
21 Aston, *Brief Supplement*, p. 7. Shadwell's letter cited in *Biographical Dictionary*, ed. Highfill *et al.*, vol. i, p. 325.
22 Anon., *Comparison Between Two Stages*, p. 18.
23 For evidence of this passion, see Otway, *Works*, ed. Ghosh, vol. i, pp. 13–14. The love-letters Ghosh discusses, apparently written by Otway to Barry, cannot be authenticated bibliographically, but the circumstantial evidence in their favour is strong.
24 Otway, *The History and Fall of Caius Marius* (1680), pp. 15, 64.
25 Otway, *The Orphan*, ed. Aline Mackenzie Taylor (1977), II.406–7.
26 For accounts of the confusing characterisation of *The Orphan*, see Laura Brown, *English Dramatic Form*, pp. 87–9, and introduction to Taylor's edition, pp. xviii, xxiv–xxvii.
27 George Granville, preface to *Heroick Love* (1732).
28 The anecdote of Barry weeping every time she spoke the line is related by Charles Gildon in *The Complete Art of Poetry* (1718), vol. i, p. 290.
29 Downes, *Roscius Anglicanus*, p. 79.
30 Nahum Tate, *The History of King Lear*, in *Shakespeare Adaptations*, ed. with an introduction and notes by Montague Summers (1922), dedication 'To my Esteem'd Friend Thomas Boteler Esq.'
31 Ibid., p. 183.
32 Aline Mackenzie Taylor, *Next to Shakespeare: Otway's 'Venice Preserved' and 'The Orphan' and their History on the London Stage* (Durham, North Carolina, 1950), p. 143.

33 Banks, *Vertue Betray'd: or, Anna Bullen* (1682), p. 48.
34 Since Marmoutier is never an integral part of any scene involving more than two people and is confined almost exclusively to the parts of the play which Dryden says he wrote later, one can infer that she was an extraneous addition. She provides a love interest and is not directly connected to anything else.
35 See *Biographical Dictionary*, ed. Highfill *et al.*, vol. I, p. 319.
36 Southerne, *Works*, vol. II, *The Fatal Marriage*, dedication, 35–6. Letter cited in *Biographical Dictionary*, ed. Highfill *et al.*, vol. I, p. 318.
37 Maynard Mack, for example, comments on the relatively small numbers of mothers, as opposed to fathers, in Shakespeare. See Maynard Mack, 'Rescuing Shakespeare', *International Shakespeare Association Occasional Paper No. 1* (Oxford, 1979), p. 8.
38 Apart from *The Fatal Marriage*, the other six are Pix's *Queen Catharine: or, the Ruines of Love* (1698), Cibber's *Xerxes* (1699), Southerne's *The Fate of Capua* (1700), Jane Wiseman's *Antiochus the Great: or, the Fatal Relapse* (1701), Dennis's *Liberty Asserted* (1703) and Rowe's *Ulysses* (1705).
39 Nicholas Rowe, *The Fair Penitent*, ed. Malcolm Goldstein, 1969, V.292–3.
40 Philip Massinger (with Ford), *The Plays and Poems of Philip Massinger*, ed. Philip Edwards and Colin Gibson (Oxford, 1976), vol. I, *The Fatal Dowry*, IV.iv.69–75.
41 Richard Cumberland, *The Observer* (1786), vol. III, pp. 273–4.
42 *The London Magazine*, vol. I (February 1825), pp. 287–8.
43 See Brown, *English Dramatic Form*, pp. 180–91.

6 THE ACTRESS AS DRAMATIC PROSTITUTE

1 The Jacobean dramatist who treats the 'fallen' woman with most sympathy is Thomas Middleton: see Angela Ingram, '*In the Posture of a Whore*': *Changing Attitudes to 'Bad' Women in Elizabethan and Jacobean Drama* (Salzburg, 1984), vol. II, pp. 336–7.
2 See Staves, *Players' Scepters*, pp. 182–9.
3 Although the play was published anonymously, most recent commentators attribute *The Revenge* to Aphra Behn (see Hargreaves, 'Life and Plays of Mrs. Aphra Behn', pp. 275–84). It would make sense for Behn rather than anyone else to develop the prostitute in a sympathetic way, since she created the potentially tragic courtesan Angellica Bianca in *The Rover* (1676).
4 Aphra Behn, *The Revenge: or, A Match in Newgate* (1680), pp. 9–10.
5 John Marston, *The Dutch Courtesan*, ed. M. L. Wine (1965), V.i.67–79.
6 Marriage to a wealthy fool is as far as Behn or any other dramatist will go by way of giving the 'whore', however unjustly she suffers, a respectable place in society. She cannot be allowed a happy marriage.
7 Behn, *The Second Part of the Rover* (1681), p. 60.
8 Hume's opinion of the end of *The Second Part of the Rover* is that it is 'romantically satisfying but simply seems a flight from reality' (*Development of English Drama*, p. 353).

9 Behn's *The City Heiress: or, Sir Timothy Treat-all* (1682), p. 41.

10 Maureen Duffy points out that this powerful love scene was used in one of the most savage satires against Behn, equating her, of course, with the character of Galliard: 'What though thou bringst (to please a vicious age) / A far more vicious widow on the stage, / Just reeking from a stallion's rank embrace / With rifl'd garments, and disorder'd face' (Maureen Duffy, *The Passionate Shepherdess: Aphra Behn 1640–89* (1977), p. 212).

11 See chapter 3, p. 81.

12 Powell, *Restoration Theatre Production*, p. 196.

13 William Mountfort, *Greenwich Park* (1691), cast list. Subsequent references given in text.

14 Although Barry did play older roles in tragedy once she began to be paired opposite the younger Anne Bracegirdle, Restoration audiences do not appear to have been concerned if a star played a much younger role. Betterton, for instance, played Hamlet well into old age (see *Biographical Dictionary*, ed. Highfill *et al.*, vol. II, p. 91).

15 Southerne, *Works*, vol. I, *The Maid's Last Prayer: or, Any, Rather Than Fail*, II.i.15–16.

16 Henry Higden, *The Wary Widow: or, Sir Noisy Parrat* (1693), p. 23.

17 Lassells apparently played only occasional minor roles after this – as Oriana in *The Traitor* and Mrs Flywife in *The Innocent Mistress* in 1697; see *Biographical Dictionary*, ed. Highfill *et al.*, vol. IX, p. 161.

18 *The Wary Widow*, preface.

19 Davies, *Dramatic Miscellanies*, vol. III, p. 121.

20 The roles which follow are all variations on the suffering mistress who speaks in some form of tragic rhetoric and suffers with tragic intensity. It should be noted, however, that Barry did occasionally play other kinds of mistress during the 1690s – notably the adulterous wife Lady Testie in Doggett's *The Country-Wake* (1696) and the temperamental courtesan Madame de Vendosme in Durfey's *The Intrigues at Versailles* (1697). Both are humorous roles.

21 John Crowne, *The Married Beau: or, the Curious Impertinent* (1694), p. 33.

22 See appendix 1 for a full list of Barry's roles at this time.

23 Mary Pix, *The Innocent Mistress* (1697), pp. 26–7.

24 Jerry Vermilye, *Bette Davis* (1974), p. 9.

7 THE ANGEL AND THE SHE-DEVIL

1 See, for instance, Catherine Belsey, *The Subject of Tragedy: Identity and Difference in Renaissance Drama* (1985), pp. 165–6; Mary Beth Rose, *The Expense of Spirit: Love and Sexuality in English Renaissance Drama* (Ithaca and London, 1988), pp. 4, 176; Pearson, *The Prostituted Muse*, p. 42. These female stereotypes have endured into the twentieth century; for example, the likenesses between the presentation of women in Restoration drama and in the early movies are particularly striking. See

Molly Haskell, *From Reverence to Rape: The Treatment of Women in the Movies* (New York, Chicago and San Francisco, 1974), and Sumiko Higashi, *Virgins, Vamps and Flappers: The American Silent Movie Heroine* (Montreal, 1978).

2 John Webster, *The White Devil*, ed. J. R. Mulryne (1970), IV.ii.87–8.

3 This has been discussed briefly in Wilson, *All the King's Ladies*, p. 97, and Rothstein, *Restoration Tragedy*, pp. 141–4, but neither critic has systematically analysed the known pairings.

4 For a full account of all the revivals of this play, see Arthur Colby Sprague, *Beaumont and Fletcher on the Restoration Stage* (Cambridge, Mass., 1926).

5 Pepys, *Diary*, vol. VII, p, 399. Although Downes, *Roscius Anglicanus*, lists Boutell as playing Aspatia in this early production, there are no records of her joining the theatre until 1670, so he is probably mistaken. But Boutell almost certainly played Aspatia in later revivals, and Downes presumably made the error because he remembered her better than he did her predecessor.

6 See Rothstein, *Restoration Tragedy*, p. 139–41.

7 William Davenant, *The Siege of Rhodes* (1663), p. 37.

8 According to Pepys' *Diary* (vol. v, pp. 33–4), she had a leading part in *The Indian Queen*. Since she played Almeria, Zempoalla's equivalent in the sequel, *The Indian Emperour*, the leading part was probably Zempoalla.

9 Dryden, *Works*, vol. VIII, *The Indian Queen*, III.i.37–8, IV.i.30. Arthur C. Kirsch suggests that Zempoalla may 'be a recollection of the dominating or unscrupulous females in Fletcherian drama', such as Evadne, or Cleopatra in *The False One* (Kirsch, *Dryden's Heroic Drama* (New York, 1972), p. 86).

10 Dryden, *Essays*, vol. I, p. 150.

11 Dryden, *Works*, vol. VIII, *The Indian Queen*, V.i.288–9.

12 Ibid., vol. IX, *The Indian Emperour*, IV.i.28.

13 Pepys, *Diary*, vol. VIII, p. 395. Derek Hughes argues that the casting of comedienne Nell Gwyn in such a serious role should be seen as part of Dryden's intention to mock the impossible ideals of other heroic dramas (*Dryden's Heroic Plays* (Lincoln, Nebraska, 1981), pp. 73, 75, 183).

14 William Davenant, *Macbeth*, ed. Christopher Spencer, *Yale Studies in English*, 146 (New Haven, 1961), I.v.25–8, II.v.93–5.

15 See also three plays of 1671, Stapylton's *Hero and Leander* (Celona and Hero), Crowne's *Juliana: or, the Princess of Poland* (Juliana and Paulina) and Settle's *Cambyses, King of Persia* (Mandana and Phedima).

16 Joyner, *The Roman Empress*, preface. (Preface also cited ch. 5, p. 111.)

17 Ibid., pp. 4, 6.

18 Dryden, *Works*, vol. XI, *The Conquest of Granada, Part I*, II.i.168–70.

19 Herbert Wynford Hill, *La Calprenède's Romances and the Restoration Drama* (Nevada, 1910), p. 82.

20 This play quickly became and remained a stock play. According to the

London Stage, it was performed on at least twelve separate occasions between 1660 and 1700, on thirty-six occasions between 1700 and 1729 and on thirty-five between 1729 and 1746.

21 Nathaniel Lee, *Works*, vol. 1, *Alexander the Great: or, the Rival Queens*, V. opening.

22 Cibber, *Apology*, p. 93.

23 Samuel Pordage, *The Siege of Babylon* (1678), p. 61.

24 Cibber, *Apology*, p. 106.

25 Aston, *Brief Supplement*, pp. 9–10.

26 Cibber, *Apology*, p. 97. See also Lucyle Hook, 'Portraits of Elizabeth Barry and Anne Bracegirdle', *Theatre Notebook*, 15 (1960), pp. 129–37. For a reproduction of the Kneller painting, see plate 12.

27 Betterton, *History of the English Stage*, pp. 22–3. Aston, *Brief Supplement*, pp. 6–7.

28 *The Female Wits*, ed. Lucyle Hook, Augustan Reprint Society Publication no. 124 (1967), p. 50.

29 See appendix 2 for full list of plays in which Barry and Bracegirdle starred together.

30 Durfey, *The Three Parts of the Comical History of Don Quixote*, p. 99.

31 See *London Stage*, Part 1, p. cxlviii.

32 See, for instance, Wycherley's *Love in a Wood: or, St. James's Park* (1671), John Leanerd's *The Counterfeits* (1678) and William Mountfort's *The Successful Straingers* (1690).

33 Wycherley, *The Plays*, ed. Holland, *The Plain Dealer*, IV.ii.343–9, 470–4.

34 Durfey, *The Marriage-Hater Match'd* (1692), p. 23.

35 Durfey, *The Richmond Heiress*, p. 31.

36 John Crowne also subverted the Barry–Bracegirdle tragic association in *The Married Beau* (1694) in which Barry, as the proud wife Mrs Lovely, and Bracegirdle, as her friend Camilla, were both attracted to Polidor. After a brief affair with the former, Polidor settled for the latter, and reformed his libertine ways.

37 Congreve, *Comedies*, title page of *The Double-Dealer*.

38 Laura Brown (*English Dramatic Form*, p. 128) also sees *The Way of the World* as 'in many respects a mature reworking of *The Double-Dealer*', combining tragic with comic conventions to create some kind of 'true fusion of moral assessment and social context'.

8 CONCLUSION: THE ACHIEVEMENT OF THE FIRST ENGLISH ACTRESSES

1 Cibber, *Apology*, p. 55.

2 Pearson, *The Prostituted Muse*, p. 31.

3 Milhous and Hume, *Producible Interpretation*, p. 47.

4 C. V. Wedgewood, quoted in Sarup Singh, *Family Relationships in Shakespeare and the Restoration Comedy of Manners* (Oxford, 1983), p. 146.

5 Belsey, *The Subject of Tragedy*, p. 193. See also Rose, *The Expense of Spirit*,

pp. 123–31 and p. 235 and, as background to both, Laurence Stone, *The Family, Sex and Marriage in England 1500–1800* (1977).

6 Robert Hume, *The Rakish Stage: Studies in English Drama 1660–1800* (Carbondale and Edwardsville, 1983), p. 183.

7 See Staves, *Players' Scepters*, pp. 113–86, Singh, *Family Relationships*, p. 157, and Hume, *The Rakish Stage*, p. 204.

8 John Webster, *The Duchess of Malfi*, ed. Elizabeth M. Brennan (1964), IV.ii.226–7. These lines are cited by Rose in her excellent account of the Duchess's heroic death (*The Expense of Spirit*, pp. 170–1).

Bibliography

In all sections the place of publication is London only, unless otherwise stated.

PRIMARY SOURCES

DRAMATIC TEXTS

If a play is an adaptation it is listed under the name of the person who adapted it.

Arrowsmith, Joseph, *The Reformation*, 1673
Baker, Thomas, *The Humour of the Age*, 1701
    Tunbridge Walks: or, the Yeoman of Kent, 1703
Bancroft, John, *Henry II, King of England: with the Death of Rosamond*, 1693
    King Edward the Third, with the Fall of Mortimer, Earl of March, 1691
Banks, John, *The Albion Queens: or, the Death of Mary Queen of Scotland*, undated, *c.* 1714
    Cyrus the Great: or, the Tragedy of Love, 1679
    The Destruction of Troy, 1679
    The Rival Kings: or, the Loves of Oroondates and Statira, 1677
    The Unhappy Favourite: or, the Earl of Essex, ed. T. M. H. Blair, New York, 1939
    Vertue Betray'd: or, Anna Bullen, 1682
Beaumont, Francis, and John Fletcher, *The Dramatic Works in the Beaumont and Fletcher Canon*, ed. Fredson Bowers, Cambridge, 1966–
Behn, Aphra, *Abdelazer: or, the Moor's Revenge*, 1677
    The Amorous Prince: or, the Curious Husband, 1671
    The City Heiress: or, Sir Timothy Treat-all, 1682
    The Counterfeit Bridegroom, 1677
    The Debauchee: or, the Credulous Cuckold, 1677
    The Dutch Lover, 1673
    The Emperour of the Moon, 1687
    The False Count: or, A New Way to Play An Old Game, 1682
    The Feign'd Curtezans: or, A Night's Intrigue, 1679
    The Forc'd Marriage: or, the Jealous Bridegroom, 1671
    The Luckey Chance: or, An Alderman's Bargain, 1687
    The Revenge: or, A Match in Newgate, 1680
    The Roundheads: or, the Good Old Cause, 1682

The Rover: or, the Banished Cavaliers, ed. Frederick M. Link, 1967
The Second Part of the Rover, 1681
Sir Patient Fancy, 1678
The Town-Fopp: or, Sir Timothy Tawdrey, 1677
The Widow Ranter: or, the History of Bacon in Virginia, 1690
The Younger Brother: or, the Amorous Jilt, 1696
Betterton, Thomas, *The Amorous Widow: or, the Wanton Wife*, 1706
The Roman Virgin: or, the Unjust Judge, 1679
Bonduca: or, the British Heroine, 1696
Boyer, Abel, *Achilles: or, Iphigenia in Aulis*, 1700
Boyle, Charles, *Altemira*, 1702
As You Find It, 1703
Boyle, Roger, Earl of Orrey, *Guzman*, 1693
The History of Henry the Fifth and the Tragedy of Mustapha, Son of Solyman the Magnificent, 1668
Mr Anthony, 1690
Two New Tragedies. The Black Prince and Tryphon, 2 pts., 1672
Brady, Nicholas, *The Rape: or, the Innocent Impostors*, 1692
Brome, Richard, *The Dramatic Works of Richard Brome Containing Fifteen Comedies Now First Collected in 3 volumes*, 1873
A Mad Couple Well Match'd, 1653
Bullock, Christopher, *Woman is a Riddle*, 1717
Burnaby, Charles, *Love Betray'd: or, the Agreeable Disappointment*, 1703
Burnaby, William, *The Ladies Visiting Day*, 1701
The Modish Husband, 1702
The Reform'd Wife, 1700
Carlile, James, *The Fortune-Hunters: or, Two Fools Well Met*, 1689
Cartwright, William, *Comedies, Tragicomedies, with Other Poems etc.*, 2 pts., 1651
Caryll, John, *The English Princess: or, the Death of Richard III*, 1667
Centlivre, Susannah, *The Basset-table*, 1706
A Bickerstaff's Burying: or, Work for the Upholders, 1710
The Busie Body, 1709
The Gamester, 1705
Love's Contrivance, 1703
The Stolen Heiress, 1703
Chamberlayne, William, *Wits Led by the Nose: or, A Poet's Revenge*, 1678
Cibber, Colley, *The Careless Husband*, 1705
The Double Gallant: or, the Sick Lady's Cure, 1708
Love Makes a Man, 1701
Love's Last Shift: or, the Fool in Fashion, 1696
She Wou'd and She Wou'd Not: or, the Kind Imposter, 1703
Three Sentimental Comedies, ed. Maureen Sullivan, New Haven and London, 1973
The Tragical History of King Richard III, 1700
Woman's Wit: or, the Lady in Fashion, 1697
Xerxes, 1699

Cinna's Conspiracy, 1713

Congreve, William, *Comedies*, ed. with an introduction by Bonamy Dobrée, Oxford, 1925
  The Judgement of Paris, 1701
  The Mourning Bride, 1697
  Squire Trelooby, with Vanbrugh and Walsh, 1704

The Constant Nymph: or, the Rambling Shepherd, 1678

Corye, John, *The Generous Enemies: or, the Ridiculous Lovers*, 1672

Cowley, Abraham, *The Cutter of Coleman Street*, 1663

Craufurd, David, *Courtship à la Mode*, 1700

Crowne, John, *Caligula*, 1698
  City Politiques, 1683
  The Countrey Wit: or, Sir Mannerly Shallow, 1675
  Darius, King of Persia, 1688
  The Destruction of Jerusalem by Titus Vespasian, 2 pts., 1677
  The English Frier: or, the Town Sparks, 1690
  Henry the Sixth, the First Part, with the Murder of Henry, Duke of Gloucester, 1681
  The History of Charles the Eighth of France: or, the Invasion of Naples by the French, 1672
  Juliana: or, the Princess of Poland, 1671
  The Married Beau, or, the Curious Impertinent, 1694
  The Misery of Civil-War, 1680
  Regulus, 1694
  Sir Courtly Nice: or, It Cannot Be, 1685

Davenant, Charles, *Circle*, 1677

Davenant, William, *Davenant's Macbeth from the Yale Manuscript: An Edition, with a Discussion of the Relation of Davenant's Text to Shakespeare's*, ed. Christopher Spencer, New Haven, 1961
  The Siege of Rhodes, 1656
  The Siege of Rhodes: the first and second parts ... The first part being lately enlarg'd, 1663

Davys, Mary, *The Northern Heiress: or, the Humours of York*, 1716

Dekker, Thomas, *The Honest Whore*, Parts 1 and 2, in vol. II and *The Virgin Martyr* in vol. III of *The Dramatic Works of Thomas Dekker*, ed. Fredson Bowers, 4 vols., Cambridge University Press, 1953–61

Dennis, John, *Appius and Virginia*, 1709
  Iphigenia, 1700
  Liberty Asserted, 1704
  A Plot and No Plot, 1697
  Rinaldo and Armida, 1699

Dilke, Thomas, *The City Lady: or, Folly Reclaim'd*, 1697
  The Lover's Luck, 1696

Doggett, Thomas, *The Country-Wake*, 1696

Drake, James, *The Sham-Lawyer: or, the Lucky Extravagant*, 1697

Dryden, John, *Amboyna: or, the Cruelties of the Dutch*, 1673
  Aureng-Zebe, ed. Frederick M. Link, 1972

Cleomenes, the Spartan Heroe, 1692
The Kind Keeper: or, Mr. Limberham, 1680
King Arthur: or, the British Worthy, 1691
Love Triumphant, 1694
Marriage à la Mode, ed. Mark S. Auburn, 1981
The Works of John Dryden, ed. E. Niles Hooker, H. T. Swedenburg *et al.*, 19
   vols., Berkeley and Los Angeles, 1954–
Duffett, Thomas, *The Amorous Old Woman: or, 'Tis Well If It Take*, 1674
   The Spanish Rogue, 1674
Durfey, Thomas, *The Banditti: or, A Ladies Distress*, 1686
   The Bath: or, the Western Lass, 1701
   Bussy D'Ambois: or, the Husband's Revenge, 1691
   The Campaigners: or, the Pleasant Adventures at Brussels, 1698
   A Commonwealth of Women, 1686
   The Famous History of the Rise and Fall of Massaniello, 2 pts., 1700
   A Fond Husband: or, the Plotting Sisters, 1677
   A Fool's Preferment: or, the Three Dukes of Dunstable, 1688
   The Injur'd Princess: or, the Fatal Wager, 1682
   The Intrigues at Versailles: or, A Jilt in all Humours, 1697
   Love for Money: or, the Boarding School, 1691
   The Marriage-Hater Match'd, 1692
   The Old Mode and the New: or, Country Miss with her Furbeloe, 1709?
   The Richmond Heiress: or, A Woman Once in the Right, 1693
   The Royalist, 1682
   Sir Barnaby Whigg: or, No Wit Like a Woman's, 1681
   Squire Oldsapp: or, the Night Adventurers, 1679
   *The Three Parts of the Comical History of Don Quixote, with the Marriage of
     Mary the Buxom*, 1729
   Trick for Trick: or, the Debauch'd Hypocrite, 1678
   *Two Comedies by Thomas Durfey: Madam Fickle: or, the Witty False One; A
     Fond Husband: or, the Plotting Sisters*, ed. Jack A. Vaughn, Cranbury,
     New Jersey and London, 1976
   The Virtuous Wife: or, Good Luck at Last, 1680
Estcourt, Richard, *The Fair Example: or, the Modish Citizens*, 1706
Etherege, George, *The Comical Revenge: or, Love in a Tub*, 1664
   The Man of Mode: or, Sir Fopling Flutter, ed. John Barnard, 1979
   She Would If She Could, ed. Charlene M. Taylor, 1972
Fane, Francis, *Love in the Dark: or, the Man of Bus'ness*, 1675
Farquhar, George, *The Beaux' Strategem*, ed. Michael Cordner, 1976
   The Constant Couple: or, A Trip to the Jubilee, 1700
   The Inconstant: or, the Way to Win Him, 1702
   Love and a Bottle, 1699
   The Recruiting Officer, ed. Michael Shugrue, 1966
   Sir Harry Wildair, 1701
The Fatal Discovery: or, Love in Ruins, 1698
The Female Wits, ed. Lucyle Hook, Augustan Reprint Society Publication
   no. 124, 1967

Bibliography

The Fickle Sheperdess, 1703

Flecknoe, Richard, *The Damoiselles à la Mode*, 1667

Gildon, Charles, *Love's Victim: or, the Queen of Wales*, 1710
  Measure for Measure: or, Beauty the Best Advocate, 1700
  The Patriot: or, the Italian Conspiracy, 1703
  Phaeton: or, the Fatal Divorce, 1698

Goring, Charles, *Irene: or, the Fair Greek*, 1708

Gould, Robert, *The Rival Sisters: or, the Violence of Love*, 1696

Granville, George, Baron Lansdowne, *The British Enchanters: or, No Magick Like Love*, 1706
  Heroine Love, 1698
  The Jew of Venice, 1701
  The She-Gallants, 1696

Harris, Joseph, *The City Bride: or, the Merry Cuckold*, 1696
  The Mistakes: or, the False Report, 1691

Hemings, William, *The Fatal Contract, a French Tragedy*, 1653

Higden, Henry, *The Wary Widow: or, Sir Noisy Parrat*, 1693

Higgons, Bevil, *The Generous Conqueror: or, the Timely Discovery*, 1702

Hill, Aaron, *Elfrid: or, the Fair Inconstant*, 1710

Hopkins, Charles, *Boadicea, Queen of Britain*, 1697
  Friendship Improv'd: or, the Female Warriour, 1700
  Neglected Virtue: or, the Unhappy Conquerors, 1696

Howard, Edward, *The Six Days Adventure: or, the New Utopia*, 1671
  The Womens Conquest, 1671

Howard, James, *All Mistaken: or, the Mad Couple*, 1672
  The English Monsieur, 1674

Howard, Sir Robert, *Four New Plays, viz: The Surprizal; The Committee; The Indian Queen; the Vestal-Virgin*, 1665
  The Great Favourite: or, the Duke of Lerma, 1668

Injur'd Love: or, the Lady's Satisfaction, 1711

Jevon, Thomas, *The Devil of a Wife: or, A Comical Transformation*, 1686

Johnson, Charles, *The Victim*, 1714
  The Wife's Relief: or, the Husband's Cure, 1712

Jonson, Ben, *Epicoene: or, the Silent Woman*, ed. R. V. Holdsworth, 1979
  Volpone: or, the Foxe, ed. Philip Brockbank, 1968

Joyner, William, *The Roman Empress*, 1671

Killigrew, Thomas, *Comedies and Tragedies*, 1664

Leanerd, John, *The Counterfeits*, 1679
  The Country Innocence: or, the Chamber-Maid Turn'd Quaker, 1677
  The Rambling Justice: or, the Jealous Husbands, 1678

Lee, Nathaniel, *The Works of Nathaniel Lee*, ed. with introduction and notes by Thomas B. Stroup and Arthur L. Cooke, 2 vols., New Brunswick, 1954, 1955

Lillo, George, *The London Merchant*, ed. W. H. McBurney (1965)

Love the Leveller: or, the Pretty Purchase, 1704

Love Without Interest: or, the Man Too Hard for the Master, 1699

Maidwell, Lewis, *The Loving Enemies*, 1680

Manley, Delariviere, *Almyna: or, the Arabian Vow*, 1707
  The Lost Lover: or, the Jealous Husbands, 1696
  The Royal Mischief, 1696, see Morgan, *Female Wits*, p. 219.
Manning, Francis, *All For the Better: or, the Infallible Cure*, 1703
Marston, John, *The Dutch Courtesan*, ed. M. L. Wine, 1965
Massinger, Philip, *The Plays and Poems of Philip Massinger*, ed. Philip
    Edwards and Colin Gibson, 5 vols., Oxford, 1976
Middleton, Thomas, *No Wit/Help Like a Womans*, 1657
Molloy, Charles, *The Perplex'd Couple: or, Mistake Upon Mistake*, 1715
Moore, Thomas, *Mangora, King of the Timbusians: or, the Faithful Couple*, 1718
Motteux, Peter, *Beauty in Distress*, 1698
  The Island Princess: or, the Generous Portugese, 1699
  Love's a Jest, 1696
  The Novelty, 1679
  Temple of Love, 1706
Mountfort, William, *Greenwich Park*, 1691
  The Injur'd Lovers: or, the Ambitious Father, 1688
  The Successful Straingers, 1690
Mr. Turbulent: or, the Melanchollicks, 1682
Norton, Richard, *Pausanias, the Betrayer of his Country*, 1696
Oldmixon, John, *The Governour of Cyprus*, 1703
  The Grove: or, Love's Paradice, 1700
Otway, Thomas, *Alcibiades*, 1675
  The Atheist: or, the Second Part of the Souldiers Fortune, 1684
  The Cheats of Scapin, 1677
  Don Carlos, Prince of Spain, 1676
  Friendship in Fashion, 1678
  The History and Fall of Caius Marius, 1680
  The Orphan: or, the Unhappy Marriage, ed. Aline Mackenzie Taylor, 1977
  The Souldiers Fortunes, 1681
  Titus and Berenice, 1677
  Venice Preserved: or, A Plot Discovered, ed. Malcolm Kelsall, 1969
  The Works of Thomas Otway, ed. J. C. Ghosh, 2 vols., Oxford, 1932
Payne, Henry Nevil, *The Fatal Jealousie*, 1673
  The Morning Ramble: or, the Town-Humours, 1673
Penkethman, William, *Love Without Interest*, 1699
Philips, Ambrose, *The Distrest Mother*, 1712
Pix, Mary, *The Adventures in Madrid*, 1706?
  The Beau Defeated: or, the Lucky Younger Brother, 1700
  The Czar of Muscovy, 1701
  The Deceiver Deceiv'd, 1698
  The Double Distress, 1701
  The False Friend: or, the Fate of Disobedience, 1699
  Ibrahim, The Thirteenth Emperour of the Turks, 1696
  The Innocent Mistress, 1697
  Queen Catharine: or, the Ruines of Love, 1698
  The Spanish Wives, 1696

Pordage, Samuel, *Herod and Mariamne*, 1673
   The Siege of Babylon, 1678
Porter, Thomas, *The French Conjurer*, 1678
   The Villain, 1663
Powell, George, *Alphonso, King of Naples*, 1691
   The Treacherous Brothers, 1690
   A Very Good Wife, 1693
Ravenscroft, Edward, *The Anatomist, With the Loves of Mars and Venus*, 1697
   The Canterbury Guests: or, A Bargain Broken, 1695
   The Careless Lovers, 1673
   Dame Dobson: or, the Cunning Woman, 1684
   King Edgar and Alfreda, 1677
   The London Cuckolds, 1682
   Mamamouchi: or, the Citizen Turn'd Gentleman, 1672
   The Wrangling Lovers: or, the Invisible Mistress, 1677
Rawlins, Thomas, *Tom Essence: or, the Modish Wife*, 1677
Revet, Edward, *The Town-Shifts: or, the Suburb-Justice*, 1671
Rhodes, Richard, *Flora's Vagaries*, 1670
Romulus and Hersilia: or, the Sabine War, 1683
Rowe, Nicholas, *The Ambitious Stepmother*, 1701
   The Biter, 1705
   The Fair Penitent, ed. Malcolm Goldstein, 1969
   The Royal Convert, 1708
   Tamerlane, 1702
   The Tragedy of Jane Shore, ed. Henry William Pedicord, 1975
   Ulysses, 1706
Scott, Thomas, *The Mock-Marriage*, 1696
   The Unhappy Kindness: or, A Fruitless Revenge, 1697
Sedley, Charles, *Antony and Cleopatra*, 1677
   The Mulberry Garden, 1668
Settle, Elkanah, *The Ambitious Slave: or, A Generous Revenge*, 1694
   Cambyses, King of Persia, 1671
   The City Ramble: or, A Playhouse Wedding, 1711
   The Conquest of China by the Tartars, 1676
   Distress'd Innocence: or, the Princess of Persia, 1691
   The Empress of Morocco, 1673
   Fatal Love: or, the Forc'd Inconstancy 1680
   Ibrahim, the Illustrious Bassa, 1677
   Love and Revenge, 1675
   Pastor Fido: or, the Faithful Shepherd, 1677
   Philaster: or, Love Lies Bleeding, 1695
   The Virgin Prophetess: or, the Fate of Troy, 1701
   The World in the Moon, 1697
Shadwell, Charles, *The Humours of the Army*, 1713
Shadwell, Thomas, *The Amorous Bigotte, with the Second Part of Tegue O'Divelly*,
   1690

Bury Fair, 1689
Epsom Wells, 1673
The History of Timon of Athens, the Man-Hater, 1678
The Humorists, 1671
The Lancashire Witches and Tegue O'Divelly the Irish Priest, 1682
The Miser, 1672
The Scowrers, 1691
The Squire of Alsatia, 1688
The Sullen Lovers: or, the Impertinents, 1668
The Virtuoso, 1676
The Volunteers: or, the Stock-Jobbers, 1692
The Woman-Captain, 1680
Shakespeare, William, *The Complete Works*, ed. with an introduction and
    glossary by Peter Alexander, London and Glasgow, 1951
She Ventures and He Wins, 1696
Shirley, James, *Dramatic Works and Poems of James Shirley*, now first collected
    in 6 vols.; with notes by the late William Gifford Esq., New York, 1966
    The Traitor, ed. John Stewart Carter, 1965
    The Traytor, with Alterations, Amendments and Additions by Anthony Rivers,
    1692
Smith, Edmund, *Phaedra and Hippolitus*, 1709
Smith, Henry, *The Princess of Parma*, 1699
Smyth, John, *Win Her and Take Her: or, Old Fools Will be Meddling*, 1691
Southerne, Thomas, *The Works of Thomas Southerne*, ed. Robert Jordan and
    Harold Love, 2 vols., Oxford, 1988
Stapylton, Robert, *The Slighted Maid*, 1663
    The Stepmother, 1664
    The Tragedie of Hero and Leander, 1669
Steele, Richard, *The Plays of Richard Steele*, ed. Shirley Strum Kenny,
    Oxford, 1971
Tate, Nahum, *Cuckolds-Haven: or, An Alderman No Conjurer*, 1685
    A Duke and No Duke, 1685
    The History of King Lear in *Shakespeare Adaptations*, ed. with an introduction
    and notes by Montague Summers, 1922
    The Ingratitude of a Commonwealth: or, the Fall of Caius Marius Coriolanus,
    1682
    The Island Princess, 1687
    The Loyal General, 1680
Taverner, William, *The Artful Husband*, 1716
    The Faithful Bride of Granada, 1704
    The Maid's the Mistress, 1708
    'Tis Well If It Takes, 1719
Theobald, Lewis, *The Perfidious Brother*, 1715
Trapp, Joseph, *Abra Mulé: or, Love and Empire*, 1708
The Triumphs of Virtue, 1697
Trotter, Catherine, *Agnes de Castro*, 1696

Fatal Friendship, 1698
Love at a Loss: or, Most Votes Carry It, 1701
The Revolution of Sweden, 1706
The Unhappy Penitent, 1701
Tuke, Sir Samuel, *The Adventures of Five Hours,* 1663
Vanbrugh, Sir John, *Aesop,* 1697
Aesop. Part II, 1697
The Confederacy, 1705
The Provoked Wife, ed. Curt A. Zimansky, 1970
The Relapse, ed. Curt A. Zimansky, 1970
Villiers, George, Duke of Buckingham, *The Chances... corrected and altered by George Villiers, Duke of Buckingham,* 1682
The Rehearsal, ed. D. E. L. Crane, Durham, 1976
Webster, John, *The Duchess of Malfi,* ed. Elizabeth M. Brennan, 1964
The White Devil, ed. J. R. Mulryne, 1970
Wilkinson, Richard, *Vice Reclaim'd: or, the Passionate Mistress,* 1703
Wilmot, John, Earl of Rochester, *Valentinian: As 'Tis Alter'd by the late Earl of Rochester,* 1685
Wiseman, Jane, *Antiochus the Great: or, the Fatal Relapse,* 1702
Wright, Thomas, *The Female Vertuoso's,* 1693
Wycherley, William, *The Plays of William Wycherley,* ed. Peter Holland, Cambridge University Press, 1981
Zelmane: or, the Corinthian Queen, 1705

NON-DRAMATIC WORKS

Anon., *A Comparison between the Two Stages, with an Examen of the Generous Conqueror,* 1702
Aston, Anthony, *A Brief Supplement to Colley Cibber Esq; His Lives of the late Famous Actors and Actresses,* 1747?
Betterton, Thomas, *The History of the English Stage from the Restauration to the Present Time, Including the Lives, Characters and Amours of the most Eminent Actors and Actresses,* compiled by Edmund Curll and William Oldys from the notes of T. Betterton, 1741
Boaden, James, *Memoirs of Mrs. Siddons,* 2 vols., 1827
Brown, Thomas, *The Works of Mr. Thomas Brown,* 3 vols., 1707–8
Chetwood, William Rufus, *A General History of the Stage From its Origin in Greece down to the Present Time,* 1749
Cibber, Colley, *An Apology for the Life of Mr. Colley Cibber,* ed. with an introduction, by B. R. S. Fone, Ann Arbor, 1968
An Apology for the Life of Mr. Colley Cibber, ed. Robert W. Lowe, 2 vols., 1889
Collier, Jeremy, *A Short View of the Immorality and Profaneness of the English Stage, together with the Sense and Antiquity upon this Argument,* 1698
Coryat, Thomas, *Coryat's Crudities: Hastily gobled up in Five Moneths Travells etc.,* 2 vols., Glasgow, 1905

Covent Garden Drolery: or, A Collection of all the Choice Songs, Poems, Prologues and Epilogues... never in Print before. Written by the refined's Witts of the Age. And collected by A.B., 1672

Cumberland, Richard, *The Observer: Being a Collection of Moral, Literary and Familiar Essays*, 5 vols., 1786–90

Davies, Thomas, *Dramatic Miscellanies: Consisting of Critical Observations on Several Plays of Shakespeare with Anecdotes of Dramatic Poets, Actors etc.*, 3 vols., 1784

Dennis, John, *The Critical Works of John Dennis*, ed. Edward N. Hooker, 2 vols., Baltimore, 1939, 1943

   Original Letters, Familiar, Moral and Critical, 2 vols., 1721

Downes, John, *Roscius Anglicanus, or an Historical Review of the Stage*, ed. Judith Milhous and Robert Hume, 1987

Dryden, John, *Essays of John Dryden*, selected and edited by W. P. Ker, Oxford, 1900

   The Letters of John Dryden, with Letters Addressed to Him, collected and edited by Charles E. Ward, Durham, North Carolina, 1942

Etherege, George, *The Letters of Sir George Etherege*, ed. Frederick Bracher, Berkeley, 1974

Genest, John, *Some Account of the English Stage from the Restoration in 1660 to 1830*, 10 vols., Bath, 1832

Gentleman's Journal, ed. Peter Motteux, 1692–4

Gildon, Charles, *The Complete Art of Poetry*, 2 vols., 1718

   The Life of Mr. Thomas Betterton, The late Eminent Tragedian... To which is added, The Amorous Widow: or, the Wanton Wife, written by Mr. Betterton, 1710

Gould, Robert, *The Works of Mr. Robert Gould*, 2 vols., 1709

Jordan, Thomas, *A Royal Arbor of Loyal Poesie Consisting of Poems and Songs*, 1664

Langbaine, Gerard the Younger, *An Account of the English Dramatick Poets*, Oxford, 1691

London Magazine and Review, 10 vols., 1825–8

Manley, Delariviere, *The Adventures of Rivella*, 1714

Pepys, Samuel, *The Diary of Samuel Pepys*, a new and complete transcription, ed. Robert Latham and William Matthews, 11 vols., 1970–83

The Spectator, ed. with introduction and notes by Donald F. Bond, Oxford, 1965

SECONDARY SOURCES

Avery, Emmett, L., 'The Restoration Audience', *Philological Quarterly*, 45 (1966), pp. 54–61

Belsey, Catherine, *The Subject of Tragedy: Identity and Difference in Renaissance Drama*, 1985

Bentley, Gerald Eades, *The Jacobean and Caroline Stage*, 7 vols., Oxford, 1941–68

A Biographical Dictionary of Actors, Actresses, Musicians, Dancers etc. in London,

1660–1800, 14 vols., ed. Philip H. Highfill Jr., Kalman A. Burnim and Edward A. Langhans, Carbondale and Edwardsville, 1973–

Bond, David, 'Nell Gwyn's Birthdate', *Theatre Notebook*, 40 (1986), pp. 3–9

Boswell, Eleanor, *The Restoration Court Stage 1660–1702*, Cambridge, Mass., 1932

Brown, Laura, 'The Defenseless Woman and the Development of English Tragedy', *Studies in English Literature*, 22 (1982). pp. 429–43

   English Dramatic Form, 1660–1760: An Essay in Generic History, New Haven and London, 1981

Butler, Martin, *Theatre and Crisis 1632–42*, Cambridge University Press, 1984

Clark, Alice, *Working Life of Women in the Seventeenth Century*, 1982

Duffy, Maureen, *The Passionate Shepherdess: Aphra Behn 1640–89*, 1977

Dusinberre, Juliet, *Shakespeare and the Nature of Women*, 1975

Ferris, Lesley, *Acting Women: Images of Women in Theatre*, 1990

Gilder, Rosamund, *Enter the Actress: The First Women in the Theatre*, Boston, 1931

Goreau, Angeline, *Reconstructing Aphra: A Social Biography of Aphra Behn*, Oxford, 1980

Gossett, Suzanne, '"Best Men are Molded Out of Faults": Marrying the Rapist in Jacobean Drama', *English Literary Renaissance*, 14 (1982), pp. 305–27

Graves, T. S., 'Women on the Pre-Restoration Stage', *Studies in Philology*, 22 (1925), pp. 184–7

Harbage, Alfred, *Cavalier Drama: an Historical and Critical Supplement to the Study of the Elizabethan and Jacobean Stage*, 1936

Hargreaves, H. A., 'The Life and Plays of Mrs. Aphra Behn', unpublished Ph.D. dissertation, Duke University, 1960

Haskell, Molly, *From Reverence to Rape: the Treatment of Women in the Movies*, New York, Chicago and San Francisco, 1974

Higashi, Sumiko, *Virgins, Vamps and Flappers: The American Silent Movie Heroine*, Montreal, 1978

Hill, Herbert Wynford, *La Calprenède's Romances and the Restoration Drama*, Nevada, 1910

Holland, Peter, *The Ornament of Action: Text and Performance in Restoration Comedy*, Cambridge University Press, 1979

Hook, Lucyle, 'Portraits of Elizabeth Barry and Anne Bracegirdle', *Theatre Notebook*, 15 (1960), pp. 129–37

Hotson, Leslie, *The Commonwealth and Restoration Stage*, Cambridge, Mass., 1928

Hughes, Derek, *Dryden's Heroic Plays*, Lincoln, Nebraska, 1981

Hughes, Leo, *The Drama's Patrons: a Study of the Eighteenth-century London Audience*, Texas, 1971

Hume, Robert D., *The Development of English Drama in the late Seventeenth Century*, Oxford, 1976

   The Rakish Stage: Studies in English Drama, 1660–1800, Carbondale and Edwardsville, 1983

Ingram, Angela J. C., '*In the Posture of a Whore*': *Changing Attitudes to 'Bad' Women in Elizabethan and Jacobean Drama*, 2 vols., Salzburg, 1984

Jardine, Lisa, *Still Harping on Daughters: Women and Drama in the Age of Shakespeare*, Brighton, 1983

Kirsch, Arthur C., *Dryden's Heroic Drama*, New York, 1972

Lanier, H. W., *The First English Actresses from 1660–1700*, New York, 1930

LeGates, Marlene, 'The Cult of Womanhood in Eighteenth-Century Thought', *Eighteenth-Century Studies*, 10 (Fall, 1976), pp. 21–39

Loftis, John, Richard Southern, Marion Jones, and Arthur H. Scouten, *The Revels History of Drama in English V 1660–1750*, 1976

London Stage 1660–1800: A Calender of Plays, Entertainments and Afterpieces Together with Casts, Box-receipts and Contemporary Comment Compiled from the Playbills, Newspapers and Theatrical Diaries of the Period.

Part I, *1660–1700*, ed. William Van Lennep, Carbondale, Illinois, 1965

Part II, *1700–29*, ed. Emmett L. Avery, 2 vols., Carbondale, Illinois, 1960

Part III, *1729–47*, ed. Arthur H. Scouten, 2 vols., Carbondale, Illinois, 1961

Part IV, *1747–76*, ed. George Winchester Stone Jr., 3 vols., Carbondale, Illinois, 1962

Part V, *1776–1800*, ed. Charles Beecher Hogan, 3 vols., Carbondale, Illinois, 1968

Love, Harold, 'The Myth of the Restoration Audience', *Komos*, 1 (1967), pp. 49–56

McBurney, W. H., 'Otway's Tragic Muse Debauched: Sensuality in *Venice Preserv'd*', *Journal of English and German Philology*, 58 (1959), pp. 380–99

Mack, Maynard, 'Rescuing Shakespeare', *International Shakespeare Association Occasional Paper No. 1*, Oxford, 1979

Maus, Katharine Eisaman, 'Arcadia Lost: Politics and Revision in the Restoration *Tempest*', *Renaissance Drama*, 13 (1982), pp. 189–209

'"Playhouse Flesh and Blood": Sexual Ideology and the Restoration Actress', *English Literary History*, 46 (1979), pp. 595–617

Meredith, George, 'An Essay on Comedy' in *Comedy*, ed. Wylie Sypher, Garden City, New York, 1956, pp. 3–57

Milhous, Judith and Robert D. Hume, *Producible Interpretation: Eight English Plays 1675–1707*, Carbondale and Edwardsville, 1985

Morgan, Fidelis (ed.), *The Female Wits: Women Playwrights on the London Stage 1660–1720*, 1981

Nicoll, John Allardyce, *A History of English Drama 1660–1900*, vol. 1, *Restoration Drama 1660–1700*, Cambridge University Press, 1952

Orgel, Stephen, 'Nobody's Perfect: Or Why did the English Stage Take Boys for Women?', *South Atlantic Quarterly*, 88 (Winter 1989), no. 1, pp. 7–29

Pearson, Jacqueline, *The Prostituted Muse: Images of Women and Women Dramatists 1642–1737*, Hemel Hempstead, 1988

Powell, Jocelyn, *Restoration Theatre Production*, 1984

Racklin, Phyllis, 'Androgyny, Mimesis, and the Marriage of the Boy

Heroine on the English Renaissance Stage', in *Speaking of Gender*, ed. Elaine Showalter, 1989, pp. 113–33

Roberts, David, *The Ladies: Female Patronage of Restoration Drama 1660–1700*, Oxford, 1989

Robinson, Ken, 'Two Cast Lists for Buckingham's *The Chances*', *Notes and Queries*, 224 (1979), pp. 436–7

Rogers, Pat, 'Breeches Roles', in *Sexuality in Eighteenth-Century Britain*, ed. Paul Gabriel Boucé, Manchester, 1982, pp. 244–58

Rose, Mary Beth, *The Expense of Spirit: Love and Sexuality in English Renaissance Drama*, Ithaca and London, 1988

Rothstein, Eric, *Restoration Tragedy: Form and the Process of Change*, Madison, 1967

Shaaber, M. A., 'A Letter from Mrs. Barry', *Library Chronicle*, 16 (1950), pp. 46–9

Singh, Sarup, *Family Relationships in Shakespeare and the Restoration Comedy of Manners*, Oxford, 1983

Smith, John Harrington, *The Gay Couple in Restoration Comedy*, Cambridge, Mass., 1948

Sorelius, Gunnar, '*The Giant Race Before the Flood': Pre-Restoration Drama on the Stage and in the Criticism of the Restoration*, Uppsala, 1966

Sprague, Arthur Colby, *Beaumont and Fletcher on the Restoration Stage*, Cambridge, Mass., 1926

Staves, Susan, *Players' Scepters: Fictions of Authority in the Restoration*, Lincoln, Nebraska, 1979

Stone, Laurence, *The Family, Sex and Marriage in England 1500–1800*, 1977

Styan, J. L., *Restoration Comedy in Performance*, Cambridge University Press, 1986

Taylor, Aline Mackenzie, *Next to Shakespeare: Otway's 'Venice Preserv'd' and 'The Orphan' and their History on the London Stage*, Durham, North Carolina, 1950

Thomas, David (ed.), *Restoration and Georgian England 1660–1788*, compiled and introduced by David Thomas and Arnold Hare, Cambridge, 1989

Tillotson, Geoffrey, '*Othello* and *The Alchemist* at Oxford in 1610', *The Times Literary Supplement*, 20 July 1933, p. 494

Tomlinson, Sophie, 'Theatrical Women: the Emergence of Women as Actors in English Theatre and Drama before the Restoration', Ph.D. dissertation, Cambridge University, in progress

Vermilye, Jerry, *Bette Davis*, 1974

Weber, Harold, M., *The Restoration Rake-Hero: Transformations in Sexual Understanding in Seventeenth-Century England*, Wisconsin, 1986

Wilson, John Harold, *All the King's Ladies: Actresses of the Restoration*, Chicago, 1958

Court Satires of the Restoration, Columbus, Ohio, 1976

Nell Gwyn, Royal Mistress, 1952

Woodbridge, Linda, *Women and the English Renaissance: Literature and the Nature of Womankind, 1540–1620*, Brighton, 1984

Index